ENGLISH SMALL TOWN LIFE

RETFORD, 1520–1642

Retford's position in the Bassetlaw Hundred: from Speed's map of 1610.

ENGLISH SMALL TOWN LIFE

RETFORD, 1520–1642

Except the Lord build the house, they labour in vain that build it: except the Lord keep the city, the watchman waketh but in vain.

Psalm 127 : 1

David Marcombe

Department of Adult Education
University of Nottingham
1993

ISBN (HB) 1 85041 067 4
      (PB) 1 85041 068 2

Printed in Great Britain at The Alden Press, Oxford

TABLE OF CONTENTS

LIST OF ILLUSTRATIONS

viii

I am grateful to the following for permission to reproduce illustrative materials in their care — Nottingham City Museums (cover illustration); the British Library (5); Retford Museum (11,12,28); Colonel Clifton (17); University of Nottingham (18); Northampton Museums and Art Gallery (20); and the Quaker Tapestry Scheme (53).

ACKNOWLEDGEMENTS

It is a great pleasure, and a special privilege, to sit down at the end of a long research project such as this and pay tribute to all of those who have helped in its successful outcome. The research on the Retford area has been under way at the Centre for Local History for eight years and it still continues, albeit in a rather different guise. If individuals have failed to receive the recognition due to them, I apologise for my oversight and point to the long and complex nature of this project as a rather feeble excuse. If the book contains errors of fact or interpretation, I take full responsibility for them since as captain of the ship my duty has been not only to correlate research findings, but also to add to them and check data already collected.

It has, indeed, been an unusual exercise when compared with the way in which more conventional academic texts are put together. Central to the effort has been the support of the members of the Archdeaconry Research Unit, whose feats of information gathering have often been prodigious. Jean Nicholson and Joy Bristow made special contributions in the area of family reconstitution; Eric Wilmshurst in demography; and Dr David Crawford in the analysis of wills. Marie Wilkinson, Jean Reid, Sue Terry, Christine Pye, John Millar, Narita Pike and Pam Stevens did sterling service on a number of fronts and William Nicholson drew the map of Retford, itself the result of considerable detective work. Special mention must also be made of my Certificate in Local History students — who undertook a project on North Nottinghamshire wills and developed an analytical methodology — and of the late Dr Norman Tyack whose work on the Archdeaconry records of the 1630s (and the bequest of that material to the Centre) has been of great value to the project.

The staffs of various libraries and record offices have been uniformly helpful and supportive and have sometimes afforded assistance over and above the call of duty. Adrian Henstock, the Nottinghamshire County Archivist, arranged the temporary transfer of Hodgkinson's transcriptions of the Archdeaconry Act Books to the University, thus enabling work to be done on them by the research team 'after hours'; Richard Beaumont, former librarian of Southwell Minster, made a similar arrangement in respect of the bishop's parish register transcripts. Dr Dorothy Johnston, Keeper of Manuscripts at Nottingham University Library, Malcolm Dolby, Curator of Retford Museum, and Dr David Smith and Chris Webb of the Borthwick Institute, University of York, have all given freely of their time and wide knowledge of the collections in their care.

A special word of thanks is called for for those whose privacy has been invaded by our research since their collections are not normally open to the public. His Grace, the Duke of Rutland generously gave permission for the use of family archives stored at Belvoir Castle and his secretary, Mrs D A Staveley, pointed me in the right direction of the major items. Similarly, my courteous reception in the offices of Jones and Co (late Jones Alexander) of Retford, solicitors, by invitation of Mr Andrew Green, allowed me to work on the private papers of John Shadrach Piercy, the nineteenth century historian of the town. Both of these sources yielded some extremely valuable information.

Not being a lover of the word processor, I owe a heavy debt to the three University secretaries, Judy Matsell, Catherine Beeston and Margie D'Arcy, who converted my manuscript into a more acceptable, and readable, form. Beyond that it was up to Lynda Prescott to create the page proofs and supervise the publication process, a task undertaken with efficiency and good humour throughout. Catherine Beeston also read the proofs and offered constructive comment on all things grammatical. Without the unstinted efforts of these individuals the book could never have seen the light of day or would have done so in a much less impressive form.

Another area of support has been from the Publications Committee of the University of Nottingham Department of Adult Education. At a time when all publishers were cutting back their lists — especially in local history — or asking for exorbitant amounts of 'sponsorship', they showed sufficient faith in this project to support it as a volume in the series *Studies in Local and Regional History*. Moreover, in 1991 the

University awarded me two terms of sabbatical leave, one of the designated projects being the writing-up of the Retford book. This was done, largely, during the term I spent as Visiting Fellow at the Borthwick Institute, University of York, where I enjoyed comfortable accommodation and unimpeded access to the records. It was with this level of institutional support that the research findings of the project were converted from a series of random jottings to the book which we see today.

Finally, my thanks are due to Professor David Loades for reading and offering comments on the typescript; to Richard Alexander, MP for Newark and Retford, for useful advice on publication; and to Snowden Houseley, a long-standing benefactor of the town, who was kind enough to offer financial backing at a time when it was thought that it would be necessary. But my most long-serving supporter has been my partner, Ann, who has lived with Retford and its little problems, on and off, for seven years now. Visits to outlandish places at strange times; tables given over to the paraphernalia of research — these are just some of the difficulties which beset a household in the grip of 'history'. For her tolerance, warmth and generosity I am eternally grateful.

The Feast of St Matthias

David Marcombe
Nottingham

Standard Abbreviations and Conventions

Acts of the Privy Council	APC
Belvoir Castle	BC
Borthwick Institute, University of York	BI
Calendar of Close Rolls	CCR
Calendar of Patent Rolls	CPR
Calendar of State Papers (Domestic)	CSP
Dictionary of National Biography	DNB
Historical Manuscripts Commission	HMC
Jones Alexander and Co.	JA
Lambeth Palace Library	LPL
Letters and Papers of Henry VIII	LP
Nottinghamshire Archives Office	NAO
Nottingham University Manuscripts Department	NUMD
Nottingham University Centre for Local History	NUCLH
Public Record Office	PRO
Retford Museum	RM
Southwell Minster Library	SML
Transactions of the Thoroton Society	TTS
Victoria County History	VCH
York Minster Library	YML

Spellings have been modernised and new style dating adopted throughout.

Introduction

The idea of a book on Tudor and Stuart Retford stemmed from the Archdeaconry Research Unit, established at the University of Nottingham Centre for Local History in 1980. The Unit, which is serviced largely by volunteers who want to learn more about history, took as its initial objective an analysis of all cases heard by the court of the Archdeacon of Nottingham between 1565 and 1610, the aim being to process these in a computer in an attempt to discover more about the early implementation of Protestantism in the county. Yet as we progressed it became plain that fewer and fewer questions were in fact being answered by the court data in isolation, and in the mid-1980s a series of community studies was embarked upon to try to place the jurisdictional information in a broader social and economic context, going back to the towns and villages to try to work out why offenders acted as they did. Individual members of the Unit selected 'manageable' village communities for study, strategically spread around the county to give a flavour of contrasts dictated by topography or known social circumstances, but we were aware that a town needed to be studied to introduce what we believed then to be the inevitable contrast between 'urban' and 'rural' communities. The size of towns here became a vital determining factor, since the volume of records associated with them was colossal when compared to the average Nottinghamshire village. Nottingham was clearly too large even for our group efforts, and in the end we dismissed Newark for the same reason. Of the ancient boroughs of the county that left East Retford, small enough to be 'manageable' and located in the far North of the county, an area which had received little attention from local historians but which had widely publicised religious connections by virtue of the fact that the Pilgrim Fathers traced their roots to the Scrooby congregation, only a few miles from the town.

Almost inadvertently we stumbled into a study which was to be more widespread, and possibly more historically significant, than at first we imagined. The only other historian to have considered Retford seriously was the non-conformist schoolmaster and antiquarian John Shadrach Piercy who wrote a history of the town in 1828. But Piercy, who used a quotation from Sir Walter Scott on his title page, was very much a product of the age in which he wrote: he was worried about 'the obscurity of the situation of East Retford', the lack of happenings of 'national' importance and the fact that he could not trace 'an uninterrupted succession of lords ... a sort of railway along which the writer had nothing to do but to drive'. Despairing of what he believed to be a lack of records, he stated:

> My task has been to traverse a wilderness, through which a path has ne'er been beaten — nay where human foot had never trod — with but little light to dissipate the gloom.[1]

Although Piercy's priorities might not be those of the modern historian, he did at least provide an explanation as to why the archive sources of the town were in such poor shape. A combination of carelessness and natural disaster was clearly to blame. When he examined the corporation records many were found to be 'scorched and mutilated...ample evidence of their having suffered some fiery ordeal'.[2] The parish chest, 'a pondrous ark of oak', contained a jumble of documents going back to the seventeenth century:

> It is much to be regretted that the contents of this chest are not so collected and arranged as to be ready at all times for reference.[3]

Piercy's achievement of sorting and making sense of some of this miscellaneous material should not be minimised — we owe him a great debt in all sorts of ways — but he failed patently to engender in the people of the town any interest in, or respect for, their past. Only two years after the completion of his book the parish chest was stolen and the contents dumped in a nearby field, and it is sad to record that documents viewed by Piercy in the 1820s now appear to have vanished, particularly the corporation books and the West Retford parish register.[4] Even today, despite an active Local History Society in the town, many residents still view the prospect of serious research with a mixture of amusement and incredulity: 'Why should anyone be interested in Retford?' they ask.

In view of this continuing wastage of archives Piercy would have been even more disheartened writing today than in 1828 but, fortunately, the goal posts of history have moved. Sources dismissed and ignored by nineteenth-century anti-quarians have become the stock-in-trade of contemporary historians, and when all is taken into account Retford is not that badly provided for if we aim at the broad mass of townspeople rather than the 'succession of lords'. Retford Museum still holds some residual corporation records, and the parish registers of two of the three town parishes have survived from early in Elizabeth's reign. In terms of legal records there is an excellent caucus of church court data at Nottingham and York, and Quarter Sessions material after 1603. One of the most important survivals for Retford, completely ignored by Piercy, is the splendid collection of probate records at the Borthwick Institute, York, many of these sources underlining Alan Macfarlane's view that 'the belief that little can be found out about ordinary people in the past is a myth'.[5] But most fortuitous, perhaps, is the survival in the offices of Jones Alexander, solicitors of Retford, of the private papers of John Shadrach Piercy. Piercy, despite his limitations by a modern judgement, was a meticulous scholar, and he continued to collect material long after the publication of his book. This means that certain classes of record which have now vanished can be consulted from Piercy's notes, particularly the missing corporation books after 1600.

As the work on Retford progressed it soon became appar-ent that there was very little context, in terms of contemporary scholarship, in which to place it. Historians such as Palliser, Phythian-Adams and Howell had conducted excellent sur-veys of larger communities, and in 1992, when our work was all but complete, Underdown's seminal study of seventeenth-century Dorchester appeared under the title *Fire from Heaven*.[6] Dorchester is the county town of Dorset and with a popula-tion of about 2,000 it fits into the classification of 'minor regional centre' rather than 'small town' in the accepted sense of the words.[7] Moreover, Underdown's revealing sociological analysis is largely constructed around seventeenth-century religious experience and for this reason the book cannot be considered to be a truly comprehensive examination of urban life. It is a book strong on anecdote, based on remarkable documentary survivals, but weak on any form of statistical underpinning of the issues raised. For these reasons it would be fair to say that Jonathan Barry's belief that the 'proper study of small towns is still in its infancy' is only marginally less true after *Fire from Heaven* than it was before it.[8] And this in spite of the obvious importance of Underdown's book and of small urban settlements. There were about 800 market towns in England and Wales during this period, and since the vast majority of the population still lived in villages these centres were important *foci* of life for buying and selling and simply having fun; lightening the tedium of a purely rural existence. Nigel Goose highlights one of the reasons for the lack of research when he says that smaller communities, unlike Dorchester, 'left fewer records'.[9] In this he is undoubtedly correct, and the case of Retford proves the point if any proof is required. Yet it is a particular disease of contemporary historians constantly to pursue archive deposits and ignore important questions which cry out for answers. A start in this direction has been made with the Small Towns Project at the Centre for Urban History, University of Leicester, but there is still a long way to go. Nevertheless, 'the importance of small towns in the urban history of early modern Europe is increasingly recognised'.[10]

That recognition involves placing small towns in the context of the debates on urban history introduced by Peter Clark and Paul Slack in their seminal and influential book *Crisis and Order in English Towns, 1500-1700*, published as long ago as 1972. In it the authors called for more detailed research on specific communities, and in 1973 Alan Everitt backed this plea by emphasising the almost complete lack of any sociological discussion of the urban environment — 'for most towns we have not even a rudimentary study of this kind'.[11] The last twenty years have seen developments of Clark and Slack's ideas, though perhaps not the major studies they hoped for, particularly relating to the smallest urban communities. These modern developments are most usefully drawn together by Jonathan Barry in *The Tudor and Stuart Town*, yet

Barry concedes that the parameters of debate introduced by Clark and Slack are still highly relevant. Basically, that view is that between 1500 and 1700 English towns faced 'a major collision of continuity and change' brought about by the impact of the Tudor rulers and the Tudor economy on an essentially 'Medieval' urban framework.[12] What survived of the old order, and the nature of that survival, has become a fruitful area of discussion. The purpose of this volume is to try to relate some of these ideas to the specific case of Retford, a community known to most people only through the carriage window of an Inter City 125 as they speed through it *en route* from London to the North of England. Because of its situation at the heart of the kingdom, and its very anonymity, it might stand as a template for English small town life.

FOOTNOTES AND REFERENCES

1. J. S. Piercy, *The History of Retford* (1828), p.vi.
2. JA, R(ed) B(ook) 1 (Chantry Lands).
3. Piercy, p.107.
4. A. A. Kidson, *History of East Retford Church* (1905), pp.132/3.
5. A. Macfarlane, *Reconstructing Historical Communities* (1977), pp. 32, 131.
6. D. M. Palliser, *Tudor York* (1979), C. Phythian-Adams, *Desolation of a City: Coventry and the Urban Crisis of the late Middle Ages* (1979), R. Howell, *Newcastle-upon-Tyne and the Puritan Revolution* (1967), D. Underdown, *Fire from Heaven: life in an English town in the seventeenth century* (1992).
7. See Chapter 1, p.19.
8. J Barry (ed). *The Tudor and Stuart Town* (1990), p.9.
9. *Ibid.*, p.72.
10. P. Clark, K. Gaskin and A. Wilson, *Population Estimates of English Small Towns, 1550-1851*, Centre for Urban History, University of Leicester, Working Paper, 3 (1989), p.i.
11. A. Everitt (ed.), *Perspectives in English Urban History* (1973), p.10.
12. P. Clark and P. Slack (eds.), *Crisis and Order in English Towns, 1500-1700* (1972), p.40.

Chapter 1

THE TOWN AND ITS POPULATION

There be two Retfords, one, the less, is called West Retford, the other is called East Retford and is the market town, as big as Rotherham and hath a church almost as fair as it. The only bridge upon the river divideth the one town from the other. [1]

When John Leland made his epic journey around the kingdom during the reign of Henry VIII the 'good market town' of Retford straddled the sleepy river Idle, ponderously winding its way towards Bawtry and the Trent by way of Mattersey priory. At this date the Idle connected up with the river Don, but following the activities of Sir Cornelius Vermuyden in draining the Isle of Axholme and Hatfield Chase for Charles I in the 1630s the river was redirected along Bicker's Dyke, just North of Bawtry, to join the Trent at West Stockwith. These works had little direct impact on Retford. Both before and after Vermuyden's improvements the river was only navigable by very small craft and goods of any substance had to be shipped from Bawtry or Gainsborough necessitating trans-shipment or an overland journey. More important, the normally tranquil Idle was liable to flooding 'whenever a fall of rain took place, or any long frost broke up', or, after the 1630s, when the Trent was affected by abnormally high tides. [2] In these circumstances 'the greatest part of the town was laid under water' a situation aggravated by the town mills which created a backlog of water built up by their dams. The low lying lands of East Retford always suffered worse in this respect than those on the West bank, and the discomfort and disease thus created must have been a major hazard to life and property. In October 1636, believing that the flooding was caused by the fact that water could not have 'free passage' down the Idle which was 'stopped and choked up' with 'divers impediments and annoyances', the corporation petitioned the King's Commissioners for Sewers who ordered that both banks should be improved at the cost of their respective landowners. Two years later the work had been completed at a cost of £105 bringing 'great benefits' to the town, but though the problem of flooding subsided somewhat, Retford had to wait until the arrival of the Chesterfield canal in 1777 for any real benefits to its water-borne trade.[3]

More important than water communications were roads, and in this respect geography had served the town remarkably well. The Great North Road, the main arterial route of the kingdom, passed a few miles to the West *en route* to Doncaster from Newark. There were local posting stations at Scrooby and Tuxford, and the obligation of the people of West Retford to provide horses for these was a matter of continuing concern.[4] Other local roads, sometimes poorly maintained, joined the town with Gainsborough, a substantial inland port on the Trent, Worksop, Sheffield and the great Cathedral city of Lincoln. Indeed, Retford's position in the Northern tip of Nottinghamshire made it a natural focus for communications with the Southern portions of Yorkshire and Lincolnshire, more so than with Nottingham itself. Nottingham, the county town, was 32 miles distant and was best reached via Newark rather than by making the more direct, but more dangerous, journey through Sherwood Forest which still formed an impenetrable barrier to the West. Sheffield (27 miles) and Lincoln (23 miles) were at least equally convenient, and Doncaster was a mere eighteen miles along the well travelled Great North Road.[5] The town, therefore, did not have a narrow 'county' orientation and it looked beyond the conventional shire boundaries for its prosperity and livelihood. In the early nineteenth century it was stated that considerable quantities of goods were brought to market in Retford from Sheffield and South Yorkshire where they were bought up by wholesalers and sold elsewhere, and this is likely to have been a pattern of trade which had very ancient roots.[6] Even before the Great North Road was diverted through Retford in 1766, visitors were commonplace, using the facilities of the town for rest and refreshment during their journeys by road. In 1638 Sir Edward Bashe wrote to the Earl of Rutland about a convivial encounter in one of Retford's many alehouses where he had managed to obtain the latest gossip about the Ship Money controversy along with other news.[7]

The soils around the town were clay and sand, prompting one sixteenth-century inhabitant to describe it as 'Retford-in-the-Clay', a form of description which was not generally adopted.[8] Indeed, the placename 'Retford' seems to signify 'the red ford', the redness being caused by the disturbance of clay, or, more romantically, the blood shed at the battle of the Idle during the Saxon period. It would be tempting to offer the alternative suggestion that the town obtained its name from 'the retting ford', but since the word 'ret' appears to have an origin no earlier than Middle Dutch, and the placename is Saxon, such an interpretation must be regarded as highly speculative.[9] To the West lay forest, and Ordsall, to the South, was described by Piercy as 'a barren wilderness'.[10] However, the land to the North and East was better, and it produced good wheat, hops and barley as well as pasture for cattle. Retford was one of six market towns in the Bassetlaw Hundred, the others being Tuxford, Blyth, Worksop, Ollerton and Bawtry. Of these Retford was the largest and most centrally situated, so, while it relied heavily on two dozen or so adjacent parishes, it might reasonably have expected to trade with places further afield. These were invariably farming communities which depended on mixed agriculture and some domestic industrial activity, the most prosperous of them lying to the East of the town in the vale of the river Trent. In 1844 the authors of White's *Directory* believed this hinterland to be in 'a high state of cultivation', a factor which helped give Retford 'an air of importance, comfort and wealth, possessed but by few country towns of the same size'.[11] This was another view which might well have been relevant to the past. The 1334 Lay Subsidy assessed the borough of East Retford at £10 13s 10d, compared with Newark's £26 0s 2d and Nottingham's £37 1s 0d:[12] however, when the suburbs of Moorgate and West Retford are taken into account also the figure for 'Retford' is increased to £16 7s 6d making it easily the third most prosperous conurbation of the county, comfortably outstripping

1: The Sun Inn, opposite St Swithun's churchyard, is a timber-framed building which probably dates from the sixteenth century.

2: An early thatched cottage which once stood on Bridge Gate: the original construction may well have been mud and stud.

centres such as Mansfield, Worksop, Blyth and Tuxford.[13] When Elizabeth I's government imposed an obligation on all towns to maintain stores of gunpowder and matches following the Armada crisis, half of the county quota fell on Newark and Retford with two parts to be provided by the larger town and one part by the smaller.[14] Similarly, in the Ship Money assessment of 1636 Retford was rated at £30, compared with Nottingham's £200 and Newark's £120. Chesterfield at once complained that Retford 'a much greater town' was under assessed, and in 1637 the sheriff, Sir Francis Thornhaugh, conceded the point when he wrote to the Privy Council suggesting that Retford was well able to pay £50 so that Newark's contribution could be reduced by £20.[15] Problems such as this were caused partly because of the confusion, in the popular imagination, between the *borough* of East Retford and the extended area of the town, but the general view that Retford was half as prosperous as Newark and a quarter as prosperous as Nottingham was well ingrained in local psychology and probably got the economic pecking order for the county just about right, despite inevitable fluctuations from time to time.

In terms of a national perspective, and this could well be an under statement, 'the historical events of Retford are neither numerous nor momentous'.[16] Princess Margaret passed close to the town in 1503 on her way North to marry James IV of Scotland and paused long enough to be greeted by the leading citizens and Charles I was there in August 1645 *en route* from Doncaster to Newmarket.[17] It was doubtless a relief to the corporation that the King confined himself to this flying visit, because the town escaped the Civil War traumas of its near neighbour Newark. But if Retford failed to make any sort of impact on national events, its role in the ongoing administration of the locality was much more significant. As the chief town of the Bassetlaw Hundred the Quarter Sessions for North Nottinghamshire met there, along with Commissioners for Musters and other important groups of officials. In 1587, as the Armada crisis approached, Brian Lassells wrote to the Earl of Rutland explaining how he intended to assemble the arms and armour of the Hundred at Retford,[18] and in 1630 the Quarter Sessions Justices thought it worthwhile to write to the Privy Council about an assault on Sir Francis Thornhaugh's son by some workmen of Sir Cornelius Vermuyden who had allegedly entered Thornhaugh's lands with 'wrongful and indecent words'.[19] Similarly, in the ecclesiastical sphere the 'corporation church' of East Retford, St Swithun's, sat at the centre of a Deanery comprising 52 parishes, and the church was used for regular meetings of the Archdeacon of Nottingham's court and less regular visitations by the Archbishop of York. Thus, in terms of the smooth running of North Nottinghamshire, Retford could not be ignored by either the civil or ecclesiastical administration, and for a time each year it became the forum for the leading men of the shire as Justices of the Peace and church officials descended on the town to do their business.[20]

The town itself was a strange amalgam and not what at first it might appear to be. Mike Bishop has pushed the origins of East Retford back to c1105, suggesting that it was a royal borough deliberately 'planted' by Henry I to compete with the trading privileges of Blyth priory and 'to exploit the market opportunities of North Nottinghamshire'.[21] If this is true, it was not as old as the adjacent settlement of West Retford, mentioned in Domesday, or the neighbouring parishes of Clarborough and Ordsall: indeed, it seems likely that the 'new' ecclesiastical parish of East Retford, which was coterminous with the borough, was deliberately carved out of Clarborough in the early twelfth century. This new borough and parish comprised about 120 acres of land on the East bank of the Idle, West Retford on the opposite side being connected by a wooden footbridge and possibly two fords for cattle. The municipal area appears to have been surrounded by a ditch, some archaeological evidence of which has come to light, though this probably marked a jurisdictional boundary only and had no defensive function.[22] Bridge Gate, or Briggate, the main way into the town from the West was 'not only low and swampy, but it was likewise very narrow'.[23] By the mid-sixteenth century this important route to the market place had been paved with a 'pitched pavement', though not without considerable ingenuity.[24] When Piercy excavated part of the area in 1828 he discovered that the road had been dug out to a depth of at least eight feet and had been filled with bundles of ling and whins, before wooden piles had been placed on top 'in preparing the swampy ground for the purposes of a road'.[25]

Retford's extensive market place was the hub of its commercial activity and in it were located the Broad Stone, or market cross, and the Moothall: during the 1590s the whole of the area was being paved.[26] Unusually for a 'planned' Medieval town the parish church did not face on to the market square but was located slightly to the North, adjacent to an open space of its own which may have served as a subsidiary, or earlier, market. The main roads of the town radiated out from this central core: Carr Hill Gate, or Carolgate, Newgate, and Churchgate, or Kirkgate, alternatively known as Chapelgate, the High Street, King Street or Kingsgate. Northgate, which like Newgate has now vanished as a street name, ran out of the town in the direction of Moorgate, the parish boundary being marked by a beck which was crossed by another, smaller, bridge.[27] Northgate, Churchgate and Newgate were respectable areas of town, paved and lined with houses and gardens, though Newgate's open sewer caused consternation to successive generations of residents. Carolgate, by contrast, was 'narrow and dirty' with most of the houses facing the street with their gable ends and a proliferation of sheds and hovels for animals. The most populous area, and also the 'most ancient' according to Piercy, was the built up block between Churchgate and Newgate crossed by Crew Yard and Twin Lane or St John's Street: it was here that the poorest inhabitants lived in houses which were 'very humble' to say the least.[28] About 50 acres of the borough was made up of the Cars and Commons, a swampy tract of communal pasture located near the river on the South side of the town. Until it was improved in the eighteenth century this area was 'of very little benefit to any of the proprietors or even to the occupiers', and the cattle sheds on Carolgate were there largely to provide overnight shelter for animals which might come to grief in this 'morass or bog' unless taken in during the hours of darkness.[29] To the North the town was connected with the hamlet of Bolham, to the East with Little Gringley and Welham and to the South with Thrumpton and beyond them with the larger communities of Clarborough, Grove, Ordsall and Babworth.

Within the narrow confines of the borough and parish of East Retford the corporation held sway under the privileges granted in a series of Medieval charters, but the real boundaries of the town were more extensive than that. West Retford, separated only by the width of the Idle and possessing its own parish church, quickly became absorbed as a suburb (despite the fact it was the earlier settlement), and by the early sixteenth century Northgate had been extended into the suburb of Moorgate, and Churchgate into Spital Hill, both of these being in the parish of Clarborough and subject to their own church about a mile distant.[30] To the South of the town the nearby hamlet of Thrumpton, in the parish of Ordsall, was close enough to be absorbed in a similar fashion, but a 'green belt' was ensured by the presence of the wet common lands. West Retford, Moorgate and Spital Hill fell outside the jurisdiction of the corporation, and it is plain that many complications stemmed from this apart from the fiscal difficulties already alluded to. Most serious, perhaps, was the dispute which followed on from the 1585 fire since the East Retford corporation went to the trouble to obtain support from the Queen and Privy Council and then complained when West Retford attempted to reap the benefits of their labour:

> They have driven into the sheriff and justices heads...that this Her Majesty's grant...is as well to their use and benefit as ours, the which (as we think) cannot be, by reason the consideration...is for and in respect of Her Highness own town of East Retford and the maintenance of her market there...they never contributing with us or once desirous to contribute with us towards the charges...we have been at for the same.[31]

A similar dispute broke out in 1638 following the improvements to the Idle. East Retford complained that West Retford had failed to pay its proper share of the costs of the work and it fell to the Commissioners for Sewers to rule that West Retford should contribute £25, though it was conceded that East Retford was the major beneficiary of the scheme.[32] Like West Retford, Moorgate and Spital Hill had different constables and churchwardens, and the difficulties in enforcing the law and church attendance were considerable.[33] The Commonwealth Surveyors of Church Lands attempted to cut the Gordian knot by suggesting the absorbtion of the Clarborough areas into East Retford in 1649, but the suggestion was not acted upon until an Act of Parliament finally altered the old boundaries in 1878.[34] As early as 1521, however, residents of West Retford and Moorgate were well aware of being part of the town, if not the corporation, and the definition of 'Retford' assumed in this study incorporates the Medieval borough along with its suburbs.[35]

The Hearth Tax returns of 1664 illustrate further the contrasting nature of the three segments of the town. From Table A it can be seen that the borough of East Retford possessed the highest proportion of large properties and the lowest proportion of small ones: at the top end of the scale this area had one house with nine hearths, two with seven, and three with six and five. West Retford and Clarborough, by contrast, had smaller proportions of large properties and larger proportions of small ones: indeed, the two parishes shared only three four-hearth houses between them as the largest properties — two in Clarborough and one in West Retford. Two conclusions emerge from this. Firstly, that the least substantial properties were in the suburbs where we might expect the poorest sections of the population to be gathered. Secondly, even the borough of East Retford does not rate that highly compared with other areas. The 1674 Hearth Tax return for Ordsall, for example, giving single hearth houses at 44%, two

Table A: **Household Size in the Extended Town, 1664** [36]

Hearths per house	East Retford	West Retford	Clarborough
One-hearth houses	59%	81%	77%
Two-hearth houses	25%	15%	12%
Three hearths and above	16%	4%	11%

hearth houses at 27% and those with three and above at 29% puts this rural parish on a higher plane of domestic comfort than its urban neighbour.[37] So, despite its superiority in the context of the extended town, East Retford was by no means rich or sophisticated.

This conclusion owes something to three natural disasters which struck the town between 1520 and 1642, all of them connected with the hearths and crowded housing already alluded to. In 1528 the town suffered a disastrous fire which destroyed 'almost the whole borough' and along with it the Moothall and possibly a portion of the parish church.[38] Out of 22 houses belonging to the town chantries seventeen were almost totally destroyed and only five were saved, a figure which, if projected to the town as a whole, would indicate that more than three-quarters of the buildings perished.[39] By 1540 rebuilding was well under way with a new Moothall 'lately builded' and the town 're-edified', but eight years later the damage was still not wholly restored and even in 1554 the proliferation of building materials left lying around the streets — principally clay and timber — indicate that many proper-ties were still not up to scratch.[40] Just when the town was on the road to recovery another fire, rather better documented, struck in 1585. By the 'especial means' of the town's high steward, Edward, 3rd Earl of Rutland, the annual fee farm and mill rents owing to the crown were relaxed and permis-sion was given for 'so much timber to be taken within the forest of Sherwood as will re-edify the late consumed houses'.[41] Moreover, letters were sent out from the Privy Council order-ing collections to be made in Nottinghamshire, Derbyshire, Lincolnshire and Yorkshire, as well as in the dioceses of York and Lincoln, and the bailiffs of the town, Edmund Spivy and Martin Billiald, travelled through these areas in an attempt to drum up support for their cause.[42] The reaction they encoun-tered was mixed. Some areas were 'very willing to satisfy our petitions', but Nottinghamshire posed a particular problem since they were 'crossed' there by the efforts of West Retford to raise money with the support of Edward Stanhope, a leading member of the commission of the peace; nevertheless, some local communities did respond, such as Worksop, which raised a collection for its near neighbours 'who had

3: Travellers enjoying a meal at an inn: Retford's inns and alehouses were an important feature of life given the town's proximity to the Great North Road.

4: A Stuart street scene: Newgate's open sewer must have been very similar to the one shown here.

lately suffered through their town having been burnt by fire'.[43] Hearing of the problems encountered in the raising of money for repairs, Rutland advised the bailiffs to petition the Assize judges at York to attempt to see that the Privy Council letters were enforced and he wrote to Mr Justice Rodes in their support. Writing to his brother John Manners at Helmsley, he requested him to assist:

> the poor men of the late burned town of Retford...in such sort as you best may amongst the justices, my good friends, with whom you are best acquainted.[44]

But despite this attempt to mobilise support for the town, progress appears to have been slow. In June 1586 the Privy Council wrote to the various sheriffs and JPs criticising their 'backwardness and coldness', and as late as 1598 a warrant was issued to the Exchequer authorising its officers to release more trees from Sherwood Forest and, also, relieving the town of six further years of rent which should have been paid to the Queen.[45] Finally, on August 19 1631, a third fire swept through East and West Retford, causing damage estimated at £1,300. On this occasion Richard Sloswicke and other inhabitants petitioned Lord Coventry, the Lord Keeper, by way of the Quarter Sessions with a view to raising money through a brief, but the response to the petition is not clear.[46]

Three major conflagrations in just over a hundred years is a startling record of misfortune for a small town, and they make Dorchester's 'fire from heaven' look small by comparison. Apart from creating serious psychological doubts about the relationship between God and the community, the fires put the town under severe financial pressure at times which sometimes coincided with national depressions. In the middle years of the sixteenth century, in the wake of the 1528 fire, several larger towns were complaining of hardship, and the period of rebuilding following the 1585 fire coincided with some of the bleakest years of the century.[47] Individuals were likely to be totally ruined by the experience, such as Richard Barker, shoemaker, who received a lease from the corporation in 1587:

> in consideration of the great losses, spoils and hinderances the said Richard Barker hath had and sustained by casualty

of fire to his great damage, loss and hinderance, almost to his utter undoing, ruin and decay.[48]

It is probable that the fires were caused by a proliferation of timber framed and thatched buildings and the existence in the town of an extensive domestic malting and candle making industry. Stores of wood bark in the tan yards must have created further problems. A special hazard might well have been the drying of flax in the malting kilns, a practice which Gervase Markham warned against in the seventeenth century. Retford's economy had shaped its fate as an urban tinderbox and given bad luck and a prevailing wind a major disaster could easily have been created out of a minor incident, especially in the dry months of summer. The will of Philip Syles, glasier, compiled just before the 1585 fire, confirms the picture of the crowded courts that made up the urban core of East Retford:

> one little house of my backside at my house end, with one shop and a parlour belonging to the same house...[and]...the little shop at my house end.[49]

No doubt it all perished in the catastrophic conflagration which Syles may just have lived to witness. Very few buildings earlier than the eighteenth century survive today in Retford, though the lines of many of the ancient burgage plots are still in place. The Sun Inn, opposite St Swithun's church, probably dates from the sixteenth century, but it is a rare survival. Local topography, therefore, provides ample evidence of the unsubstantial nature of the early town and the devastating impact of the three fires.[50]

Considerable attention has been paid in recent years to the question of demography not least as it applies to towns. Penelope Corfield has set down a 'numerical index' which aims to classify towns in terms of their population. These towns varied considerably in their demographic profiles, but a community needed to at least double its population between the 1520s and 1700 to keep pace with national trends of population growth.[52] The problems of assessing urban population are considerable, but the Centre for Urban History at the University of Leicester has made a useful start with a recently published work on small town demography.[53] The sources

Table B: **English Towns in relation to their Population**[51]

Designation	Population Estimate	Estimated number
Leading Provincial Centre	5,000+	31 or 32
Minor Regional Centre	2,000 - 5,000	40-50
Small Market Centre	Under 2,000	About 730

used for the earlier period are the obvious ones, such as the diocesan surveys of 1563 and 1603 and the Protestation Returns of 1642, with appropriate multiples applied.[54] According to the Leicester estimate, based on the 1603 survey, East Retford comes out with a population of 846 which, by the time of the Compton Census in 1676, had fallen to 600, a level of population which appears to have been in decline or was, at the very best, static.[55] The 1603 figure for Retford, if it was correct, would place the town on a par with communities such as Lutterworth in Leicestershire and Bakewell in Derbyshire and would make it smaller than its Nottinghamshire counterparts of Blyth (1,020) and Worksop (1,050).[56] If this sounds unlikely for the principal town of the Hundred, the authors suggest one reason for possible error:

> The most widespread single difficulty attending estimates of the kind attempted here concerns the geographical unit being observed. Settlements in general, and towns especially so, were no respectors of administrative boundaries. Some of our small towns (60 in all) comprised more than one parish. Other towns appear to have been coterminous with a single parish. But the commonest case was for a town to have made up a part of a parish — and an indeterminate part at that. What makes this particularly important is that most of the data before 1800...refers to the parish and not to the town.[57]

This is the very problem encountered in the case of Retford where the town was not coterminous with a single parish but spread out over three. This is why the Leicester estimates — based only on the parish and borough of East Retford — need to be revised.[58]

It is considered generally that parish register analysis provides the best estimate of population during this period, and register entries have been extracted for East Retford and Clarborough from the beginning of their records (in 1573 and 1567 respectively) up to the Civil War.[59] West Retford poses a major problem since the register is lost before 1772 and all that remains is a series of incomplete bishop's transcripts covering the years 1622-41. This is particularly frustrating because when Piercy was writing in 1828 the register certainly *was* extant: moreover it was said to commence in 1538 and was 'in most excellent preservation'.[60] The East Retford and Clarborough registers are reasonably well kept and in fair condition with the exception of a series of gaps in the East Retford burial register during the years 1587-88, 1593-95 and 1626-30. To provide a rural comparison with the urbanised areas, the Ordsall register was also examined. This turned out to be the best of the set with baptisms commencing in 1538, burials in 1556 and marriages in 1557: all continued through to the Civil War without interruption.

The Clarborough register provided some important clues which suggested lines of enquiry, and caveats, for the demographic study of the town. Firstly, between 1613 and 1633 the scribe had included the abode within the parish of all children born in Clarborough from which it was calculated that baptisms at Moorgate and Spital Hill made up 28% of the parish total.[61] This was valuable since it indicated that the urbanised portion of the parish — Moorgate and Spital Hill — comprised a significant proportion of the population, perhaps as much as a third when unmarried working people were taken into consideration. Secondly, a comparison of the Clarborough register with the surviving bishop's transcripts for the early seventeenth century revealed a number of anomalies which soon cast doubt on the accuracy of both sources. On occasion the transcript provided additional information (abodes being given on the 1608/9 transcript, for example, and abodes and occupations on that of 1613/14) but, in sixteen cases between 1620 and 1640, events recorded on the register did not get through to the transcript. All of this made it seem less likely that the fragmentary West Retford transcripts would yield much useful information.[62]

Cambridge Group *pro forma* PEF I, II and III were used to extract a record of events in the four parishes under study and, on that basis, graphs were drawn up relating baptisms, marriages and burials in the individual parishes.[63] In East Retford the death rate peaked dramatically in 1586-88, 1591 and 1616; there was also a sustained plateau of high mortalities over the period 1634-1647 with the period of the war being particularly badly affected. For 1587 and 1593-95 the register of burials is unreliable, and this is particularly frustrating because, in each case, it occurs close to a major mortality. The reason for this is impossible to determine, but it may be that in both cases we are dealing with extended mortalities which were, in fact, much worse than is indicated by the records. With people dying in large numbers the keeper of the register might well have grown lax in his duty of recording events accurately.[64] On several other occasions burials outstripped baptisms in a less dramatic fashion, notably in 1573-4, 1576, 1580-1, 1583-4, 1586, 1601-2 and 1607-08: during the period 1622-30 baptisms fell to a dangerously low level, though mortality appears to have been held in check, an interesting phenomenon which was to warrant further investigation. The adjoining and partially urbanised parish of Clarborough reflects, to some extent, this pattern of increased mortalities in 1588 and 1591; the East Retford increase in 1616 being delayed until 1618. In Clarborough there is no parallel to the increased plateau of deaths post-1634 as in East Retford. Burials outstripped baptisms in 1569, 1572, 1574, 1592-3, 1596-7, 1599, 1602, 1624-5, 1629, 1631 and 1633 but never on a very significant scale. Clarborough experienced a nadir of baptisms in 1616, but not the prolonged decline that affected East Retford in the next decade. The comparison between these two parishes and Ordsall is very striking. Here there was a significant mortality between 1557 and 1561 (which Piercy picked up in the vanished West Retford register) recording 82 deaths for that community between July 22 and October 12 1558.[65] During the whole year of 1558, at the height of the epidemic (which coincides with a national visitation of influenza) Ordsall suffered only sixteen deaths, a reflection of the greater virulence of disease in a more crowded urban setting. Piercy put down the mortality:

> to the low and swampy situation of part of the town, and from
> the noxious effluvia arising from the stagnant waters — the
> remains of the frequent floods of the river Idle.[66]

Had the registers of East Retford and Clarborough survived
for this early date we may well have seen a similar pattern and,
if the level of West Retford mortality was repeated, this was in
all likelihood the most devastating plague to hit the community between 1520 and 1642. Once Ordsall had recovered from
the mortality of 1557-61 it is notable that, thereafter, there were
no major peaks except for small increases in 1613 and 1619;
there was an imbalance of burials over baptisms in 1566, 1568,
1571, 1573, 1575, 1591, 1601, 1607, 1617, 1623 and 1625, and
Ordsall, like East Retford, has a notable, but slight, trough in
the level of baptisms between 1623 and 1630. However, this
community escaped entirely the high death rates which beset
East Retford and Clarborough around 1590.

Jonathan Barry suggests that there is little evidence that
urban mortalities were caused by starvation, but rural people
might well have moved into the towns during periods of
hardship and succumbed more readily to diseases to which
townsmen were immune.[67] The worst years of dearth and
high food prices in Elizabethan England were 1586/7 and
1594-98. It is interesting that the beginning of the first Retford
mortality corresponds closely with the first of these, which
was also a period of depression in the cloth trade. Deaths
began to rise sharply in East Retford during September 1586
and reached a peak in January 1587 with fourteen burials,
hardly an epidemic, but well above the average for the town:
between February and April they declined again to the levels
of the previous autumn and then, between May 1587 and
March 1588, the record becomes defective. When the register
takes up again, in April 1588, burials remained at a relatively
high level until the end of the year. In Clarborough the
mortality for 1586 was slight and only began to increase
appreciably after January 1587, peaking twelve months later
with ten mortalities (January 1588) and remaining a significant problem for the remainder of that year. In both cases this
was a fairly extended, but not devastating, mortality which
was at its worst in the winter months. What sort of people
were affected? The Clarborough register is much more help-

ful in this respect, because it enables us to differentiate between children and adults and to establish family relationships: it also occasionally includes a description of the deceased person and sometimes a note of unusual circumstances. From this information it can be deduced that about
half of the deaths in 1587 and 1588 were of children and that
six widows died in the latter year: on January 12 1588 four
females comprising two married women, a widow and a child
were interred at East Retford, a rare occurrence for Clarborough
parishioners even when they came from Moorgate or Spital
Hill.[68] It is open to speculation whether it was inclement
climatic conditions or fear of contagion which led to this
unusual expedient. Of the child burials, it was quite usual for
more than one child from the same family to perish, and
sometimes one or more parent would follow within a short
period. John Metcalfe, for example, lost three children in
January 1588, Ann, Alice and an unnamed son; William
Acreley lost his son William and his daughter Elizabeth in
April, and the Smyths were virtually destroyed as a family
unit, William Smyth losing his wife and two daughters during
the years 1587/88.[69] The 1591 mortality at Clarborough
followed a similar pattern: half of the deaths were of children,
often family units were involved, and four widows died.[70]
The only other clue as to the origin of the mortality is that
several 'strangers' were buried between 1587 and 1592, one of
them being 'found dead in the snow' in January 1587.[71]

It is more difficult to reconstruct what went on at East
Retford because the register is less informative. Though there
were families that suffered more than one bereavement — the
Blanckleys in 1586, the Moults in 1587, the Hydes in 1588, the
Bishops in 1591, for example — there is less of an emphasis on
family-linked mortality than at Clarborough.[72] The phenomenon seems rather more random, striking down the town
vicar, Christopher Say (April 1587) and obscure characters
such as John Brislechurch (November 1586) who do not fit into
the traditional name patterns of the locality.[73] It would be
speculative to attempt an interpretation based on such scanty
evidence, but it seems likely that the beginning of the problem
in East Retford was linked with the disastrous fire of 1585,
followed by a bad harvest and high food prices in 1586, a

depression in the cloth trade, and harsh weather conditions in the winters of 1587 and 1588. The fire deprived a substantial section of the population of proper housing; it also may well have destroyed food stocks, and its demoralising effect on the communal psychology will have been very considerable indeed. In these circumstances, with the population unable to obtain fresh supplies of food because of shortages, and people huddled together in overcrowded squats or living under canvas, it was likely that infection would have spread and the harsh winter weather would have picked off the weakest — classically widows and young children. The nature of the disease at work, if indeed it was a single disease, is now impossible to determine, but typhus, scarlet fever and diphtheria might be possible contenders. It is likely that the same set of circumstances affected East Retford and Clarborough, though in different degrees. The hypothesis is strengthened when we recall that Ordsall escaped entirely from any abnormal mortality during the years 1586-91.[74]

The mortality of the late 1580s is comparatively well documented, but over a more extended time scale it assumes less significance alongside other demographic crises which can only be hinted at because of a lack of records. In the absence of parish registers mortality peaks can be highlighted by a comparison of numbers of wills brought to probate over five year periods, and when this test was applied to the extended urban area of Retford the register data was confirmed and new problems were revealed.[75] The mortalities of the late 1580s and 1616-18 showed up clearly, with a marked increase in people making wills in the latter crisis.[76] A new peak was revealed in the early 1520s, declining, and then rising to a plateau in the early 1540s when Thomas Marshall left a legacy to the poor of Welham Moorhouse 'weekly during the plague time'.[77] However, the real crisis came in the late 1550s as recorded in the Ordsall register and discussed by Piercy for West Retford. On the evidence of wills there is no doubt that this crisis was equally serious in East Retford, probably more so, since the total of 47 probates for the five year batch is made up of 26 from East Retford, sixteen from West Retford and five from Moorgate and Spital Hill. Many of these wills were made by people of less substance than those who normally

5: A countrywoman rides to town with her wares: Retford's relationship with the surrounding villages was vital to the economic well-being of the community.

6: Men at work: the town took on the appearance of a permanent building site following two disastrous fires in the sixteenth century.

made wills, and a high proportion were drafted by married men with young families: an awareness in them of the possibility of sudden or multiple death was commonplace, illustrated by Bartholomew Nickerson's gloomy resignation in October 1558 'if it please God to call me and my wife forth of this world or my children'.[78] In 1560 John Wymoke left property for the support of 'visited houses with plague or extreme sickness', but whether he meant by this dwellings specifically reserved for infected persons, or merely plague-stricken households, is not clear. Nevertheless, the mortality of the late 1550s must have been uppermost in his mind when this legacy was made.[79]

In an attempt to arrive at a better overview of population during the period of the registers, and assess the impact of the 1585 fire and its consequences, five year averages were calculated from the PEF data for East Retford, Clarborough and Ordsall.[80] But in order to obtain an accurate assessment of the town in its entirety the following adjustments were made. Firstly, 35% of the Clarborough figures were added to East Retford to compensate for Moorgate and Spital Hill. Secondly, a round average figure of 250 was added to represent West Retford: this was arrived at by assessing the five year averages for 1627-31 and 1632-36, along with a figure derived from the diocesan survey of 1603.[81] The resultant graph[82] shows the real population of the town at about 1,150 in 1603 rather than the 846 suggested by the Leicester estimate: this would put it on a par with Mansfield in Nottinghamshire or Ashby-de-la-Zouch in Leicestershire, and would make it slightly larger than Blyth and Worksop, its immediate competitor market towns in the Bassetlaw Hundred.[83] But, more interesting than this is the dramatic fluctuation revealed in the population of the town between 1576 and 1640. Already in excess of 1,400 in 1576 — representing a good recovery after the 1528 fire and the 1558 plague — the population remained constant until it collapsed in the wake of the 1585 disaster, falling to 1,050 by 1600. A short period of recovery and relative stability in the early years of the seventeenth century was followed by a further dramatic collapse between 1616 and 1630 which cannot be ascribed either to mortality or known natural disaster. The only explanation is that people were moving away from Retford in considerable numbers, or not marrying and raising families there. The reason for this is postulated in Chapter 4.[84] The population of the town reached its nadir in the late 1620s — at about 850 souls — but thereafter it recovered swiftly to exceed its 1576 figure on the eve of the Civil War. This view fits well with the complaints of Chesterfield in 1636 that Retford was 'a much greater town'. By then the population was approaching 1,500, comparable to that of Chesterfield at the time of the Hearth Tax returns.[85] Allowing for some special pleading on the part of the Chesterfield burgesses, who might have compared Retford's buoyant prosperity with their own faltering trade, the statement is just about acceptable. And, indeed, the same assessment which valued Newark at twice as much as Retford, also works out quite well in terms of the revised population estimate of the town.[86] Retford's recovery also helps to explain why there was such doubt about its true worth: there would be a tendency amongst many people, particularly outsiders, to see it as it was (and this was no doubt an illusion the burgesses were happy to preserve) rather than what it had become in very recent years. Though still quite firmly a 'small market centre' by the standards of Corfield's template, the experience of Retford confirms her belief that urban population growth was 'not necessarily continuous'.[87] What East Retford had suffered in the years between 1585 and 1630 was the 'relative eclipse' that was common amongst small towns: the experience of the 1630s proved that the town was able to replenish its population by attracting new migrants from its hinterland as economic prospects improved. The notion of inter-relationship between town and countryside is confirmed by the five year averages for Ordsall which show a steady decline setting in after 1590 and then a recovery from the 1620s onwards, a pale reflection of what can be seen in Retford. Clearly, more analysis work is required, even within this limited area, before firm conclusions can be reached on the important question of who drew migrants from whence, when and why.

Retford was, therefore, a substantial market and administrative centre during the Tudor and Stuart period and one which defies a county-based analysis: its horizons were always much wider than the shire of which it was a part. For the historian one of the major problems is one of definition, since the Medieval borough, which enjoyed extensive corporate privileges, was only a part of the 'town' as it was generally viewed. Contemporaries tended to try to use this confusion to their advantage as circumstances changed, happy to utilise the cheap labour provided by the surburbs when times were good but closing ranks around their borough privileges if they felt at all threatened. Those same contemporaries would have been aware of being part of a community in a perpetual state of flux. Fire, pestilence and economic depression took its toll on the town at an alarming rate and denied it the luxury of sustained growth. Indeed, what is remarkable is not that Retford failed to reach national targets of 'expansion', but that it held its own during a period in which the cards seemed inexorably stacked against it. Many townsmen came from the surrounding country areas and maintained interests there once they had settled in Retford. The 'urban psychology' of the place might, therefore, seriously be called in question because, despite its civic panoply, its close inter-relationship with the rural hinterland was to remain the base-line of its prosperity, mentality and *raison d'etre*.

FOOTNOTES AND REFERENCES

1. L. T. Smith (ed), *The Itinerary of John Leland*, 4, p.16.
2. J A, B(lack) B(ook), f.178.
3. *Ibid.*, RB 2, ff.27/8, F. and J. White, *History of Nottingham* (1844), pp.47/8, 667.
4. H. H. Copnall, *Nottinghamshire County Records* (1915), p.113.
5. White, p.660. For the geographical context of the town see Appendix, Map 1.
6. *Ibid.*, p.667.
7. HMC, *Rutland*, 1, p.502.
8. BI, P(robate) R(egister) 15, pt.3, f.665.
9. Piercy, pp.5/6, E. Ekwall, *The Concise Oxford Dictionary of English Place-Names* (1966), p.385. For the appeal of linking the placename to the processing of flax, see Chapter 4,

pp.102-4.

10. Piercy, p.9.

11. White, p.660.

12. R. E. Glasswell (ed.), *The Lay Subsidy of 1334*, Records of Social and Economic History, New Series II (1975), p.233.

13. *Ibid.*, pp.227, 228, 234.

14. JA, RB 2, f.25.

15. PRO, SP 16/347/75, *CSP Dom, 1635-36*, p.253, *1636-37*, p.288, *1637*, p.158.

16. White, p.666.

17. C. E. Long (ed.), *Diary of the Marches of the Royal Army*, Camden Society, 74, 1859, p.227.

18. *HMC, Rutland*, 1, p.234. See also *CSP Dom, 1619-23*, p.427 for a later example. In 1627 a considerable stock of arms and armour was moved from the house of Gervase Markham to those of Leonard Cosin, bailiff, and William Jepson 'a dresser of armour'. NAO, DD 3P, 17/1b.

19. *CSP Dom, 1629-31*, p.355.

20. Out of 68 JPs for Nottinghamshire 31 sat at the Quarter Sessions at Retford between 1603 and 1642: these included Sir Henry Pierrepoint (1603-15), John, Earl of Clare (1625-37), Robert, Earl of Kingston (1633-41), and Sir Gervase Clifton (1609-32). NAO, QSMI/1-12.

21. M. W. Bishop, 'The Origins of East Retford', *TTS*, 82, 1978, p.26.

22. JA, BB f.178. For a detailed plan of the town see Appendix, Map 2. I am grateful to Malcolm Dolby for his observations on the town ditch.

23. *Ibid.*

24. *Ibid.*, BI, PR 14 f.283.

25. JA, BB f.178.

26. BI, PR 16 f.170.

27. *Ibid.*, PR 23 f.851: JA, BB ff.173-79, RB 2 ff.85-99: NAO, Mee, 1/88. 1F/3. Why Northgate has become the modern Churchgate, and the ancient Churchgate Chapelgate, defies a ready explanation.

28. JA, BB f.175.

29. *Ibid.*, ff.148, 173.

30. The derivation of Spital Hill is interesting since it implies the existence in the town of a Medieval hospital. This is not generally acknowledged, but Piercy noted a Hospital of St. Oswald founded by Robert de Beck in the twelfth century and

granted to Thomas, 1st Earl of Rutland, by Henry VIII. If this is correct it may also explain the 'chapel' of Chapelgate. JA, BB f.174.

31. BC, Letters, 26/4/1585.
32. JA, RB 2 f.27/8.
33. See Chapter 9, Chapter 4, pp. 120-1.
34. Kidson, p.95.
35. BI, PR 9 f.230.
36. W. F. Webster (ed), *Nottinghamshire Hearth Tax, 1664:1674*, Thoroton Society, Record Series, 37, 1988, pp. 25/6, 48.
37. *Ibid.*, p.128.
38. A. H. Thompson, *The Chantry Certificate Rolls for the County of Nottingham*, TTS, 17, 1913, pp.113, 160: Kidson, p.14.
39. JA, RB l (Chantry Property). An unusual inscribed stone was set up in the parish church to commemorate this event and the consequent rebuilding. Piercy, pp.98/9.
40. JA, RB 2 ff.85-99, *TTS*, 17, p.160, Smith, 4, p. 16.
41. *CSP Dom, 1581-90*, p.235, BC, Letters, 26/4/1585.
42. *APC, 14*, pp.160/61, BC, Letters, 26/4/1585.
43. *Ibid.*, Kidson, p.17.
44. BC, Letters, 16/7/1585.
45. *APC, 14*, p.160, *CSP Dom, 1598-1601*, p.133. This privilege caused complications because in 1627 the town was called to account by the King's Receiver for Nottinghamshire and Derbyshire to explain arrears in the fee farm payments. Piercy, p.23.
46. NAO, QSMI/7, Mee, 1/22. 1E/16.
47. Barry, p.53.
48. RM, Ancient Deeds (1587).
49. BI, PR 23 f.104.
50. Pevsner describes the Sun as 'a low, basically timber-framed building, now stuccoed, probably sixteenth century'. N. Pevsner, *Nottinghamshire* (1979), p.297. It is possible that more evidence of early building survives beneath more recent frontages and in 'backsides'.
51. Barry, p.49.
52. *Ibid.*, p.52.
53. Clark, Gaskin and Wilson, *op.cit.*
54. Houses 5.75: households/families 4.25: commicants (male) 3.0: communicants (male and female) l.5: individuals/souls etc. l.0. *Ibid.*, p.v.

55. *Ibid.*, pp.129/30 and *Corrigenda*.
56. *Ibid.*, pp.29, 101, 129.
57. *Ibid.*, p.iii.
58. In 1947 A. C. Wood stated of Retford,'We have no figures from which to estimate its population, but even in the middle of the seventeenth century it was still under a thousand'. A. C. Wood, *A History of Nottinghamshire* (1947), p.159.
59. For a general discussion see E. A. Wrigley and R. S. Schofield, *The Population History of England 1541-1871* (1981). The data for the parish register analysis can be consulted at NUCLH.
60. Piercy, p.181. For the years 1623-26 and 1637-39 all or part of the transcript is missing. SML, West Retford BT.
61. Clarborough 35%: Moorgate and Spital Hill 28%: Little Gringley 22%: Welham 14%: Bolham 0.8%.
62. SML, BTs for East Retford, West Retford and Clarborough.
63. See Appendix, Graphs 1, 2, 3.
64. This argument is counteracted somewhat by Piercy's observations on the missing West Retford register: if the mortality had been a really devastating one it would certainly have spread to West Retford and presumably provoked a comment from Piercy. Piercy, p.181.
65. *Ibid.*
66. *Ibid.*
67. Barry, p.16.
68. NAO, C(larborough) P(arish) R(egister),(1587/88).
69. *Ibid.*
70. *Ibid.*, (1591).
71. *Ibid.*, (1587/88, 1591).
72. *Ibid.*, E(ast) R(etford) P(arish) Register), (1586/88, 1591).
73. *Ibid.*
74. Little can be said about the mortality of 1616 except that it claimed 43 lives in twelve months, most of them perishing between January and September: this may suggest a shortage of food from the previous year, though the high proportion of will makers who died implies that this mortality was not associated with the very poor and was therefore not famine related. NAO, ERPR, CPR (1616).
75. See Appendix, Graph 4.
76. The general trend, highlighted by the graph, is that more people were making wills as the period progressed. Whether this reflects a steadily growing population or a greater

fashion for will making is more difficult to determine.

77.   BI, PR 11 f.666.
78.   *Ibid.*, 15c f.420.
79.   *Ibid.*, 16 ff.144/5.
80.   See Appendix, Graph 5.
81.   1603, 222: 1627-31, 255: 1632-36, 312. The actual average derived from these figures is 263, adjusted down to 250 to allow for a margin of error.
82.   See Appendix, Graph 6.
83.   Clark, Gaskin and Wilson, pp.101, 129.
84.   See pp.112-3.
85.   Clark, Gaskin and Wilson, p.29.
86.   Newark was estimated at 2,602 in 1603. *Ibid.*, p.129.
87.   Barry, p.45.

Chapter 2

CIVIL DIFFERENCES

*We have already found their new devised innovations very
dangerous, some of their new found faction continuing still
so mutinous by occasion of their discontented humours and
sundry complaints.[1]*

East Retford was a royal manor and on the eve of the
Reformation its civic government rested on a conglomeration
of Medieval charters built up since the reign of Richard I,
usefully precied in Piercy's 'recapitulation of ancient grants'
and set out in the extant confirmation from Elizabeth I obtained in 1562.[2] After 300 years East Retford was considered
'a free town of itself', governed by 'bailiffs and burgesses' or
'bailiffs, burgesses and commonality', if a wider definition
was employed.[3] In either event the burgesses, or free townsmen, played a vital role, since in 1279 the town was granted
to them in fee farm by the King on condition they paid £10 *per
annum* for the privilege.[4] This 'King's rent' continued to be
paid throughout the period under review, and the Exchequer
quittances for the years 1597-1604 still survive in the town
museum.[5] Townsmen were, therefore, conscious of being
inhabitants of a 'royal' borough, and the bailiffs took some
pride in their perceived role as 'King's bailiffs' of the town.[6]
Burgesses enjoyed a monopoly of trade and after 1571, when
the privilege was revived, they had the right to vote in
Parliamentary elections: moreover, they were exempt from
all foreign service, had an entitlement to 'gates' on the Cars
and Commons and as late as 1655 certificates were issued
proving their freedom from 'any toll, pannage or murrage'
anywhere in England.[7] The precise extent of burgess rights
was sometimes a subject of heated debate, and by 1606
Richard Welch, butcher, had had many 'suits and variances'
with the corporation over the occupation of stalls in the

Moothall and market place. Welch believed that his freedom entitled him to free stallage and that he could rent out these stalls if he decided not to use them himself. The respected local gentleman, Sir John Thornhaugh, was called in to arbitrate, and he ruled that Welch should pay for his Moothall stall 'as a stranger shall do' but that he could let out his market stall 'to some sufficient victualler' if he wished, at his own profit.[8] The corporation, despite its deference to Thornhaugh, was not at all pleased with this decision, and when Welch's son, Thomas, came to receive his freedom in 1620 he was made to swear that he would never revive his father's claims and would not rent out his market place stall 'but only to stand there himself, if he so think good'.[9] But most important, from a political point of view at least, was the right of a burgess to participate in the internal government of the town, which he did through the election of bailiffs and the holding of minor office.

The number of burgesses at any given time is difficult to determine, and it fluctuated as the fortunes of the borough ebbed and flowed. In 1388 twenty burgesses entered into the agreement for the new Moothall:[10] 47 were involved in the petitions to the Earl of Rutland in 1598;[11] and 85 voted in the contested Parliamentary election of 1624, by far the best guide since this was a situation in which not a single voice was wasted.[12] If the population of East Retford at this date stood at about 500 — excluding the suburban areas of West Retford and Clarborough where none of the inhabitants, in theory, had burgess rights — approximately half of the adult male population of the borough enjoyed burgess status, a figure which falls to 30% in the context of the extended town. This coveted privilege was obtained in one of three ways. Firstly, by serving an apprenticeship in the town: secondly, by being the eldest son of a burgess born after his father had received his freedom; and thirdly, by redemption, or the payment of an agreed sum into the town chamber. Redemption costs could vary considerably, but in 1608 it was ruled that it should be no less than £1 6s 0d.[13] In any event the new burgess was expected to take an oath 'to maintain all laudable ways and customs of this town', and if at any future date he failed in his obligations he could be disfranchised 'and for ever taken and reputed as a foreigner', unless he compounded with the chamber for readmission.[14] The rights of the 'commonality' — who comprised all townsmen of non-burgess status — were undefined, but they were clearly regarded as possessing some sort of voice in local affairs: they were mentioned as part of the incorporation of the town in 1518, though such references became increasingly rare as the sixteenth century progressed.[15]

The bailiffs were elected on Michaelmas Day from amongst the burgesses assembled in the Moothall, the centre of civic government. The Moothall, occasionally but less commonly referred to as the Guildhall, was located at the Northern end of the market place and for a small community was an impressive focus of local pride. Originally built in 1388 of timber and slate, it was replaced after the 1528 fire when Leland referred to 'a goodly house or Moothall lately builded in Retford'.[16] Its ground floor was given over to a market hall and in the upper story, approached by an external stairway, courts, elections and public meetings were held. From a cupola perched on the roof top a bell gave warning of impending happenings, such as the commencement of fairs and markets, and petty offenders were exposed in a 'stock house' beneath the stairway. For certain purposes its location was not central enough to the heart of the market place, so when royal proclamations and other important information needed to be announced by the bellman this was done from the upper chamber of a shop near the Broad Stone over which the corporation reserved rights of access.[17] In 1279 the burgesses had obtained authority to elect 'their own proper bailiffs... who shall keep the same town and exercise the office of bailiff there' and on election days the Moothall surged with activity as new officers took their oaths and old ones rendered up their accounts.[18] Generally two bailiffs were chosen to serve for a year, but quite commonly in the sixteenth century there appear to have been three. Two burgesses were also selected as chamberlains to supervise the town chamber, or treasury, and between them the bailiffs and chamberlains were entrusted with the keys of a chest in which the 'bonds and evidences' of the town were kept. Once installed these officers were expected to work in close co-operation with the wardens of the companies, and a council of twelve burgesses, 'according to ordinances from time to time by them established'.[19] To create these ordinances a court of orders met quarterly or as often as the bailiffs thought appropriate 'for the good government thereof [i.e. of the town] and the better execution of the ancient orders here'.[20] Membership of the court was made up of the bailiffs, wardens and council, a group of no more than eighteen and no fewer than twelve burgesses, who had the effective control of the borough.[21] This was a form of government which had become customary by the second half of the sixteenth century, but its details were nowhere spelt out in the Medieval grants. It was government by 'our old and ancient orders', as the corporation put it, a form of oligarchic control which had been devised largely by the townsmen themselves. Given a comparatively small number of burgesses, it was probably broad-based enough to allow anyone with serious political ambitions to obtain a foothold in local government, but it was not designed to cope with concerted opposition or a legalistic investigation of its *raison d'etre*.

The elected officers were supported by permanent officials who received patents from the corporation. The high steward was the principal of these, but there was also a learned steward, or recorder, who was generally a professional lawyer. Since there were no borough Quarter Sessions the learned steward, in fact, had little to do, and as the corporation saw it he was there merely:

> to help us in doubtful matters in law arising in our court, and such like accidents concerning law wherein the bailiffs should demand his opinion.[22]

The town had been granted extensive civil and common law jurisdiction during the Middle Ages, and it appears that the day-to-day running of this was entrusted to a deputy steward, or town clerk, appointed under a separate patent by the corporation. When William Watson was appointed in 1587, for example, he was empowered to hold all courts 'according to the custom of the said town time out of mind used', along with all fees and emoluments as of 'ancient time', and power to nominate deputies: the office was granted for life with a fee of 40s *per annum*.[23]   In practice this probably meant the supervision of the court leet and court baron of the town which had cognizance of a wide range of offences, as illustrated by the only surviving court roll of 1554.[24] Retford was too small a community to require extensive legal facilities of its own, and it is clear that crimes of a more serious nature were dealt with in the county Quarter Sessions, which often met at Retford, or at the Assizes. Finally, the corporation employed two sergeants-at-mace as enforcement officers; a bellman or town crier; and waits to provide entertainment on festive occasions.[25] It was an establishment which was quite adequate, and indeed possibly over-complicated, for a small town in which the panoply of power tended to obscure the reality.

The town chamber drew income from three sources; from the exercise of its legal and commercial privileges and from the management of property. The court leet and court baron imposed small fines (generally of 2d and 4d) for a wide range of transgressions, and it also enforced contributions of 3d from the burgesses towards the King's rents:[26] this custom ceased in 1622 when it was decided that the fee farm should be paid out of the profits of the town mills.[27] In addition, the court of orders, under the bailiffs, received payments for burgess admissions and compositions, and half of the fines imposed by the companies traditionally went to the town chamber.[28] The borough also had the right to tax its inhabitants, but the details of this are obscure though it appears that a levy might have been imposed on a burgess's estate following his death:[29] possibly the principle was similar to that which existed at Oxford in 1608:

> We think it lawful and reasonable to use taxation of the citizens for any such purpose, if need be. And for relief of all such as are visited with the plague, and for watching to keep them in their houses or other places when they are removed, we use taxation of freemen and all inhabitants towards their relief and keeping.[30]

Commercial income rested on the revenues of three fairs and a Saturday market. An eight day fair was held in March around the feast of St Gregory the Bishop: a six day event in July based on the feast of St Margaret: and a four day fair in September around the feast of St Matthew the Apostle. These must have brought a substantial income, usefully spaced out to coincide with the spring, summer and autumn trading cycles.[31]

The town estate in 1530 comprised thirteen houses in Retford and 48 acres of land in Ordsall and Clarborough.[32] The events of the Reformation added to this a further ten houses in the town, originally the property of the St Mary and St Trinity chantries, and the fee farm of the Idle mills, previously in the hands of Welbeck abbey.[33] More controversial was the corporation's management of the grammar school endowment after 1551, a position of trust which was to cause acrimonious dissention as late as the nineteenth century.[34] Despite this, the sixteenth century saw a substantial rise in the volume of property for which the chamber was responsible. It was leased generally for periods of 21 years (and sometimes more) after 'a competent sum of money' had been paid as a fine: tenants of burgage property were obliged to maintain it 'with thatch, mortar, lath and nail at his own proper costs', with 'great timber only' the responsibility of the landlord.[35] In leases of school lands tenants were bound, in addition to their rents, to provide geese or capons for 'the dinner of the great leet', a festive occasion which was, no doubt, keenly anticipated by the whole corporation. This event was probably the 'venison feast' for which the waits were called out to provide entertainment.[36]

Out of the money collected in this way certain sums were earmarked for the personal use of the bailiffs and chamberlains. In 1600, for example, the chamberlains were entitled to the 2s stall rents charged on butchers in the basement of the Moothall, along with other rents totalling £3 2s 8d.[37] Out of this they were expected to fund the miscellaneous costs of their offices as set out in an account of 1666.[38] After the costs of the school had been met and appropriate salaries and fees paid, the residue was placed in the town chest, or hutch, to await any extraordinary demand on communal funds, such as the cost of obtaining the new charter of 1607 or of prosecuting the case in Parliament in 1624. Legal costs were indeed the major drain on any surplus the town might have been able to build up, because with so many and varied interests controversies were bound to arise. In the 1540s the corporation had to answer suits in Chancery alleging wrongful imprisonment and seizure of goods, a problem which recurred in 1604 and

1617.[39] In 1601, which must have been a fairly typical year, the corporation was defending itself against Henry Parnell, a burgess, who alleged that his malt had been unlawfully taken as a toll by the sergeant-at-mace, and prosecuting Gervase Markham who was refusing to pay taxes, duties or King's rents and encroaching on Newgate Green.[40] It was at times like this that the learned steward came into his own and, indeed, the high steward too who might be asked to consider 'some course as his Lordship shall think of to defend them'.[41]

To what extent did the corporation perceive of the needs of the community over and above its own oligarchical control of the town? The grammar school and the corporation almshouses, discussed elsewhere, were the main public institutions of Tudor Retford, and the Moothall was, no doubt, an important social axis where wedding feasts and similar occasions might be celebrated. A common brewhouse and bakehouse was supported, and the 'still' mentioned in 1588 may well be connected with the former.[42] Private enterprise occasionally weighed in to bolster civic provision, but such intrusions were rare. In 1571 Sir John Hercy gave to the town 'one house ready framed as it lieth in the park to set over their cross', and in 1578 Nicholas Pettinger II contributed a met of rye to the corporation 'to the buying of their bell'.[43] Frances Rose suspected the inertia with which new initiatives were likely to be greeted when she made the following bequest in 1605:

> I give 6s 8d to the making of a common washing stool for the benefit of the poor of the town if the town of East Retford will lay the same money to it, or else the legacy to be void.[44]

If the bailiffs, then, were far from innovative in their approach to town government, at least they did their best to maintain the *status quo* and prevent the worst excesses of anti-social behaviour on the part of their neighbours. The court roll of 1554 records an active preoccupation with the maintenance of pavements and drains, and also a determination to prevent the blockage of the streets by muck heaps, clay heaps, ling stacks, piles of timber and clogs, and the offensive 'issues' from pig sties and maltings.[45] Baking, brewing and candle-making were restricted to prescribed places, as much because of the fire risk as the protection of the manorial monopoly perhaps, and butchers and tanners were similarly prevented from plying their anti-social trades in

7: The market place and old town hall in 1848: despite its classical appearance, the old town hall shared the same location, and basic plan, as the sixteenth century Moothall.

8: Edward Manners, 3rd Earl of Rutland, who used his influence as high steward to arbitrate in the disputes which divided the burgesses in the mid-1580s.

public. People guilty of encroaching on common lanes or common ground were punished, as were those 'for disobedience' (presumably to the bailiffs) or for undertaking violent frays. Unusual offenders were Robert Drayton 'for sending not for the ale tasters': Henry Webster 'for wheels binding in [the] street' and Nicholas Wilson 'for keeping unlawful games in his house on Michaelmas day last and divers other times'.[46] By the mid-sixteenth century offences such as these must have been prosecuted in Retford for centuries, and at this level town government owed little to the Reformation or the policies of the Tudor rulers. The corporation too was remarkably resistant to change, basking lazily in the protection of its ancient charters and doing just as little as was needed to survive. However, the more complex central administration of the sixteenth century was placing new demands on town government, for example the supervision of the grammar school and its lands, and it remained to be seen whether or not the traditional administrative system would be able to cope with these changes.

The oligarchical nature of the old corporation is well illustrated by Sir George Chaworth's belief that he could obtain his own way in the town by keeping on the right side of two brothers: David Watson, bailiff in 1586 and 1590, and William Watson, deputy steward and town clerk after 1587; 'friend Watsons, as I have found you mine assured', he wrote to them in 1590, '... as my last request of all friendship that ever hath been between us'.[47] The Watsons were indeed influential in supporting the Rutland interest, but theirs was not a position won without opposition. Their protagonist was Thomas Symcock, son of a Somerset gentleman, who had settled in Nottinghamshire. Symcock, a lawyer of the Middle Temple, had become learned steward of the borough soon after 1588, probably through the influence of the Earl of Rutland since he served the Countess as a legal and electoral agent in 1591/2.[48] However, he also had contacts with Gilbert Talbot, 7th Earl of Shrewsbury, which placed him in an interesting position in the context of the covert intrigues going on with regard to the high stewardship and Parliamentary seats of East Retford after 1588.[49] Symcock, who was a JP for Nottinghamshire and obtained property in Retford, was clearly determined to make a mark in local affairs and he viewed his learned stewardship as an obvious vehicle of advancement.[50] It is likely that he exploited latent opposition to the oligarchs already evident within the town, because even before the death of the 3rd Earl of Rutland in 1587 a 'new found faction' had been 'impeached' before the high steward:

> who so sharply in the presence of many admonished them to take heed ... for if at any time after he should understand them any more thereof to be complained on, he would not only thrust them out of the company but also move the bailiffs to disfranchise them.[51]

The reason for this confrontation is not clear, but it may have been connected with radical religious opinion or controversies arising from the monies collected as a result of the 1585 fire. Rutland was also possibly concerned about the existence in the town of an embrionic Talbot faction which over the long term might have been detrimental to the influence of his family. Alternatively, Rutland's ambiguous use of the word 'company' might indicate a commercial dispute, since at this time textile towns, such as Retford, were becoming divided over the 'new draperies' and the corporation always had a high proportion of mercers and drapers in it.[52]

The best clues we have to the motives of the 'new found faction' are to be seen in William Spivy, one of its leading members. Spivy was a draper and a well connected man in the town, his father, Edmund Spivy, having been one of the bailiffs who had travelled around collecting money under the Privy Council mandate following the 1585 fire.[53] Yet the Spivys were in all likelihood viewed with some suspicion since their family roots were in West Retford and not in the borough. William Spivy's mother was Anne Denman, niece of Sir John Hercy, which meant that he was a nephew of the influential West Retford puritan clerics William and Francis Denman and cousin of John Denman who married the sister of the puritan divine, Walter Travers.[54] William Spivy's sister, Isabel, married in turn into the noted Protestant families of Pettinger and Sloswicke; indeed, his cousin John Denman and his brother-in-law John Sloswicke were to turn out to be amongst the leading religious radicals of the town.[55] Spivy's firm Protestantism, and probable puritanism, is borne out by the preamble of his will, written, as he says:

> considering the frailty of man and how necessary it is to be in a continual readiness whensoever the good pleasure of Almighty God is to call...And first I give and bequeth my soul unto the hands of Almighty God hoping by the only merits of Jesus Christ his son and by his death and passion which he suffered for me to be saved and my body to be buried in the parish church of Grantham...from whence my trust is that my body shall arise and see the glorious coming of my saviour Christ and be partaker of his heavenly kingdom prepared for all true believers.[56]

Spivy's impeccable puritan credentials were combined with an eye for profit which meant that by the time of his death in 1603 he was certainly one of the wealthiest citizens of the town. All of this, no doubt, prompted resentment and envy amongst other, less successful, men. It is possible that in his business practices Spivy was thought to have been profiteering from the cheap lightweight materials which the older and more traditional merchants regarded as anathema, the so-called 'new draperies' which were causing a stir in other fabric producing centres at about this time. What is beyond doubt is that after the mid-1580s puritans were feeling themselves more overtly under threat because of the activities of Archbishop Whitgift, a situation intensified in Retford because of the death of their main local protector William Denman, rector of Ordsall and lord of West Retford, in 1587. Worst of all, perhaps, for the established burgesses of the town 'the new found faction' might have been regarded as savouring too much of *West* Retford in terms of its family connections and maverick attitude to traditional commercial regulation. In the years after the fire this had a special significance since East and West Retford were in direct competition for the relief funds available and one of the major collectors for the borough — Edmund Spivy — might have been seen to have had divided loyalties. It would not have taken such a great leap of the imagination to have seen in the 'faction' an attempt from the West to subvert the corporation of East Retford and somehow make it subject to the old enemy. All manner of desperate thoughts could have been encouraged by the situation of utter desperation, the result of fire and plague, which characterised the town in the late 1580s and in this Retford may well have suffered a crisis of conscience similar to that noted by Underdown in seventeenth-century Dorchester.

By 1592 the corporation was concerned that the animosity between Symcock and the Watsons was getting seriously out of hand, an ironic situation since they had helped to create it by appointing both men as their officers. The dispute hinged on the town courts, and, in particular, the relationship between the manorial jurisdiction and the court of orders, and what role, if any, the learned steward had to play in this. The corporation was emphatic that Symcock was there for advice only:

> not that he should intrude and thrust himself to meddle with the alteration of our ancient orders, civil government and choice of our magistrates.[57]

But to a trained lawyer, such as Symcock, the constitution of the town must have seemed a mess, with little legal justification for many of the things that went on inside it and mounting criticism of the management of the grammar school endowment and the exclusion of the 'faction'. Particularly galling was his own lack of a specific role except that provided by his office and independent status as a JP which, presumably, entitled him to hear cases, under the authority of the Queen, quite independent of either of the town courts. William Watson, as deputy steward, stood to lose most from this, and as the battle of jurisdictions went from bad to worse the Watsons were seen to epitomise all that was bad in the old order. By 1592 the dispute had got as far as Chancery, and in October commissions were about to be sent out for the examination of witnesses in Retford. This sent the corporation into a panic, and they wrote to Roger Manners for help:

> lest this controversy now grown betwixt them who are acquainted with the secrets of our town by reason of their offices might grow dangerous unto us, our government or commonwealth, by open disclosing of any secret in our charter or by breeding mutinies, contentions or divisions amongst ourselves being examined one against another. Wherefore we are warned by the examples of other

corporations, our neighbours, to prevent such attempts or beginnings as might by any colour prejudice us, our commonwealth or liberties.[58]

The corporation requested that Manners use his influence to 'stay' Symcock, and they for their part would 'command Watson to cease'. Commenting on the situation in 1598 the Earl of Rutland believed that the jurisdictional dispute was 'the particular...whereon...much of the general ariseth'.[59]

The judgement was an astute one, because by 1598 the government of the town had become deadlocked as factions gathered around the protagonists. The Watsons were supported by a clear majority of the burgesses who regarded themselves as the upholders of traditional values — 'the ancients', as they self-consciously styled themselves.[60] Symcock, on the other hand, had a much smaller following comprising 'mischievous and factious members', seeking, according to the 'ancients', such 'innovations and alterations from our old orders as their young heads have devised'. These 'malcontent brethren', of which Edmund and William Spivy, Robert Wharton and John Sloswicke were the principal, were joined in bonds of kinship and faith and often had links outside of the borough. Not only was there the West Retford connection to contend with, but, worse still, William Spivy had married the widow of Thomas Russell, a Grantham draper, causing him to extend his business interests out of the town. For that reason, apparently, he was thought 'neither fit to be one of our council or of our company...keeping no hospitality at all with us at Retford', an assertion which would seem to have little basis in truth since Spivy remembered the town generously in his will in 1602.[61]

Although Watson's supporters put down the activities of the opposition to headstrong young men who did not have the true interests of the town at heart, it is significant that between 1586 and 1600 no member of the opposition faction served as bailiff, in sharp contrast to the years 1584 and 1585 when Sloswicke and Edmund Spivy served in turn. This suggests that something happened c1586 necessitating the intervention of the Earl of Rutland and excluding the 'faction' from the government of the town. All of the bailiffs between 1586 and 1600 were drawn from the 'ancients', with William

Thornton serving three times and David Watson and John Mason twice each.[62] Clearly, the bailiffs, as the main executive officers of the town, had a vital significance in the context of the dispute between the learned steward and the deputy steward, so to return amenable bailiffs might be regarded as a piece of gamesmanship which would give a particular protagonist the edge. Whatever went wrong, the Spivys and their allies blamed the Watsons for undermining them and also for having 'drawn and moved many of the burgesses and inhabitants to mutiny and to join with them'. They echoed the legalistic arguments of Symcock when they stated that the Watsons:

> rather respecting their own private satisfaction than the safety and public benefit of the said town, have sought the utter perverting of this order of government, to the end they might live at liberty and as they list without restraint of any order or law other than such as they should from time to time allow as for their own private respects.[63]

By 1598 Symcock's supporters had seven places on the council. With little backing amongst the burgesses they were unable to carry an election for bailiff, but they were well placed to make the town virtually ungovernable by concerted action.

The crisis came on Michaelmas Day 1598 at the elections in the Moothall. When the old bailiffs, Geoffrey Bailey and Hercy Cobb, called for the keys of the town chest 'according to their ancient order and custom', William Spivy, who possessed a key 'not by right...[having] had the keeping of the said key too long', refused to hand it over:

> but besides that used very contemptuous and unseemly words unto the said bailiffs about the same, and so presently departed out of the said town whereby the said bailiffs...were enforced...to break open the lock of the said chest which when we had done...both the said ancient book of orders and also the bond we were then to use was missing and not there to be found...saying they are in betters hands than ours, where they shall be kept despite of Mr Bailiffs.[64]

William Thornton and John Mason were duly elected as the new bailiffs, but the incident was a public display of the rift within the corporation and the removal of the sensitive book of orders (which might have been used in litigation) was an alarming development which raised all of the phobia of the old guard concerning 'the secrets of our town'. There was now no alternative but for both sides to make direct appeals to the Earl of Rutland in the hope that he could defuse the situation before it became totally out of hand:

> First, they insult against us at home with unseemly and quarrelsome terms: secondly, conspire together and embezil our books of orders and other evidences concerning our town from us; and lastly they trouble your honour with such variety of complaints as their own unstable brains doth breed, which is in truth the occasion of all or the most of our civil differences.[65]

Having received representation from 40 burgesses supporting Watson and seven supporting Symcock, Rutland wrote to John Manners and John Thornhaugh in November 1598 asking them to resolve the matter as his deputies after hearing representations from both sides, 'and I am in hope you may more easily do it, because both parties do like of my choice of you'.[66]

The arbitration of these gentlemen has not survived, but certainly it was made and it went a long way towards resolving the difficulties in the town. It is clear that on hearing the matter they believed that the minority group had a good case, because their position was stronger after the arbitration than it was before it. By 1600 a group of twelve aldermen, made up of the old councillors had been formed, though what their rights were is not apparent. However, these probably anticipated those enshrined in the 1607 charter, because the practical impact was that between 1600 and 1604 a member of the 'faction' was always elected as one of the bailiffs, giving them the voice in civic affairs which they had lacked in the 1590s.[67] In 1599 new regulations were approved for apprentices and in 1600 new rules were laid down for the management of the town companies, suggesting that the disputes may have had a commercial edge connected with the 'new draperies', as mentioned above.[68] David Watson died in 1599 and William Spivy probably cut his links with the town at about that time having moved to Grantham, but William

Watson lived on and continued to be a thorn in the side of the corporation.   In 1600 a bill was exhibited against him in Chancery 'for all such records, court rolls, books, writings and evidences as have been and are come into his hands or custody', and though his deputy, George Lane, resigned in 1601, it seems unlikely that Watson did so because of his life interest in his patent: in April 1604 he was contemplating action against the town, and he may well have remained in office until the granting of the new charter in 1607.[69] Symcock, on the other hand, assisted the corporation in its attempt to give permanent stability to the arbitration and clear the muddy waters of ancient government. In 1600 he was sent to seek the advice of Sir Edmund Anderson, Lord Chief Justice of Common Pleas, 'that his Lordship may consider...what is right therein to be done'.[70] The advice of this learned judge, whose family seat was near Gainsborough, has not survived, but it probably touched on the enhancement of the power of the bailiffs and the obtaining of a new charter: certainly in 1602 the corporation was keen that the bailiffs become JPs for their year of office, and one year after 'if it may be', and by the following year the renewing of the charter was actively under review.[71] At last, in April 1604, Symcock was authorised to procure a new charter with a shopping list of requests approved by the corporation. Authority was to rest with the bailiffs, aldermen and council who were to 'govern the same [town] and the affairs thereof' according to the recent arbitration: it was particularly requested that the bailiffs should enjoy the status of JPs with power to take knowledge of statutes, to hold a court of orders and to appoint the wardens of companies, 'or else such of them as can be obtained'.[72] Symcock was given full authority 'to do and deal for the renewing and confirming thereof as he shall think fit', and his expenses were to be reimbursed out of the town chamber.[73]

Over three years later, on November 25 1607, the new charter was sealed by James I, a major landmark in the history of the town by any standard.[74] It confirmed all of Retford's ancient privileges and with them the position of the burgesses, but placed its government in the hands of a common council of twelve aldermen to be selected by the burgesses 'or the major part of them'. The first bailiffs were named in the

9: Sir Edmund Anderson, Lord Chief Justice of Common Pleas: he adjudicated in many important state trials and was the probable architect of the charter of 1607.

10: The ancient seal of the borough showing two birds combatant: its continued use was authorised following the new charter.

charter, and it is clear that the aldermanic body of 1600 (itself the successor of the old council) was simply perpetuated, allowing for replacements in the meantime. Once appointed an alderman remained in office for life, and when he died (or was for some reason removed) a replacement was selected by the council and burgesses from two nominated freemen. The common council not only assisted in the day-to-day government of the town, it also played an important part in the election of the bailiffs, a process which was regularised to avoid the chaos of 1598. Now there was to be two bailiffs — a senior and junior — selected on the first Monday in August and taking up office on Michaelmas Day. The senior bailiff was chosen by the aldermen from amongst their own number, and the junior bailiff was selected by the aldermen and burgesses from two freemen nominated by the common council. Once elected, there was little to separate the senior and junior bailiff in terms of his authority. Each was a JP *ex officio*, and each remained in office for twelve months without a proviso for progression from junior to senior status. Over the vexed question of the law courts, the charter provided for a learned steward, or recorder, an 'honest man to be instructed in the law of England', who was also a JP. He was to be selected by the bailiffs and common council and was to remain in office at their pleasure, with power to appoint a deputy steward or town clerk. The steward, or his deputy, or the bailiffs if they felt so inclined, were obliged to hold a court for civil cases every third Monday, or more often if necessary. Thus, all of the town's legal officers, with the exception of the deputy steward, were JPs, a move which brought the community into line with the legal mainstream of the kingdom and ensured that its officers were more readily accountable to the crown.

Some historians have alleged that urban government became narrower and more oligarchical after the Reformation, as central government asserted its desire to have more manageable hierarchs in control of local affairs. Indeed, Clark and Slack have stated that:

> the continuous growth of oligarchic magistracy is the most obvious theme in English urban history from 1500 to 1700.[75]

Is this view borne out by the experience of East Retford? Certainly in the sixteenth century, and probably before, the management of the town was already in the hands of a narrow group of its citizens. The problem was that the election of bailiffs remained in the hands of a much broader group of burgesses. Hence bailiffs could be returned who did not reflect the wishes of the governing *élite*. This was, it seems, the essence of the administrative problem of the 1590s. Why the ancient *modus operandi* suddenly became considered unacceptable, and moreover alterable, is an interesting question. It had something to do with the impact of personalities — principally Symcock, perhaps — but underlying that was the impulse given by the Protestant Reformation to the common law and the notion that the individual had the right to have his voice heard above the crowd. This is why a small group of burgesses was determined enough to hold out against the majority of 'traditionalists' and in the end bring their ideas to fruition in the form of a legally manageable constitution for the town. What the 1607 charter did was to restrict the rights of the burgesses in the election of bailiffs in order to create a more workable system. In this process the burgesses were weakened but not fundamentally undermined, because they retained the right to elect aldermen (the leading figures in elections) and also to choose between two of their own number to serve as junior bailiff. Thus, the aldermen always reflected the wishes of the burgess body, and, in case they became out of touch, there was always one non-aldermanic burgess on the common council in the form of the junior bailiff. It would, therefore, be difficult to uphold the view that Retford became notably less 'democratic' as a result of the new charter — principally, it became more orderly. The only group to vanish completely in the new charter was 'the commonality', though active participation by the commons, if it had ever existed, was already a dead letter by the sixteenth century. The burgess republic of Retford maintained its fundamental identity after 1607, but its electoral rights were channelled along more circumscribed lines. As if to emphasise this continuity, the charter named the last bailiffs of the old order as the first of the new. Significantly, these were William Thornton, a leading member of the 'ancients' during the 1590s, and Nicholas Watson, son of David Watson and nephew of the now discredited deputy steward. With Spivy and many members of his faction now dead, it was an obvious attempt to heal the rifts of dissention.

After the granting of the charter it only remained for the corporation to consolidate certain details which had been left obscure. Sir Richard Williamson, a Master of Requests, became learned steward and appointed Robert Browne as his deputy.[76] Thornton and Watson were 'dignified with the prime and chief places of aldermen' since they were the first JPs ever to serve in the town, and at a 'common hall' in 1608 it was decided that the old device of two birds combatant should be retained as the seal of the borough.[77] Sir Gervase Clifton, elected high steward in 1616, gave the town a silver/gilt mace bearing the royal arms to be carried in processions, and the aldermen obtained purple robes trimmed with fur to wear when they attended church and on other ceremonial occasions.[78] But as civic pomp increased in the wake of the new grant, it is also evident that old suspicions did not suddenly die. Ghosts of the 1598 controversy were resurrected in 1612 with a disagreement as to who was to have keys to the town hutch, a detail not touched on in the charter. Eventually it was decided that four keys were to be spread amongst the aldermen and one held by the bailiffs, a decision which again endorsed a commitment to the fairly broad based constitution conceived in 1607.[79]

Corporation books dating from about 1600 existed in the 1820s when Piercy viewed them and noted some of their contents. Though the originals have now disappeared, Piercy's notes enable us to obtain some sort of impression of the work of the new civic body.[80] Much of this was of a routine nature, recording the admission of new aldermen and bailiffs, but from this information a picture of a typical *cursus honorum* can be built up, though we are hampered by possessing little data about minor officers such as chamberlains and company wardens. The usual route, however, was for an aspiring town elder to begin by serving the office of churchwarden as a young man; to progress through company and minor town office to the rank of junior bailiff; and then to be elected on to the common council as an alderman, serving as senior bailiff perhaps once before his death. It seems clear from a number of cases that the office of junior bailiff was a necessary prerequisite to election to the aldermanic bench, though some, for example, Thomas Cade (1631) and Robert Smeeton (1639) managed to short circuit the established form. A fairly typical career is illustrated by the case of Francis Moody, born in the town in 1582. Moody was a shoemaker who served as churchwarden in 1616 and as chamberlain between 1620 and 1622. In 1625 he was elected an alderman, and finally became senior bailiff in 1636/37 at the aged of 54, a year before his death.[81] Another local man was Robert Wharton, born in 1589. Because he came from a family of wealthy mercers and woollen drapers heavily involved in local affairs, his promotion was swifter than Moody's and he served the churchwarden's office in 1616 at the age of only 26. Junior bailiff in 1620/21, Wharton was elected an alderman immediately his term of office ended and was senior bailiff three years later in 1624/5. Had his life not been cut short in 1631, aged only 42, he would, no doubt, have gone on to serve additional terms.[82] By contrast, other aldermen were strangely inactive or failed to make the grade either through personal choice or some assumed weakness in character. Robert Hudson did nothing between his election in 1609 and his death in 1616, and William Moody was similarly inactive between his appointment in 1616 and his resignation eleven years later.[83] Despite difficulties in persuading men to serve minor office, the bailiffs' positions seem to have been keenly sought, with only one man filling the same office twice after 1607.[84]

Once elected aldermen usually served for life, though some were permitted to resign with the consent of the council. William Thornton, a stalwart upholder of local government for well over 30 years, finally resigned in 1622, 'on account of his age and infirmities' having been bailiff five times, and if an alderman moved to West Retford or Clarborough, as William Billiald did in 1621, his civic career would be cut short.[85] Richard Reynolds, elected in 1642 'and not being in his place to take on him the said office', was fined twenty nobles, but this was suspended 'until he should appear' when William Parnell assured the council he would be 'forthcoming'.[86] More serious were the cases of Henry Parnell (1608) and Thomas Draper (1622) who were deposed because of 'miscarriage and evil judgement': unfortunately the nature of this is not described in either case, though Parnell's character is hinted at by the fact that he had pursued a law suit against the corporation in 1601, and he was indicted in the Archdeacon's court in 1608 for allowing a servant guilty of fornication to depart unpunished.[87] The only other officer dismissed by the corporation after 1607 was its learned steward, William Fletcher. Appointed in 1615 in succession to Williamson, he was deprived in 1621 because he had been absent from the town for twelve months: his replacement was the local gentleman Sir Hardolph Wastneys who held the office until his death in 1649.[88] This is hardly a startling record of civic disobedience, and it indicates that the charter was broadly successful in establishing an effective and reasonably coherent system of local government.

If there was a problem it was connected with the perceived lowly status of many of the burgesses, which was hinted at before 1607 and continued to cause concern after that date. In 1620 due to a 'want of sufficient men to be chosen chamberlains' it was decided that the existing incumbents:

> should stand the office two years and that in future all chamberlains should stand the same period unless they should be elected bailiffs.[89]

During the 1624 election campaign one of the Wortleyites:

> affirmed, and that with a great oath,...that there was twenty of them [burgesses] and he would be hanged if all of them were not worth a pot full of pottage.[90]

William Ingleby, one of the most turbulent citizens of the town, abused George Earle in 1625 as 'a base shitten and beggarly alderman', and went on to suggest that the whole of the council, except four or five, were 'base shitten and beggarly aldermen' with other language 'equally reprehensible'.[91] Ingleby, who had been on the fringes of the inner ring as a churchwarden and chamberlain, was 'utterly disfranchised' for his outburst, but he obviously touched a raw nerve. Although all of these comments were made at a time when Retford was suffering a deep economic depression and the fortunes of many of its citizens were at a low ebb, Ingleby's assessment that less than half of the aldermen seemed to justify their positions in terms of wealth and status re-echoes the old problem of a town with privileges and immunities out of proportion to its size, the division being between aldermen such as Francis Moody and Robert Wharton cited above. Whereas mercers were able to carry off their offices with some *aplomb* this might not always have been so easy for a shoe-maker, yet this was an inevitable problem with over 10% of the burgess body serving company or civic office in any given year.[92] And Ingleby's attitude along with the changes of 1607, bred a certain cynicism amongst the burgess body as a whole. By 1642 so few freemen were attending the elections of the bailiffs that the corporation was obliged to impose a fine of £5 for each default, a startling turnabout in view of the hotly contested campaigns of the 1590s but, for some, a vindication of the new order within the town.[93]

The hierarchy of the town was united by links of kinship, belief and commerce, but it was not so far removed from the rest of the burgesses, socially and economically, to establish its identity as an elevated and detached *haute bourgeoisie*. Many of the bailiffs and aldermen were linked by ties of kinship, and, with the notable exception of the Spivy clan, those links were invariably rooted in East Retford rather than the suburbs. In the 1600 council no family provided more than one alderman: in the 1607 list the Parnells provided two: and in 1624 the Whartons accounted for three.[94] By 1640 five of the aldermanic families of 1607 had provided additional aldermen — the Parnells, Whartons, Masons, Bellamys and Tupmans — and many of these can be identified as sons of previous members of the council.[95] Moreover, new names appearing after 1607 often turn out to be related to old councillors by way of marriage. The Drapers, for example, were related to the Taylors and Parnells, and the Dunstons had contacts with the Parnells and Bellamys.[96] The apparent unity of the corporation in the seventeenth century owed much to inter-relationship, but at the same time it was possi-ble for an ambitious outsider to break into the charmed circle provided he managed to raise sufficient support amongst the burgesses. The Earles and Kirkes are examples of families who entered the common council after 1607 without family roots in

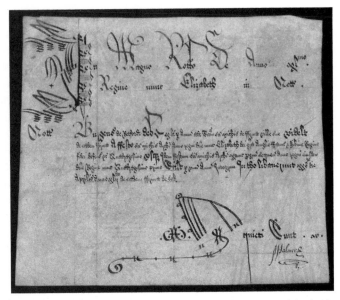

11: Quittance from the Exchequer for payment, by the burgesses, of the fee farm of the borough owing to the crown (1598/99).

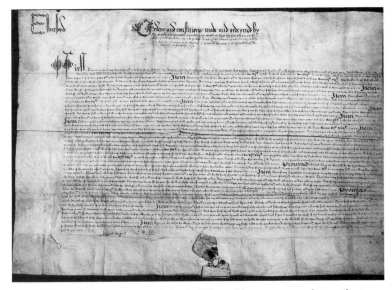

12: Orders and Constitutions of the bailiffs and burgesses regulating the town companies (1599).

Retford or traceable relationships with the dominant groups, and in each case they were quite capable of pursuing respectable civic careers.[97] Thus the government of the town was continually refreshed by new forces coming in from outside. It is possibly best described as semi-oligarchical, because although some families had huge advantages of wealth, relationship and long standing connections with the town, they were never numerous enough — and rarely survived long enough — to achieve a lasting domination, assuming that they aspired to this in any case. There was always space for popular and active burgesses to move in, even if their economic position sometimes set them ill at ease with their aldermanic colleagues and prolonged exposure to the corrosive comforts of the inner ring caused them to become conservative and self-satisfied.

Protestantism was another force which bound the ruling *élite* together and transcended the more particular bonds of family relationship. Will preambles indicate that members of the common council were solidly conformist in their views, reflecting the attitudes of the town in general, though in four cases after 1607 there is a specific mention of predestination and therefore a hint at something more than conventional Anglicanism.[98] William Mason, for example, who died in 1641 commended his soul to God:

> trusting in the mercies and in the merits of Jesus Christ, his son, my only saviour, to receive full remission of all my sins and to be received into the heavenly and everlasting joys prepared for his elect.[99]

This godly, Calvinistic awareness amongst families such as the Whartons, Parnells and Bellamys only rarely translated itself into the preoccupations with charity and education commonly associated with more advanced Protestants. There were no outstanding charitable ventures or puritan lectureships in Retford as there were in other — generally larger — towns before 1642, for example. Most aldermen left respectable, if not over-generous, legacies of about 40s to the poor, and only Nicholas Watson showed any sense of civic pride by leaving £4 'towards repairing the Moothall' in 1623.[100] There were no notable book owners amongst the aldermen, and only John Jepson demonstrated a concern for the education of his daughters by stating the hope that his wife 'will be very careful for their good education and profits'.[101]   The most outstanding example of public-spiritedness, in fact, came from that much-maligned member of the old corporation, William Spivy, who died in 1603.   Not only did he leave detailed instructions for the education and bringing up of his own children, but he also demonstrated a real awareness of the problems of the town in a wider sense.   Special endowments were set aside for the maintenance of 'the most needful places' in St Swithun's church and for the augmentation of the income of the minister and churchwardens.   Similarly, the bailiffs and chamberlains each received small additions to the funds from which they were expected to underwrite their offices and 'the poor people of the almshouses' also received a legacy.[102] Most imaginative of all, perhaps, was Spivy's scheme to provide loans for poor tradesmen who were encountering difficulties or struggling to set themselves up in business.[103] It should be said that none of these endowments were permanent, being either for 21 years or until such time as his son reached his majority, and Spivy's legal and financial difficulties may in the end have nullified some of his good intentions. But his was a bold gesture offered to a town which had sought to reject him. William Spivy's quite different window on the world was a result of his wealth, his puritanism, and, not least, the sense of *noblesse oblige* he felt as a scion of the Denmans and the ancient house of Hercy. These were connections that few of his fellow burgesses were able to demonstrate in quite so direct a fashion.

Aldermen were drawn from a wide range of trades, but mercers, tanners and shoemakers pre-dominated, reflecting the preoccupations of the three town companies. By contrast, John Earle was a maltster, John Ellis a haberdasher and Richard Elsam a miller.[104]   However, there was a growing tendency in the seventeenth century for aldermen to disguise what they actually did by the use of the impressive status descriptions of 'alderman' or 'gentleman', a piece of snobbery which no doubt further irritated malcontents such as Ingleby. A classic case was William Mason who described himself as gentleman/alderman but was in fact a tailor, occupying a workroom over the shop of George Wharton in the market place.[105] Nevertheless some of the hierarchs were able to demonstrate a modest affluence. William Spivy, with his lucrative interests in Grantham, may be regarded as something of an exception in this instance, but amongst more 'conventional' aldermen John Wharton left his daughter a dowry of £200 and Nicholas Watson, who adorned his fingers with a seal ring and a 'hoop ring', could afford the wages of several servants.[106] Income from trade obviously accounted for much of this, woollen draperies in the case of Wharton and Watson, but aldermen also raised a significant income from property in the town as well as in adjacent villages. Some of this was purchased or inherited, but aldermen were especially well placed to use their positions of influence to exploit the town estate. Because of its relatively small extent this was never likely to become a damaging abuse, but several members of the council have been traced as lessees of town property in East Retford, Moorgate, Little Gringley and Ordsall.[107] Widespread occupation of land amongst the aldermen, and close proximity to commons, closes and open fields, meant that they invariably depended upon the same diversified form of income as the burgesses.[108] William Mason owned a shop with 'all my bellows, smithies hammers, vice and other my tools and implements' along with a kiln house and equipment for malting, despite his trade as a tailor:[109] Richard Elsam, a miller, similarly owned a kiln house and a quantity of malt, but he also had pigs, bees and spinning wheels.[110] His inventory, made in 1628, indicates that he occupied two houses, one in East Retford 'next the street' and the other at Welham. The Retford house comprised four downstairs rooms and three upstairs chambers: by contrast, the Welham house was slightly larger with four downstairs rooms, four upstairs chambers and a garret. Both houses included outbuildings — a coalhouse, hay loft, stable and kiln house at Retford, and a workhouse and brewhouse at Welham. Despite the plurality of residences and the modest comfort implied by the arrangement of rooms, Elsam's possessions were of no great value. They provide a picture of a practical and simple household with little visible sign of sophistication, possibly one of the 'base shitten and beggarly' aldermen lampooned in 1625.

The fact that so many of the aldermen were so close to their neighbours in terms of wealth and status, meant that they shared equally — or almost so — in the jurisdictional hazards which were likely to fall upon the burgesses and commons. The court roll of 1554 records the bailiffs, Christopher Jackson and William Rossell II, amongst the offenders, as well as leading members of the council such as John Wymoke and John Twels.[111] William Smyth, bailiff in 1586, found himself the subject of an ongoing *cause célèbre* before the Archdeacon's court, and of the twelve aldermen named in the 1607 incorporation four had been the subject of church court prosecutions already, and two were to appear again after their appointment.[112] Another two aldermen made initial appearances before 1620, a total of half of the common council culpable before the canon law for offences as widely dispersed as sexual malpractice, failure to receive communion and abusing the Sabbath. Although this might have raised the wrath of Archbishop Sandys who stated that 'he is unmete to govern a city that can not govern his own household',[113] it indicates that a small town like Retford was far removed from the ideal and polarised society that the reformers sought, and some historians believe to have actually existed. In Retford townsmen and town governors were so close in terms of relationship and status that the position of common councillor, or even bailiff, did not guarantee an immunity from prosecution if they ignored the general social and religious mores laid down by the clergy and the broader community of the town. The aldermen were true delegates of the burgesses in local government, and not a closed and dominant *élite*. Money, marriage and motivation constantly opened up new routes of advancement, and such was the complexity of even small town administration that the voice of the ordinary citizen was never wholly stifled.

Another question closely linked to this is the extent to which urban government was seriously involved with 'national' issues in the years leading up to the Civil War. There is little evidence in Retford that the corporation gave consideration to issues other than purely local ones in the choice of their MPs or in the government of the town. By rights the town should have supported the King in the Civil War since it was an ancient royal borough, dependent on successive monarchs for its privileges, a bond which had been tightened in 1607 by the new charter and the elevation of three town officers to the position of JP. Moreover, the high steward, Sir Gervase Clifton, was a notable follower of the King in the Short and Long Parliaments, and the new town vicar, Henry Bate, who arrived early in 1641, was a royalist and a man of apparently ambivalent religious views.[114] Yet when the Protestation arrived in Retford in July 1642 most of the corporation was violently opposed to it. Bate wrote to Clifton in an attempt to see if these two gentlemen between them could find a cure for what he termed 'the King's evil':

> I find our aldermen (save two or three) are so utterly averse from subscribing to the Protestation...that they have dissuaded as many as they can from subscribing it themselves. Therefore, good Sir, be pleased...to intimate your disaffection to this their denial. Sir, a word of yours...will prevail more than hundreds of mine to make them fear God and honour the King.[115]

It is clear from the Protestation return itself that in the end most of these dissidents swallowed their pride and signed, a reflection of how easily overawed a small town corporation such as this was.[116] But their initial hostility is significant, and is probably explained by the impact of four areas of royal policy since 1607. Firstly, James I's inept intervention in the economy, by way of the Cockayne project, which created the deepest recession in Retford since 1520. Secondly, the disillusionment with the established church by way of two unpopular town vicars (Watt and Bate) and the revived energy of the ecclesiastical jurisdiction in the 1630s. Thirdly, the demands of Ship Money, and in particular the raising of Retford's contribution in order to 'ease' Newark. Finally, the drainage schemes of Vermuyden which brought direct benefits to an old commercial rival, Bawtry, but did very little for the ancient borough of Retford. All of these areas were directly attributable to the Stuart Kings, particularly to Charles I, and it seems clear that local happenings were liable to rebound on to central government if it could be held to blame. This was hardly a protest of principle, but of injury to pride and purse over a long period of time. Despite the fact that the corporation was successfully re-modelled in 1607 to create a closer alignment with the crown, these advantages were almost squandered by the insensitivity of royal policy over the next 25 years. What finally pulled Retford back into line was not goodwill to the royalist cause, but its inability to resist the pressures imposed by individuals whose social and economic influence it was unable to withstand.

FOOTNOTES AND REFERENCES

1. BC, Letters 22/10/1598.
2. Piercy, pp. 27-31, RM, 1562 Charter.
3. Piercy, p.32.
4. *Ibid.*, p.28.
5. RM, Ancient Deeds.
6. BI, PR 9 f.287.
7. NAO, DP 47/4.
8. JA, RB 2 f.136.
9. *Ibid.*, f.3. For the Welch family, see Chapter 5 pp.147-8.
10. Piercy, p.20.
11. BC, Letters 22/10/1598, 3/11/1598.
12. NUMD, Cl. LP. 52.
13. Piercy, pp.55/6.
14. JA, RB 2 f.163.
15. Piercy, p.20.
16. *Ibid.*, p.18.
17. JA, RB 2 ff.138/9.
18. Piercy, p.32. For a list of bailiffs see Appendix, Table 1.
19. BC, Letters 3/1/1598.
20. RM, Ordinances 1600.
21. *Ibid.*
22. BC, Letters 22/10/1598.
23. JA, RB 2 f.101.
24. *Ibid.*, ff.85-99.
25. The town waits turned out to welcome Princess Margaret when she passed along the Great North Road *en route* for her marriage with James IV of Scotland in 1503.
26. JA, RB 2 ff.85-99.

27.   *Ibid.*, f.5.
28.   RM, Ordinances 1600.
29.   JA, RB 2 f.161, BI PR 16 ff.144/5.
30.   Quoted in R. C. Richardson and T. B. James (eds.), *The Urban Experience* (1983), p.86.
31.   Piercy, pp.27-31.
32.   NAO, DP 47/24.
33.   See Chapter 8 pp.229-30.
34.   See Chapter 7 pp.204-5.
35.   NAO, DP 47/2, JA, BB f.26, RM, Ancient Deeds, 1532, 1587, 1614.
36.   JA, RB 1 (Grammar School), 2 ff.20-4.
37.   *Ibid.*, ff.1/2.
38.   *Ibid.*, ff.20-24, 79/80.
39.   PRO, *Early Chancery Proceedings*, File 1134. l5, JA, RB2 f.163/4, Copnall, p.46.
40.   JA, RB 2 ff.137/8, 161. In 1608 the corporation was prosecuted at the Quarter Sessions 'for a defective measure bound with a chain'. Copnall, p.47.
41.   JA, RB 2 ff.163/4.
42.   BI, PR 23 f.85l.
43.   *Ibid.*, 16 ff.48/4, AR 31 f.84.
44   NAO, Wills (Frances Rose, 1606).
45.   JA, RB 2 ff.85-99. Clogs were tree roots.
46.   *Ibid.*, ff.86, 88, 97.
47.   BC, Letters 22/2/1590.
48.   *The Visitation of Nottinghamshire*, Harleian Society, 4 (1871), p.156, *HMC Rutland*, 1, pp.299, 306, 314. Alexander Radcliffe was still learned steward in September 1588, so Symcock's appointment must have come after that as a result of Radcliffe's resignation since he did not die until 1616. JA, RB I (Members of Parliament).
49.   *Catalogue of the Arundel Castle Manuscripts ... [and] ....Calendar of Talbot Letters*, Sheffield City Libraries (1965), p.203. See Chapter 3, pp.69-72.
50.   NAO, Wills (John Mason, 1607: Hugh Smith, 1610).
51.   BC, Letters 22/10/1598.
52.   Did the Earl mean the 'company' of councillors, or a trading company? For Retford's fabric trade, see Chapter 8 and for Spivy see NAO, Mee, 1/64. 1R/2.
53.   See Chapter 1, pp15-7.

54.   See Appendix, Table 9.
55.   See Chapter 6, p.184.
56.   PRO, PROB 11/101.
57.   BC, Letters 22/10/1598.
58.   *Ibid.*, 31/10/1592.
59.   *Ibid.*, 3/11/1598.
60.   This was a form of description employed by senior guild members in Coventry. Clark and Slack, p.59.
61.   BC, Letters, 22/10/1598, PRO, PROB 11/101.
62.   See Appendix, Table 1.
63.   BC, Letters, 3/11/1598.
64.   *Ibid.*, 22/10/1598.
65.   *Ibid.*
66.   *Ibid.*, 3/11/1598.
67.   William Woodrough (1600/01): Henry Mason (1601/02): Thomas Tupman (1602/03): John Sloswicke (1603/04): Robert Wharton (1604/05).
68.   RM, Orders and Constitutions 1599, Ordinances 1600.
69.   JA, RB 2 ff.101, 161, 163. The date of William Watson's death is not clear. Elizabeth, the widow of a William Watson, died in February 1604 at Clarborough. The dates of their children correspond well with the deputy steward, though in April 1604 Watson was threatening action against the town. He may therefore have been the William Watson buried at East Retford in 1618. NUCLH, F(amily) R(econstitution) F(orms), NAO, ERPR (1599, 1618), CPR (1604).
70.   JA, RB 2 f.161. Anderson had already involved himself in the affairs of the corporation by approving the new orders for the town companies in April 1600.
71.   *Ibid.*, ff.162/3.
72.   *Ibid.*, f.163.
73.   *Ibid.*, f.135.
74.   RM, 1607 Charter, *CSP Dom, 1603-10*, p.382, Piercy, pp.31-49.
75.   Clark and Slack, p.25.
76.   JA, RB 2 ff.2, 101.
77.   *Ibid.*, f.2. The identity of these birds has given rise to intriguing debate, but today they are generally considered to be choughs.
78.   Piercy, p.91.
79.   JA, RB 2 f.2.
80.   *Ibid.*, ff.1-5, 144.

81. NAO, ERPR (1582, 1638), Wills (Francis Moody, 1638), JA, RB 2 f.144.
82. NAO, ERPR (1589, 1631), Wills (Robert Wharton, 1631), JA, RB 2 f.144.
83. *Ibid.*
84. Robert Stockham: senior bailiff, 1608/09 and 1628/29
85. JA, RB 2 ff.5, 144.
86. *Ibid.*, f.6.
87. *Ibid.*, ff.137/8, NAO, DDTS 11 f.54.
88. JA, RB 2 ff.4/5. The deputy stewards to serve Sir Hardolph Wastneys were Robert Butler (1626-29) and James Lane (1629-42).
89. *Ibid.*, f.4.
90. NUMD, Cl.LP. 52.
91. JA, RB 2 f.6.
92. This calculation does not include the offices of constable, overseer and churchwarden which were probably open to non-burgesses. However, burgesses often served them, and if *all* offices are taken into account the proportion rises to 20%.
93. JA, RB 2 f.5.
94. *Ibid.*, f.144, NUMD, Cl. LP.52, Piercy, p.78. Yet by the time of the Protestation (1642) there was no Wharton alderman. W. F. Webster (ed.) *Protestation Returns 1641/2: Notts/Derbys* (n.d.), pp.10/11.
95. For example, John Wharton (1621) and John Bellamy (1640). NAO, Wills (Robert Wharton, 1628: William Bellamy, 1631).
96. Ibid, (Martin Taylor, 1622: William Bellamy, 1631).
97. NUCLH, FRF.
98. NAO, Wills (Richard Parnell, 1626: William Bellamy, 1631: John Wharton, 1631: William Mason, 1641).
99. *Ibid.*
100. *Ibid.*, (Nicholas Watson, 1623).
101. *Ibid.*, (John Jepson, 1617).
102. PRO, PROB 11/101.
103. See Chapter 4, pp.108-9.
104. NAO, Wills (John Earle, 1631), BI, PR 36 f.292, NUMD, PB 339 (1620).
105. JA, RB 2 f.138/9, NAO, Wills (William Mason, 1641).
106. *Ibid.*, (John Wharton, 1631: Nicholas Watson, 1623).
107. Richard Parnell in Little Gringley: Nicholas Watson in East

Retford: Richard Elsam in Moorgate: William Spivy in Ordsall. RM, Ancient Deeds 1614, NAO, Mee, 1/64. 1R/2, Wills (Richard Parnell, 1626: Nicholas Watson, 1623: Richard Elsam, 1625).
108.   See Chapter 4, pp.95-7.
109.   NAO, Wills (William Mason, 1641). The blacksmith's equipment was probably used by his son, William Mason.
110.   NAO, Wills (Richard Elsam, Inventory 1628).
111.   JA, RB 2 ff.85-99.
112.   For Smyth, see Chapter 5, pp.136-7.
113.   Barry, p. 236.
114.   For Clifton, see Chapter 3, pp.75-6. K.S.S. Train (ed.), *Lists of the Clergy of North Nottinghamshire*, TS, Record Series, 20, 1961, p.155. Sir Hardolph Wastney's, the learned steward, was also a royalist.
115.   NUMD, Cl. C.17.
116.   *Protestation Returns*, pp.10/11. In East Retford there was 'non denying'.

Chapter 3

A ROTTING BOROUGH

*And fearing that...the town should receive a memorable
blemish to have a burgess place thus bought and sold...that
if they were sure it would turn to the utter overthrow and
undoing of the town, yet they would do it.[1]*

It was customary for the borough of East Retford to appoint
a high steward 'as their protector', an office which was said to
have existed 'time out of mind' in 1624.[2] In 1537 Henry VIII
granted the manor and lordship to George Talbot, 4th Earl of
Shrewsbury, and on this basis Piercy believed that the 4th Earl
and his son Francis Talbot, 5th Earl of Shrewsbury, succes-
sively enjoyed the high stewardship.[3] However, on the death
of the 5th Earl in 1560 the succession becomes doubtful,
because by the 1570s the high stewardship had fallen into the
hands of the Manners Earls of Rutland. It is possible that in
1560 Henry Manners, 2nd Earl of Rutland, Lord Lieutenant of
Nottinghamshire and Lord President of the Council of the
North, was selected as the new high steward, a shrewd choice,
since he was a man more in favour with the new Elizabethan
regime that the Talbots, but a short- lived appointment since
he died in 1563 leaving a minor as his heir under the wardship
of Sir William Cecil. On the other hand, George Talbot, 6th
Earl of Shrewsbury, might have succeeded to the stewardship
and handed over the office to his nephew, Edward Manners,
3rd Earl of Rutland, after he came of age in July 1570. The 6th
Earl of Shrewsbury and the 3rd Earl of Rutland maintained a
friendly working relationship in the Midlands, but why the
Talbots should have voluntarily given up such a potentially
important office is puzzling. Perhaps it is more likely that the
high stewardship changed hands in 1560 than later, but
certainly by the 1570s the Rutland influence stood unchallenged.[4]

High stewards were generally appointed for life with an annual fee of £4 and they were expected to assist the corporation in any way in which they were able.[5] This might involve help in the obtaining of grants and charters: support and advice in law suits: or arbitration in any controversies the town might find itself embroiled in. Successive high stewards were fulsome in their offers of support — 'you shall be most assured of more honourable assistance in all your good causes'; 'be most assured of my best help and assistance'; and:

> I wish you to be assured no pleasure in my power shall be less cheerfully and freely afforded the town...whensoever your occasions present an opportunity.[6]

The reason why these grandees employed such deference towards the tanners and shoemakers of Retford was not because of the monetary value of their office — which was negligible — but because the borough commanded two seats in the House of Commons 'which being all the courtesy the town hath been able to afford them'.[7] These seats had first been taken up in 1315, but they had lapsed in 1330 because of the poverty of the electorate.[8] However, the privilege was revived for the 1571 Parliament when East Retford returned two MPs, probably on the prompting of the Earl of Rutland, without waiting for a writ: although the election was questioned, the town's right was upheld and thereafter East Retford elected two burgesses to every Parliament until the privilege was removed by legislation in 1830.[9] By then the town had become a national scandal as a classic 'rotten borough', yet even in the sixteenth and seventeenth centuries the franchise was very narrow. Voting was restricted to the burgesses — a group of between 50 and 100 men — who could easily be manipulated by powerful forces from outside. Indeed, it is a significant point that before 1642 the constituency failed to return a single townsman to represent it, suggesting that the lack of substantial men, given as the reason for non-election in the fourteenth century, was every bit as valid 300 years later.

The influence of the 3rd Earl of Rutland after 1571 is illustrated by a letter to him from the bailiffs in 1586 explaining how they were 'in duty bounden' to uphold the Earl's candidates:

> understanding...that your Lordship's request is to have the election of one or both of them [i.e. Members of Parliament]

...and therefore it may please your Lordship to make choice and nominate at your good Lordship's pleasure and we will ratify; yet if it pleased your honour to think well of Mr Denzil Holles we would be very glad, if not at your Lordship's pleasure.[10]

Almost all the town's representatives before 1586 were indeed clients of the Earl, a man who made a significant impact on Elizabethan politics and died as Lord Chancellor designate in 1587:[11] the most outstanding was Job Throckmorton (1572) a notable puritan and opponent of Mary, Queen of Scots, who was sent to the Tower in 1584 and may well have been the author of the Martin Marprelate tracts.[12] Two early members, however, hint that other forces may have been at work in the borough, and this is confirmed by the ambivalence of the bailiffs in 1586 as to whether Rutland had the nomination of 'one or both' of their MPs. In 1624 the town clerk stated that the high steward had 'always...recommended to the town some gentleman of worth for *one* of their burgesses', and the truth of the matter was probably that if another forceful representation was put to it (other than by the high steward) the corporation was prepared to consider it.[13] Henry Draycot (1571) was a Derbyshire man who possibly had contacts with George, 6th Earl of Shrewsbury, and Denzil Holles (1585 and 1586) had a foot in both the Talbot and Manners camps.[14] Interestingly, Holles was a candidate of whom the Retford corporation expressed approval. The grandson of a London mercer, his family had settled at Haughton, Nottinghamshire, where he had gained the reputation of a good landlord: this 'sad and wise man' was nevertheless a notorious lecher, and his illegitimate daughter, Susan, was to become the wife of George Bradley, a Retford alderman.[15] Which of these characteristics endeared him particularly to the corporation is not clear, but his acceptability by both the Shrewsbury and Rutland interests may not be insignificant.

The death of the 3rd Earl of Rutland before his 40th birthday introduced a period of instability into the politics of the region. His successor John, the 4th Earl, was dead by the end of 1588, leaving as heir his son Roger, the 5th Earl, an eleven year old boy who was to remain a ward of Lord

Burghley until his majority in 1597. These developments coincided with the death of George Talbot, 6th Earl of Shrewsbury, in 1590, and the efforts of his son Gilbert, the 7th Earl, to build up a more coherent following in the region. The 7th Earl of Shrewsbury was a quarrelsome man who took up residence at Welbeck in Nottinghamshire, and commenced a feud with Sir Thomas Stanhope which split the area into factions and culminated in the bitter county election campaign of 1593 which became 'a trial of strength between the two camps'.[16] Retford, with its two Parliamentary seats and a tradition of involvement by both the Manners and Talbots, was not likely to emerge unscathed from such a confrontation, especially at a time when Shrewsbury's Cavendish relatives were making inroads into the borough by their purchase of local tithes and advowsons.[17] In 1588, following the death of the 4th Earl of Rutland, Lord Gilbert Talbot wrote to the corporation in support of Alexander Radcliffe, their learned steward, to be an MP being:

> very honest and sufficient, whom I will undertake shall afford his best travail for the advancement of any benefit towards your town.[18]

The request was backed by Peter Roos of Laxton to whom the seat had already been promised, but he agreed that:

> I will for this time yield...for that his Lordship may much more and many ways do more good to your town than I can.[19]

Radcliffe was, in fact, a remarkably uncontroversial candidate. Not only was he learned steward, which gave him a legitimate moral claim to one of the seats anyway, but he was also in the service of the Countess of Rutland and had the backing of the well respected Roos family. With credentials such as this 'the first request that ever he [Lord Talbot] made unto you' could hardly go unanswered.[20] More sinister, so far as the Rutland interest was concerned, was the parallel effort which was being made by the Talbots to secure the high stewardship of the borough. It seems that the 4th Earl of Rutland was briefly high steward, but following his unexpected death it was decided to put forward Sir George Chaworth as a stop gap in view of the minority of the 5th Earl. Chaworth, who came from an ancient Nottinghamshire family, was a kinsman and servant of two Earls of Rutland and had served the Manners as their electoral agent in a succession of Parliaments, taking care not just of East Retford but also of seats such as Nottingham, Grantham and Lincoln.[21] In his campaign for the high stewardship Chaworth placed his faith particularly in the influential burgesses, David and William Watson, to whom he later gave thanks and said:

> I am not ignorant you were greatly laboured...for your stewardship and not unlikely incurred some unkindness for placing me therein.[22]

The opponent was the same Lord Gilbert Talbot who was currently trying to raise support for the election of one of the town MPs. Peter Roos hinted at the clandestine nature of the affair, and in particular his suspicion of the Watsons, when he requested that his letters to the bailiffs and burgesses be kept 'closed...so that I may have the same again if cause so require'.[23] Chaworth duly secured his election to the high stewardship, along with the nomination of a relative, George Chaworth, as one of the town MPs,[24] but the pride of the Talbots was salved somewhat by a decisive role in a Parliamentary election, their first clear nomination since 1571.

Sir George Chaworth did not live long to enjoy his high stewardship. Early in 1590, feeling that death was near, he had gone to London to consult the College of Physicians and being 'in weak estate' he took steps to wind up his affairs. He was determined that the high stewardship of Retford, so recently won, should not pass out of the Rutland sphere of influence, and in February 1590 he wrote to the corporation pointing out that he had merely served as a 'substitute' for 'my young Lord Roger, the now Earl of Rutland' and that it would prove 'to your town's best avail...to continue your former affection to the house of Rutland'. Chaworth made it clear that he would resign only in favour of the Earl:

> Therefore I pray you make no delay to make speedy choice of him for your high steward...and upon receipt of his patent I will return you mine own.[25]

Chaworth's understandable caution had been tempered by many years of experience and the knowledge that once more the Talbots had their hats in the ring with a hope of election.

The argument employed against the Earl of Rutland was that he was still only fourteen years of age and because of this could not do the best job for the town, but Chaworth responded by pointing out that he enjoyed the support of Lord Burghley, whose ward he was, and that he could also rely on the backing of Roger Manners, his great uncle and godfather and an influential man at court. Indeed, letters were procured from Burghley and Manners proving these points to be true, 'and therefore I wish you to do it both speedily and willingly that my Lord Treasurer may take it more thankfully'.[26] In Retford itself Chaworth fell back on his old allies in the hope that they could once more influence the corporation, and he wrote to David and William Watson asking that they should go to the Countess of Rutland 'secretly and with speed'. On their meeting he advised the Countess that:

> You will do well to accept them at your table with some kind courtesies which you know best how to deliver, for they are the men who can and must strike the chief stroke.[27]

Chaworth's machinations had the desired effect and the 5th Earl of Rutland was duly elected, though the bailiffs evidently had some doubts since they wrote to Roger Manners in 1592 stating how they had rejected 'others both honourable and worshipful...the which we hope in the Lord we shall never have cause to repent'.[28] The events of 1587-90 underline the high value placed on borough seats by competing families of aristocrats, and the lengths to which they were prepared to go to secure Parliamentary patronage. These competitions had repercussions in the internal politics of the town, since the Watsons became controversial figures and their problems are more fully explored in Chapter 2.

The words of the corporation were prophetic, because they probably lived to regret their support for the 5th Earl of Rutland. In the early years of his stewardship Lord Burghley certainly had a voice in the use of the young Earl's patronage, because in 1593 Anthony Cooke of Gidea Hall, Essex, became one of the members for the town. Cooke was a relative of the Cecils, and this 'impoverished gentleman', a soldier in Spain and Ireland, used his influence in Parliament to promote a bill to circumvent a conveyance settling the inheritance of his

13: Elizabeth, Countess of Rutland, who was advised to deliver 'some kind courtesies' to the representatives of the town in 1592.

14: Roger Manners, 5th Earl of Rutland: his long minority, and abortive involvement in the Essex revolt, weakened the influence of his family.

lands, only passed due to the intervention of the Lord Treasurer.[29] Other MPs during the 1590s were more local in their origins and upheld causes which might have been closer to the hearts of the townsmen. Roger Portington (1593 and 1597) owned lands in South Yorkshire and at Everton and served on committees concerning monopolies and horse theft;[30] John Roos (1597) was the nephew of Peter Roos of Laxton and served on committees concerning the Poor Law and soldiers and mariners.[31] Portington's patron is not clear, but Roos was related to both the Manners and Cecils and was possibly a servant of the 5th Earl of Rutland. The 5th Earl had indeed become a power to reckon with by 1597. Well educated and well travelled, he was emerging as a leading supporter of Robert Devereux, Earl of Essex, Queen Elizabeth's last favourite and a determined opponent of the Cecils. When Essex attempted to seize London and with it the person of the Queen in 1601 Rutland was amongst his followers, a blundered act of treason which must have caused dismay to his clients and supporters, especially in a town such as Retford which prided itself on its links with the crown. When the writs for the 1601 election were issued Rutland was already in disgrace, but nevertheless one of the Retford seats was filled by Roger Manners, a younger son of John Manners of Haddon Hall, Derbyshire.[32] If this appointment may have represented a compromise between the Manners and Talbot interests, the second Retford seat, which went to Robert Kydman, was a more clear cut example of Shrewsbury's growing power. Kydman, who came from a Norfolk family, was secretary to the 7th Earl of Shrewsbury and was nominated as a result of the Earl's direct intervention with the corporation, overthrowing an earlier promise to Sir John Thornhaugh made on behalf of Rutland.[33] Hasler asserts that this marked the end of Rutland's influence in the borough and that 'the high stewardship returned once more to the Talbots',[34] but in this he is incorrect since Rutland was still high steward when the next election was held in 1603, returning two non-controversial gentlemen with strong local connections, Sir John Thornhaugh of Fenton and Sir Thomas Darrell, father of Edward Darrell of West Retford and a relation of the Denmans.[35]

On the Earl of Rutland's death in 1612, however, the time was ripe for change, and Gilbert Talbot, 7th Earl of Shrewsbury, was duly elected high steward having intrigued for the position for quarter of a century.[36] The election for the Addled Parliament of 1614 followed hard on the heels of Shrewsbury's appointment, and he was now able to write to the corporation with the full authority of his position:

> Whereas it is like we shall have a Parliament very shortly, I am bold to commend unto your election for one of the burgesses of your town of Retford my dearly beloved nephew Sir William Cavendish, who what he shall want in the gravity of grey hairs to do your town any good or to defend it from any prejudice I dare undertake will be supplied in the love and good affection that he beareth unto the welfare thereof and unto all you his good neighbours the inhabitants there, wherein he shall be most assured of my best help and assistance.[37]

Despite this forceful plea, Cavendish, whose father owned the rectory and was soon to become first Earl of Devonshire, does not appear to have been elected, though he did represent Derby in Parliament after 1621.[38] The replacement was Nathaniel Rich, a merchant adventurer with colonial interests and a relative of Robert Rich, 2nd Earl of Warwick, and the Nottinghamshire knight Sir Gervase Clifton.[39] What lay behind this shift is not clear, but it seems unlikely that Shrewsbury's wishes were openly defied in a contested election. The other Retford seat was filled by Sir Richard Williamson of Gainsborough, the learned steward, who wrote to the corporation in March 1614 requesting nomination 'by your kind and free election', but stating that if some other had been chosen he would 'rest satisfied'. If 'strangers' were elected, he pointed out, it might be thought that the town had a steward:

> either unwilling or unworthy to be employed...which may be some disreputation to myself but (which I more regard) some disgrace to the body of your incorporation.[40]

Rich and Williamson were duly elected to serve in this most shortlived and negative of Stuart Parliaments.

Shrewsbury did not live long to enjoy his position and he died in 1616. For a replacement the town did not turn either to a Talbot or a Manners but, unusually, to Sir Gervase Clifton 'being a near neighbour and one from whom the town had received many favours'.[41] What these favours were is not clear, but Clifton's hand had possibly been evident in the 1614 election with the nomination of Nathaniel Rich. At the time of his appointment Sir Gervase was 29 years old and a member of one of the county's most ancient and prominent families: he was a JP, had served as sheriff and was member of Parliament for the shire in 1614. Thoroton was struck by his pleasant manner and easy going charm, a man 'of a sound body and a cheerful facetious spirit', and the ladies evidently valued these assets too because Clifton was to be married seven times.[42] But although two of these wives were the daughters of Earls and Clifton built up a considerable fortune by settlement, none of this disguised the fact that as a high steward of the borough he was not in the same league as his predecessors. At the end of the day he remained a Nottinghamshire baronet, not a great peer of the realm. It is possible that having obtained the new incorporation of 1607 the town did not feel as vulnerable as it did before that date, and hence the need for aristocratic protection was seen to recede. Moreover, Clifton was elected at a time of unprecedented economic depression in Retford, and the corporation might have felt that a loyal friend on the county bench was of more use than a more remote aristocratic ally. Whatever the reason, Clifton's high stewardship was not to be without its problems.

For the Parliament of 1620 the nominees were Sir Nathaniel Rich (presumably on the recommendation of Clifton) and Edward Wortley, the son of Elizabeth, Countess of Devonshire by her first husband Sir Robert Wortley. Although the Wortleys had established an interest in the town as early as 1565, this nomination coincided with the purchase of extensive estates in Ordsall by the Countess in favour of her son, a deliberate attempt to use money and influence to create a new gentry presence on the outskirts of the town.[43] Three years later Parliament was summoned again, and although Rich was nominated for a third time the destiny of the other seat evidently provoked some debate though the names of the contenders are not known. What is clear is that on August 2 1623 the corporation met and 'disabled' fifteen named burgesses from voting in future elections because they had moved away from the town 'and therefore did not pay anything to the support thereof'. Residence for a full year was required if they wished to recover their privilege in the future.[44] The man returned was John Holles, son of Lord Haughton and grandson of Denzil Holles, MP in the 1580s, a candidate who probably had the strong support of the burgesses because he was to represent the town in four Parliaments.[45] It seems likely that Sir Edward Wortley stood again in this election but was displaced by Holles, a blow which he and his Cavendish backers cannot have regarded with much relish. The situation was put back into the melting pot when Sir Nathaniel Rich announced that he was abandoning his East Retford seat in favour of Harwich. Clifton, who had been returned once more as a member for the county, was in London early in 1624 for the opening of Parliament and he had determined to use his influence as high steward in support of John Darcy, the youthful son of John, Lord Darcy of Aston.[46] On January 14 1624 John Darcy expressed his gratitude to his patron in his cramped schoolboy hand — 'worthy knight...I heartily thank you for praying on my behalf for that temporal blessing which I most want'.[47] With Wortley's supporters still smarting under the defeat of 1623, this latest move by the 'upstart' Clifton could not be allowed to go unchallenged.

On February 24 Clifton presented a letter to the corporation nominating John Darcy, but on the following day Philip Spurling, an agent of the Countess of Devonshire, arrived in Retford requesting that Sir Edward Wortley should have the vacant seat. Caught between two powerful forces the bailiffs were unsure what to do and the only alternative was to proceed to a contested election, vividly described in an account written for Clifton by Robert Browne, the town clerk.[48] The bailiffs and the majority of aldermen supported Clifton, but the Countess of Devonshire gained active support from the vicar, John Watt, two serving aldermen, Richard Elsam and Martin Taylor, and an ex-alderman, Thomas Draper.[49] With these 'confederates' Spurling set about 'secretly to undermine the burgesses'. In this task he fell back on three weapons. Firstly, the authority of the vicar in preaching from

15: The arms of the Manners Earls of Rutland, hereditary high stewards of East Retford.

16: Gilbert Talbot, 7th Earl of Shrewsbury: he made determined efforts to exercise influence in Retford and eventually became high steward in 1612.

the pulpit, though this turned out to be a mixed blessing since Watt was not well liked in the town.[50] Secondly, the power of rumour, particularly spreading stories about the possible consequences of incurring the wrath of the Countess. Clifton too was attacked in this respect, it being suggested that he had not given his wholehearted support to his candidate, and that he was unworthy of the office of high steward:

> That Sir Gervase was not great enough, for he could not speak to the King for the town if need be.[51]

Thirdly, bribery and 'treating' was employed on a large scale, and, if Browne is to be believed, considerable sums of money were laid out. The alehouses of the town overflowed as the Wortleyites:

> spent bravely and entertained their burgesses that they won with brave merriments at the tavern...And doubtless they have kept a good house for by their own report they have spent £40.[52]

Votes were bought for £2, £3 or £4 each, and on the night before the election 'it was a common talk over the town what the price of a burgess voice was...*Ten pounds for three voices'*. Spurling viewed many of these new converts with understandable suspicion, and felt that a degree of discipline was needed to keep his followers in line:

> They would not trust them upon their bare words, but enforced them to give it under their hands because they should not start back, and if at any time after they found them wavering then they threatened them with the Star Chamber because they had given it under their hands.[53]

Having been subjected to several days of intense and sometimes riotous electioneering on the part of Spurling, the bailiffs, William Dickons and George Earle, evidently felt that the contest was slipping away from them. Not only did they resent this open challenge to their authority and to the Clifton interest, but also the fact that the 'poorer' burgesses, often backed by the unfranchised commons, were actually exercising their right of choice, and not simply toeing the line of the town hierarchs: 'yet these fellows now carry themselves bravely with money in their purses', said Browne with an obvious hint of resentment. With Wortley moving into the lead, attention focused on the fifteen 'disabled' burgesses of 1623: of the fifteen, ten had already been restored by the time of the election, but the permanent disappearance of five meant that the town was below its normal voting strength.[54] If these voices could be restored a decisive advantage in favour of Darcy might be won. Accordingly, a special court was summoned by the bailiffs 'warily' at which eleven new burgesses were created: these were exclusively the sons of pro-Darcy aldermen who were free by virtue of their parentage. When Wortley's supporters demanded similar treatment, their appeals were rejected because they had failed to give notice of their intention to the aldermen and had not obtained the appropriate certificates from the parish register. When this decision was announced the Moothall erupted in disorder:

> And the burgesses of that faction being about 30 or 40...began to make a great uproar, some saying it were a good deed to pull their gowns off their backs, meaning the bailiffs and town's clerk, others crying 'A Wortley! A Wortley!' that there was such a confused noise and outcry raised that they in the town, nay in their houses, were sore affrighted, thinking we had been all together by the ears, and some others verily conceiving that they heard a great cry of 'Murder! Murder!' And the truth is that the disorder and uproar was such that the bailiffs were informed in all haste to adjourn the court and speed themselves away for fear of some mischief.[55]

Feeling themselves cheated by the legal chicanery of the corporation, some of Wortley's supporters began to affirm that 'if they could not carry it with voices they would have it with the sword', and when election day dawned, on March 9, the bailiffs feared another 'commotion'. 'To prevent the worst', as Browne put it, or to intimidate the opposition as Spurling would have had it, armed guards were placed at the door of the Moothall where voting was to take place, and Sir George Lassells and Sir Ralph Hansby, 'well wishers to Mr Darcy', patrolled the market place 'whose presence, as they thought, might do well to stay the multitude'. Only voting burgesses were admitted:

Yet for all this they of the faction would needs have had others
up, and in the end got up one, whereupon all the hall was in
a hurly burly till that man that had not his wedding garment
was taken and sent to prison.[56]

When the assembled burgesses had settled and the doors
were shut the bailiffs entered with truncheons concealed
beneath their cloaks and the town clerk proceeded to the
reading of the writ. But:

> as it was plotted beforehand, all the poor of the town with
> some others of the commons were brought into the market
> place accompanied with Vicar Watt and Welch his wife who
> emboldened and encouraged them to cry 'A Wortley! A
> Wortley!' telling them that if it were not a Wortley they and
> all the town were undone. Hereupon began a great cry and
> noise with whooping and shouting so loud that we in the hall
> could not hear one word when the King's writ was in reading,
> and so enforced to give over till the noise was appeased. And
> then beginning to read the writ again there began a second cry
> and noise as ill as the first, and thereupon the town's clerk
> enforced again to give over the reading of the writ.[57]

Eventually the votes were recorded at 47 for Darcy and 36 for
Wortley. Clifton's candidate had won the day but only by the
eleven new burgess voices created at the controversial meeting before the poll.

  When the result was known Clifton wrote to the corportion
with obvious relief and gratitude, acutely conscious of the
loss of face which a defeat of his candidate would have
involved:

> I never endured to be unrespecting of my friends and therefore
> have not the patience any longer to contain my thankfulness
> to yourselves and all my constant friends...which gives me
> just cause to redouble my thanks to yourselves, the aldermen
> of your consort and all the like burgesses, for not only
> granting my desire and tendering it so carefully...but even by
> effecting the same, preserving my reputation with all which
> hath ever been of more esteem with me than all I possess, and
> by this indirect course must needs have suffered.[58]

In order to forestall such problems in the future and re-
establish authority over the town, both Clifton and the corpo-

ration were agreed that some 'exemplary punishment' was required to prevent:

> this tumultuous and corrupt carriages of elections...and to render the inferior sort to terms of better conformity towards the principal magistrate.

Clifton's anti-democratic venom was directed 'against Spurling his fellow solliciths and the rabble of bruted burgesses' who needed to be:

> taken off from demeaning themselves in such intolerable manner...in which quarrel as I am deeply interested so I will join all my power.

The corporation suggested a case before Star Chamber, but Clifton believed that the Committee of Privileges was the proper place to determine such a dispute, and in deference to him the town borrowed £60 to pursue their complaint in Parliament.[59]

Accordingly the corporation presented a petition accusing Spurling and others of 'undue practices...and...divers misdemeanours', only to be counter-petitioned by Wortley's supporters who accused the town clerk of mishandling the election and asked for a new writ to be issued.[60] The corporation's case centred around the bribery and treating employed by Spurling and Richard Welch, one of his leading burgess supporters, and the attempts of the vicar to raise a tumult amongst the non-voting commons. But Wortley too had legitimate grounds for complaint, not always evident from Robert Browne's one-sided account of the contest quoted above. Henry Bishop, the sergeant-at-mace, had used his authority to arrest two prominent Wortley supporters, and armed force had been used to overawe the opposition on election day, particularly when Darcy's friends paraded in the market place in 'a brave'. But most important of all was the creation of the eleven new burgesses just before the poll. It was alleged that of these only one should have been given the vote, as a householder, the others being merely 'foreigners and sojourners'. This point employed the definition of a burgess enshrined in the Statute of Apprentices, not that traditionally accepted in the town, and though Wortley might have felt genuinely aggrieved by the fact that civic authority was manipulated in favour of the Clifton interest he was on weak ground when he sought to prove that the corporation had acted illegally. Nevertheless, the committee showed more sympathy to his petition than that of the town, many of whose points did not stand up to scrutiny or were deemed to be but 'slenderly proved'. In the end only four people were thought to have committed misdemeanours (Spurling, Welch, Bishop and Watt), and those were 'not very enormous and for the most part proved by a single testimony'. The fact that John Darcy died on April 21 took a good deal of the heat out of the situation, because it meant that a new writ had to be issued thus giving Wortley's supporters another opportunity. The Journal of the House recorded: 'concerning East Retford, Lord Darcy his son returned who died, to let this sleep and pass it over'.[61] When the third election for this Parliament was held the victor was Sir Francis Wortley, brother of Sir Edward, suggesting that Clifton had gracefully permitted the Countess of Devonshire to have her way in order to avoid any further 'indirect and insufferable proceedings' which could only act to the discredit of established authority and the encouragement of plebians.[62]

Indeed, the most notable point to emerge from the complicated story of the 1624 election is the determination of 'authority' to dictate the nomination of MPs and the fears unleashed when a contested election actually led to the burgesses exercising their legitimate powers of choice. The whole incident had uncanny echoes of the elections for bailiffs in the 1590s when burgess power had still been a force to reckon with in the town. Since 1607 the aldermen had been able to 'manage' these elections by selection of candidates, and the uproar and tumult of 1624 certainly convinced some individuals that some further control of the Parliamentary process was also called for. Given their heads in a supposedly 'free' election why did people vote as they did? Interestingly, Robert Browne sent to Sir Gervase Clifton a note of all votes cast for Darcy and Wortley in the second election of 1623/24, from which we are able to identify townsmen who were prepared to stand out against the high steward and the corporation and try to work out why they voted as they did. Amongst 'the rabble of bruted burgesses' which voted for Wortley were some highly respected citizens, such as William Thornton and William Mason both of whom had served as JPs by virtue of having been bailiffs since 1607: Thornton, indeed was one of the most venerable inhabitants of the borough and had retired as an alderman in 1622 only because of old age and frailty.[63] The leaders of the Wortley faction hint at an interesting mixture of motives. John Watt who, of course, as vicar, had no vote, was a nominee of the Cavendish family and looked to them for further preferment. The serving aldermen, Richard Elsam and Martin Taylor, broke ranks with the corporation for similar motives. Elsam's family came from Ordsall, where the Cavendishes were actively buying up land. He occupied property at Welham, in Clarborough, where they owned the rectory. Taylor had married Elizabeth Turvin in 1587, probably the sister of the previous vicar, so the ecclesiastical connections of the Cavendishes may well have carried some weight here too.[64] Taylor was also the father-in-law of another prominent Wortley supporter, Thomas Draper. Elsam and Taylor had both been bailiffs of the town, so they were hardly marginal characters in local politics, and Draper enjoyed that office in 1614: however, in 1622 he was deposed as an alderman 'for his miscarriage and evil government' which doubtless left him with a grudge against the corporation. It is significant that Draper was one of the Wortley supporters locked up by the sergeant-at-mace during the election campaign.[65]

It was also a sense of grievance against the hierarchy which motivated the Welch family, the leading Wortleyites amongst the burgesses. Richard Welch, a butcher, and Thomas, his son, had been involved in a long and bitter dispute with the corporation over commercial premises in the Moothall and market square and were likely to espouse any cause directed against their would-be oppressors: Richard's wife, Amy, showed considerable spirit by helping John Watt to whip up support from the paupers in the market place on election day.[66] Thus, Spurling looked to two sorts of person to spearhead his attack. Firstly, those who were traditionally loyal to, or wary of, the Countess of Devonshire; and secondly, those who had some grudge against Clifton

17: Sir Gervase Clifton: a major protagonist in the disputed election of 1624 and high steward from 1616 to 1666.

18: John Holles, 1st Earl of Clare: his great wealth, and traditional links with the town, secured one of the Parliamentary seats for his son John, Lord Haughton, in the 1620s.

and the corporation which might not have any relevance whatsoever to the election. Given the loyalty of a nucleus of activists, it was then down to bribery, threats and promises to build up enough votes to win the day. Wortley's burgesses were not significantly inferior to those who supported Darcy — the Masons, indeed, were one of the more substantial families of the town[67] — but the losers would inevitably fall victim to a tirade of patronising rhetoric designed to undermine their credibility and question their motives. What is clear is that the election was dominated entirely by local personalities and issues, without a thought for the vexed question of the royal prerogative or any of the other issues of state which concerned the Parliamentarians of Westminster. It speaks well of Retford's 'openness' and tolerance, that even those who came out for Wortley in 1624 were not disabled from making their mark in local politics and serving as aldermen and bailiffs during the next decade. Clifton's compromise with the Countess of Devonshire was mirrored by a similar truce in local affairs.

The elections of 1625, 1626 and 1627 were less controversial, with John Holles, Lord Haughton, retaining one of the seats and the other being occupied by the Wortley brothers, Sir Francis in 1625 and 1627 and Sir Edward in 1626.[68] These elections, and particularly that of John Holles, son of the wealthy first Earl of Clare, illustrate how open both Clifton and the borough were to representations made on behalf of the sons of the aristocracy of the region.[69] The same was true in 1640 after eleven years of personal rule by Charles I. In the elections for the Short Parliament Clifton was lobbied by William Cavendish, first Earl of Newcastle, to give the Retford seats to his son, the fourteen year old Lord Cavendish, and Endymion Porter, poet and confidant of Charles I.[70] However, it soon became apparent that on this occasion Clifton intended to occupy one of the borough seats himself, and Robert Pierrepont, first Earl of Kingston, wrote independently to the corporation requesting the election of his son, Francis.[71] A potentially damaging confrontation between Newcastle and Kingston was avoided when Lord Cavendish was accepted for Nottingham, thus leaving Clifton and Francis Pierrepont as the Short Parliament members for East Retford.

When fresh elections were soon held for the Long Parliament, Clifton and young Lord Cavendish occupied the borough seats. In view of the Parliamentarian sympathies of the corporation, it is ironic that almost all of its representatives, and the men pulling the strings behind them, were notable supporters of the royalist cause. Only Francis Pierrepont, whose election his father hoped would 'decrease his humour of melancholy', became a Parliamentarian and rose to be a colonel in the army and a friend of John Hutchinson.[72] Lucy Hutchinson, with her usual insight, characterised him as:

> a man of good natural parts, but not of education according to his quality, who was in the main well affected to honest men and to religious liberty: a man of very excellent good nature and full of love to all men, but that his goodness receive a little alloy by a vain glorious pride which could not well brooke that any other should outstrip him in virtue and estimation.[73]

It is a peculiarly modern view to suppose that a member of Parliament should reflect the views of the people he represents. However, given the attitude of the corporation to the Protestation in 1642, there must have been many people in the town who instinctively warmed to the politics, and direct action, of the puritanical Colonel Pierrepont.

In East Retford the Parliamentary franchise sank as low as it was likely to fall in sixteenth and seventeenth England, and people enjoyed the vote there who would not have come even close to such a privilege in the shire. Generally speaking the corporation was prepared to be deferential to its high steward or any other local magnate who might make an uncontested recommendation, and with no competition elections were non-events requiring little effort or outlay by the protagonists. The burgesses had a clear preference for local men who might have been better able to represent the interests of the town, but beyond that they paid little attention to who was elected or what he did once he arrived in Parliament: two of the members for the borough during this period were only in their middle teens, and what good they could have done for the town must have been seriously debated, even in the context of seventeenth century politics. It was only when an election became contested, as it did in 1624, that the towns-men came into their own, to the obvious resentment not only of their high steward but also their own governors. Here, with the sons of noblemen paying court to humble tradesmen, was a dangerous vision of the world turned upside down, the politics of the 1650s presaged as if in a dream. But, although the upshot was the same both in terms of the experience and the conservative backlash it provoked, the townsmen of Retford in the 1620s were hardly motivated by the same altruistic causes which often moved the democrats of the Cromwellian era. Election to a national assembly was governed by bribery and local issues as trivial as the occupation of butchers' stalls in the shambles. This was the true measure of a borough which was to become rightly regarded as one of England's most rotten, over-represented in the years before the Civil War and for the most part too weak to make that representation work to its benefit.[74]

FOOTNOTES AND REFERENCES

1. NUMD, Cl. LP. 52.
2. *Ibid.*
3. JA, RB 2, f.98, Piercy, p.20.
4. P. W. Hasler, *The House of Commons, 1558-1603* (1981), 1, p.223/4: *DNB.*
5. JA, RB 2 ff.2, 3, NUMD, Cl. D. 1632: the grant to Sir Gervase Clifton (1616) still bears a splendid impression of the seal of the corporation.
6. BC, Letters, 22/2/1590; RM, 667. 85; NUMD, Cl. C. 378.
7. *Ibid.*, Cl. LP. 52.
8. Piercy, p.51.
9. JA, RB 1 (Members of Parliament).
10. BC, Letters, 22/9/1586.
11. *DNB*, Early Rutland clients were Thomas Broxholme (1571): George Delves (1572): Thomas Wade (1585): John Conyers (1586). Hasler, 1, pp.502, 643, 2, p.29, 3, p.560.
12. *DNB*, Hasler, 3, pp.492-4.
13. NUMD, Cl. LP. 52.
14. Hasler, 2, pp.55, 330.

15. JA, RB 1 (Members of Parliament), RB 2 ff.144. See also A. C. Wood (ed.), *Memorials of the Holles Family, 1493-1656*, Camden Society, 3rd Series, 55, 1937.

16. Hasler, 1, pp.222/3, P. Seddon, 'A Parliamentary Election at East Retford, 1624', *TTS*, 75, 1972, pp.26-8. For a wider discussion of this issue see, W. T. MacCaffrey, 'Talbot and Stanhope: an episode in Elizabethan politics', *Bulletin of the Institute of Historical Research*, 33, pp.73-85.

17. See Chapter 6, p.165.

18. JA, RB 1 (Members of Parliament).

19. *Ibid.*

20. *Ibid.*, Hasler, 3, p.267, *The Visitation of Nottinghamshire*, pp.111/12. The copy letter in the Piercy Mss. names Peter Rook (which baffled Piercy), but this is almost certainly a mistranscription for Peter Roos.

21. Hasler, 1, pp.595/6, *TTS*, 75, pp.26/7, BC, Letters, 24/9/1586.

22. BC, Letters, 22/2/1590.

23. JA, RB 1 (Members of Parliament).

24. Hasler, 1, pp.595/6.

25. BC, Letters, 22/2/1590.

26. *Ibid.*

27. HMC, *Rutland*, 1, p.280.

28. BC, Letters, 31/10/1592.

29. Hasler, 1, pp.643/4.

30. *Ibid.*, 3, pp.238/9.

31. *Ibid.*, p.304.

32. *Ibid.*, p.9.

33. LPL, Shrewsbury Mss. 708 ff.115/6, Hasler, 2, pp.425/6. Kydman was described as 'a noted papist' in 1591.

34. Hasler, 1, pp.223/4.

35. JA, RB 2 ff.2, 164, *The Visitation of Nottinghamshire*, pp.90/1. In 1606 Rutland was duly paid his fee as high steward, probably at the house of Sir John Thornhaugh at Fenton.

36. JA, RB 2, f.2.

37. RM, 667. 85.

38. *DNB*.

39. *Ibid.*, *TTS*, 75, p.28.

40. JA, RB 1 (Members of Parliament).

41. *Ibid.*, RB 2 f.3, NUMD, Cl. D. 1632, LP. 52.

42. For some details of his career, see P. R. Seddon, 'Marriage and Inheritance in the Clifton Family during the seventeenth century', *TTS*, 84, 1980, pp.33-43.

43. The estates were purchased from Thomas Cornwallis Esq, Piercy, p.210. In 1565 William Swift received licence to alienate monastic property in East Retford and Clarborough to Francis Wortley and Mary, his wife. *CPR, 1563-66*, p.298.

44. JA, RB 2, f.5.

45. V. Gibbs (ed.), *The Complete Peerage*, 3, p.248.

46. J. W. Clay (ed.), *Dugdale's Visitation of Yorkshire* (1907), 2, p.79. Darcy was stated to be only fifteen or sixteen years old.

47. NUMD, Cl. C. 149.

48. *Ibid.*, Cl. LP. 52. See also *TTS*, 75.

49. Also one Daintry, the Countess's bailiff of Ordsall. This could be Tristram Daintry, who was a churchwarden of East Retford in 1615. JA, RB 1 (Churchwardens).

50. For the role of Watt in this election, see Chapter 6, pp.188-9.

51. NUMD, Cl. LP. 52.

52. *Ibid.*

53. *Ibid.*

54. Of the ten 'disabled' burgesses who voted in 1624 six voted for Darcy and four for Wortley. They were probably restored before the campaign, having compounded with the town chamber. It remains a matter of speculation whether or not they regarded this as a straightforward commercial transaction i.e. the cost of composition set against the bribes likely to be received in a contested election campaign.

55. NUMD, Cl. LP. 52.

56. *Ibid.*

57. *Ibid.*

58. *Ibid.*, Cl. C. 378.

59. JA, RB 1 (Members of Parliament). Ironically the corporation borrowed from Thomas Cornwallis who had sold his Ordsall estate to the Countess of Devonshire!

60. J. Glanville, *Reports of Certain Cases...in Parliament, 21 and 22 James I* (1775), pp.128-32.

61. *Journal of the House of Commons*, 1, p.797.

62. NUMD, Cl. LP. 52.

63. JA, RB 2 f.5.

64. UNCLH, FRF.

65. JA, RB 2 f.5.

66. *Ibid.*, ff.3, 136.

67. For a partial pedigree, see JA, RB 3. The family came from Yorkshire, and there was a link with the Huttons of Houghton-

le-Spring, Co Durham, descendants of Matthew Hutton, Archbishop of York.

68.   *TTS*, 75, p.33.

69.   John Holles, 1st Earl of Clare, was reputed to have paid the Duke of Buckingham £15,000 for the Barony of Haughton and Earldom of Clare. Gibbs, 3, pp.247/8.

70.   NUMD, Cl. C. 344, 606. *DNB*. Porter had been active in the attempt to negotiate a Spanish marriage for Charles in the 1620s: during the 1630s he was used by the King as one of his agents to build up his collection of pictures. He sat in the Long Parliament for Droitwich and resisted the attainder of Strafford. For the 1640 elections in the county, see P. R. Seddon, 'The Nottinghamshire Elections for the Short Parliament of 1640', *TTS*, 76, 1972, pp.26-34.

71.   NUMD, Cl. C. 294, 295, 684, 715.

72.   B. D. Henning, *The House of Commons, 1660-1690* (1983), 3, pp.242/3.

73.   Quoted in JA, RB 1 (Members of Parliament).

74.   For a town election later in the seventeenth century, see P. R. Seddon, 'An East Retford Parliamentary Election of 1670', *TTS*, 88, 1984, pp.42-46.

Chapter 4

PROSPERITY AND POVERTY

And so as that town...for ever may be...a town of peace and quietude, to the dread and terror of evil delinquents, and reward of the good...in their offices, functions, services, trades and businesses.[1]

Like all market towns Retford depended for its prosperity on its relationship with its hinterland, the definition of which was variable according to time and circumstance. Sitting at the centre of the Bassetlaw Hundred the town, 'consisting wholly of artificers', had the potential to act as a trading centre for North Nottinghamshire, and indeed beyond the county boundaries, but effectively Retford sustained it closest relationship with a cluster of parishes grouped within a five mile radius of the town, the distance a countryman could travel to market without suffering notable ill effects on the journey. Clarborough was often in trouble before the Quarter Sessions for the condition of its roads, which had the danger of damaging Retford's trade, and in 1613 it was stated that the road from North Wheatley was 'far gone in decay, so that passengers cannot go that way without peril to their lives'.[2] Benevolent townsmen such as Brian Thornton occasionally did something to try to relieve this problem; he provided money to prevent the flooding of Thrumpton Lane in 1604, but it was really beyond simple amendment.[3] With the exception of the considerable boon of the Great North Road, Retford was destined to pursue its economic life with a communications system which was poor on land and virtually non-existent on water.

The trade of the borough fell under the supervision of the corporation who, for the sake of convenience, delegated its authority to the wardens of a number of companies. In 1600, under new regulations approved by Sir Edmund Anderson, these companies were 'reduced' to three, the companies of mercers, tanners and shoemakers which were supposed to incorporate all of the trades in the town.[4] Each company had two wardens elected annually by the membership on the Friday before Michaelmas Day in the Moothall 'upon the ringing of the bell'. The companies enjoyed a monopoly of trade in the town, except during 'open fair' when outsiders were welcomed, and in return for this considerable privilege the wardens were expected to shoulder certain responsibilities such as regulating apprentices, enforcing regulations in a court of orders, and keeping accounts. In none of these activities did they have much freedom of action independent of the bailiffs and aldermen who were determined — at least after 1600 — to retain ultimate control of the companies. The continual emphasis on penalties for non-performance of duties implies a long standing difficulty in galvanising the wardens or their membership into concerted action. Apart from these purely economic functions the companies had a social role too. When a freeman married, or when one of his immediate relatives or servants died, for example, every householder of the same occupation was expected to attend church, and if any member of a company was to 'fall into poverty or decay' by reason of fire or sickness, 'and not through...folly', he was to be relieved at the discretion of the wardens. Indeed, at the end of the year when all fines and income had been collected in by the various companies, the proceeds were to be split evenly between the wardens and the town chamber for the use of 'decayed persons', the defence of the liberties of the corporation 'and other needful and expedient uses'.

The regulation of apprentices was, potentially, the most time consuming and troublesome aspect of a warden's work, and the corporation was obliged to issue a set of guidelines in this respect in 1599, repeated under the seals of the Assize judges in 1639.[5] They were emphatic that apprentices were to serve for no less than seven years, that they were to be bound within 40 days of entry and that they were to be enroled before the bailiffs. Once indentured no apprentice was to depart without licence and no master was to 'sell the years of his apprentice': if a master died before the agreed term was completed, the apprenticeship was to be transferred to his widow or another member of his family, if possible. In the event of a dispute between master and apprentice, both parties had recourse to the bailiffs and wardens who could determine the matter upon 'hearing both parties with their proofs and witnesses'. Two matters, in particular, called for special attention, and these must have been highlighted as a result of many years of experience: theft and disordered conduct. If an apprentice stole more than 6s 8d from his master, in money or goods, he was to be punished according to the law, but if his crime was not encompassed in the definition of felony he was to be dealt with by the bailiffs and wardens and not released from prison until a fine of 20s had been paid. If the apprentice was a haunter of alehouses, 'or other infamed or suspected house', a gamester, 'or do lie forth by his master or mistresses house', he was to be imprisoned for 24 hours on bread and water for the first offence and for 48 hours for the second. A single offence of theft and a third offence of disordered conduct caused an apprentice to lose his freedom of the town, and this could only be restored for a 'new admission' which would cost £5. An apprentice could not obtain a house or commence trading until three months before the end of this indentured term, and then he was obliged to pay a fee 'at his first upsetting before he shall keep shop'. No one not apprenticed in the town was to share this privilege, unless he had been apprenticed 'in some ancient city of this realm' or was specially licensed by the bailiffs and wardens. The need to underline these regulations so vigorously implies that the corporation feared that traditional attitudes towards training and social discipline were in danger of breaking down towards the end of Elizabeth's reign, a feeling shared in other urban centres at this time. This may indeed have been so in view of the growing awareness of poverty and vagrancy and the disputes amongst the town hierarchs over the nature of their incorporation: as suggested in Chapter 2, these quarrels may well have had a dimension which included the enforcement of traditional apprenticeship regulations and necessitated a tight control over the town companies.[6] In this context, of course, there was always the loophole of West Retford and Moorgate where corporation regulations had no force whatsoever.

To gain an overall impression of Retford's economy a total of 384 occupational descriptions was extracted for the three parishes between 1550 and 1642, largely derived from wills and Quarter Sessions' records. Of these a high proportion (68%) were status descriptions, and the remainder (32%) related to specific trades and occupations.[7] The status descriptions were not very helpful in explaining what a person actually did, since it soon became plain that a 'yeoman' (the most common terminology accounting for 40% of the sample) might as easily be a tradesman as someone connected wholly or partly with agriculture. Indeed, status descriptions were interchangeable to such a degree that it was sometimes difficult to be sure that one was actually dealing with the same person. Childers Keyworth, for example, was a yeoman/husbandman, William Bend a husbandman/labourer, and William Day a labourer/yeoman.[8] The occupational descriptions were more helpful, but still prone to an interchange with status descriptions, Thomas Noddle being a tanner/labourer and Richard Tong a blacksmith/husbandman.[9] In general the town trades were what would be expected to service a rural economy. Excluding the specialised leather and fabric trades which will be considered later, 30% of tradesmen fitted into a miscellaneous category covering a wide range of service, supply and retail agencies — coopers, chandlers, pedlars and blacksmiths. These were the sort of trades needed to supply Retford's needs and also those of country people who came into town on market days seeking services not available in their own villages, the specialised occupation of glass working (which required furnaces and other equipment) being a good example of this. Medical help too was available and the town supported a surgeon in 1585 and 1637.[10]

The problem of inconsistent and dual description is related, at least in part, to the fact that many townsmen pursued more than one occupation and that their status was debatable in the eyes of their neighbours. Sons of men of established burgess, or 'yeoman' stock, who worked as wage labourers might be difficult to account for: did their contemporaries judge them on what they did or accord them the status due to their families? Henry Marshall, tailor, owned a house and land that he let out on lease, and William Smyth, shoemaker and ex-bailiff, also owned and leased property, kept pigs, and brewed his own ale, possibly for sale.[11] Given the inter-relationship implicit in a small town and the diversity of activity needed just to guarantee survival, the vagaries of description appear to be less surprising. One of the most widespread activities pursued alongside a primary occupation was malting and the brewing of ale. Although there were many professional maltsters in Retford, many quite ordinary dwellings had kilnhouses attached to them for the production of malt from barley, and malt figures significantly as a legacy in a number of wills:[12] in 1542 Thomas Marshall bequeathed 36 quarters of it, and in 1605 Jonie Oxenforth bestowed a more modest fourteen and a half quarters along with 'four metts and strykes' of malt.[13] Both of these testators came from Moorgate which appears to have been the centre of malting activities. A wealthy clergyman such as Nicholas Pettinger II had his own kiln and malting equipment at West Retford, but George Turvin had to put out his barley to be malted elsewhere; in 1617 he owed 2s 8d for the making of three quarters of malt, and at the time of his death he had another two quarters with the maltster valued at 40s.[14] The next step on from malting, of course, was the brewing of ale, and in the seventeenth century both the Archdeacon's court and the Quarter Sessions testify to the problems caused in the town by the proliferation of alehouses, often opened by poor people in an attempt to bolster their paltry incomes. Alehouses were attacked because they consumed barley, which it was thought should have gone for the production of bread, and also because of the drunkenness and irreligion they were believed to foster.[15] So widespread was the problem that the corporation was obliged to direct a specific order against bailiffs engaging in this activity in 1646:

> not only to the great scandal of the said office but also to the hinderance and obstruction of the due administration of justice, and the evil example of others, and the encouragement of offenders.[16]

The only perceived benefit of the town's alehouses was that they helped keep poor ale sellers above the poverty line. It is impossible to state whether Retford produced sufficient malt to enable its export, or simply to cater for the alcoholic requirements of its own inhabitants. These were considerable if the churchwardens presentments of the 1620s and 1630s are to be believed.

The large number of tradesmen in the town meant that many young people were employed as apprentices or servants, the latter term referring as often to an 'industrial' servant as to one who worked in the household. The cost of an apprenticeship varied considerably. Dorothy Watson left Daniel Sharpe 20s 'to bind him to prentice', but Robert Speighte provided Robert Barker with 40s 'to be bound prentice': Henry Atkinson, shoemaker and erstwhile bailiff, had received £5 from the grandmother of his apprentice, Joseph Bold.[17] No doubt much depended on the trade and the master, but a wealthy burgess and draper, such as William Spivy, would almost certainly be considered an ideal choice to take in hand the training of a younger kinsman. The pattern of debts which existed between Spivy and the parents of his apprentice, Francis Denman, is not clear, but in his will in 1602 he remitted them whilst leaving another apprentice, John Wilsbie, the not inconsiderable sum of £10.[18] The Quarter Sessions, as well as the companies of the town, were keen to enforce indentured apprenticeship and in 1639 Henry Turner was prosecuted for plying the trade of a butcher without proper training.[19] As both justices and bailiffs were well aware apprenticeship had as much to do with imposing discipline on the young as it did with maintaining high standards of workmanship, delaying their marriage and teaching proper respect for their elders. It is notable that when testators gave a legacy to an apprentice, be it a horse or a sum of money, it was invariably to take effect after the apprenticeship was completed, to avoid any risk of dislocation of the training in hand.[20] The majority of apprentices traced have been male and the assumptions in the regulations seem to confirm this, but in 1524 Agnes Richardson was provided with a legacy on the completion of her apprenticeship and in 1592 Joan Leake was apprenticed to William Key, a tailor.[21] Despite rules designed to deal with crises, relationships between masters and servants, be they apprentices or not, were commonly harmonious, revealed by legacies, such as those of William Spivy, and instructions left in wills. William Dunstan, tanner, gave his apprentice 40s:

> provided that he serve my executor, having meat and drink
> and all things necessary for an apprentice until the leather be
> wrought up in the yards.[22]

Similarly, John Day left his apprentice all his clothing and
'one wymble, one thixell, a joynter, a whittell and an old
axe'.[23] Non-indentured servants could be treated just as well.
Edmund Seyton gave to Peter Savile:

> his house which he now dwelleth in rent free for sixteen years
> so that he shall be diligent and friendly to help my wife and
> children with his labour for their reasonable wage.[24]

Philip Syles, glazier, gave to George, 'my man', his vice and
working tools and 'the little shop at my house end' for the
duration of his lease.[25] Elizabeth Smith, 'my late wife's
kinswoman and now my servant', possibly did best of all
when she received a share of the residual estate of John Earle,
maltster, in 1632.[26] But the relationship again underlines the
close social proximity of people in a small town such as
Retford. Occasionally testators mention children who had
gone off to work for masters elsewhere, and they are generally in villages within the five mile radius.[27] This mutual
exchange of children and kinsfolk as apprentices and servants could guarantee considerate treatment or at least the fear
of retribution if things went too badly wrong.

But of course servants could equally well be drawn from
amongst the mobile underworld of the poor, and those
lacking the social discipline of an apprenticeship might rebel
when faced with authority they were not prepared to put up
with. In these circumstances the Quarter Sessions was obliged
to step in to enforce agreements or bargains struck at hirings.
In 1635 the town suffered a minor epidemic of disordered
servant girls when Margaret Watson and Joan Mullins both
left their masters. Mullins claimed she had been sent away by
Richard Parnell because she was pregnant, but Watson left
William Moody of her own accord, though there was a
suspicion that she too was with child. Watson survived for a
while with temporary work, but Mullins became a vagrant
wandering aimlessly about the town. Neither was a situation
the justices were prepared to tolerate, and both girls were sent
back to their masters to serve out the terms of their contracts.[28]

Thomas Bishop, rector of West Retford, also found himself in the position of enforcing a contract against a reluctant servant. In 1640 he hired John Craggs for a year as a farm labourer, but no sooner had he done this than Craggs became tenant of a cottage at Babworth owned by Christopher Coe who also desired his services. Craggs, afraid of losing his house, left Bishop's employment after only a month, but the justices upheld the initial contract and ordered the constable of Babworth to deliver him up if he refused to comply.[29] These incidents prove that there was plenty of legislation to fall back upon if working relationships fell apart: they were designed to help servants, as in the case of Joan Mullins, just as much as they were to uphold the rights of masters. As in the case of the ecclesiastical jurisdiction, however, swift movement away from the town rapidly rendered all such sanctions null and void since the mechanism, or the will, to pursue offenders simply did not exist.

If 30% of the town's trade was made up of miscellaneous occupations, the remaining 70% was trade of a specialised nature connected with the processing of leather and fabrics. The leather trades, ranging from butchers, through tanners to shoemakers and glovers, comprised 45% of all stated occupations. The fabric trades, comprising spinsters, weavers, mercers, drapers and tailors, comprised 25%, though it will be shown that this is not necessarily a fair reflection of the place they held in the local economy in general. Within these groups the most important trades were tanners and shoemakers (comprising 65% of the whole), and mercers and tailors (comprising 55% of the whole). It was no coincidence that the three companies selected to regulate the trade of the town were connected with these dominant occupations. These trades held pride of place in the economy and administration of Retford from the close of the Middle Ages up to the Civil War, the leather trade remaining fairly consistent in its prosperity but the cloth trade being subject to dramatic fluctuation dictated by England's relationship with the Low Countries and other factors far out of the control of the townsmen. In each case production was beyond the scale required to service the town and its hinterland and surpluses must have been available for export, nationally and perhaps internationally.

19: Preparing hides in a tanyard: the tanneries on the banks of the Idle were one of the major industries of the town.

20: Shoemaking was one of the Retford's most important industries, but the craftsmen themselves rarely achieved great prosperity.

Although it is impossible to determine the scale and relative importance of these more widely disseminated goods, Retford's position on the line of the Great North Road to London and proximity to Gainsborough, a port with trade links with the Low Countries, should not be forgotten.

In the nineteenth century Piercy noted that to the South and East of the town, in the valley of the Trent, lay some exceptionally fine grazing land.[30] Livestock had been a feature of the area since earliest days, cattle being produced to the East of the town and sheep on the less fertile lands to the West: indeed, the large number of sheep bestowed as legacies in the sixteenth century is one of the abiding impressions of a large number of Retford wills. Edward Slater, a Retford butcher, provides an insight into how the local livestock trade operated by virtue of a dispute he had with John Savage, rector of Fledborough, in 1614. Slater occupied pasture land at Fledborough, on the banks of the Trent, where he reared fat cattle and sheep which were taken to Retford for slaughter.[31] The killing of animals other than in authorised places was an ongoing nuisance, and in 1554 James Atkinson was fined by the town court for 'killing flesh' and pouring blood in the street.[32] Although the meat of these animals was retailed by the butchers of the shambles, some of it perhaps having been salted, it was for their by-products that they were principally valued and it was ordered in 1599 that no butcher living outside of the town was to sell flesh in Retford 'unless he or they bring with them the hide and tallow thereof'.[33] Given a regular supply of water from the Idle and bark from nearby Sherwood Forest, Retford was an obvious base for the tanning industry, and in the 1554 court roll many more prosecutions were brought for 'washing skins' than for the unlawful slaughter of animals.[34] Indeed, Piercy noted in the 1820s that:

> It will be found on digging rather deep in all the gardens lying along the margin of the river Idle, from Bridgegate to the Car, that the land is full of hooves and horns and in many instances the hair of animals has turned up as fresh as when it was first buried.[35]

Tallow was used for the production of candles, and the 1554 court roll once more provides ample evidence of this activity being carried out at places other than authorised centres of production.[36]

With regard to the meat and tanning industries John Wymoke stands out as a man of considerable commercial importance. Wymoke, a drover, who died in 1560, was one of the town's wealthiest inhabitants and was active in local government as early as the 1530s, serving as bailiff in 1541: Robert Wymoke, a butcher, was probably his brother.[37] In conjunction with a Mrs Mason, he leased a farm at Fenton in the Trentside parish of Sturton-le-Steeple where cattle were raised. Wymoke also bought in livestock from a wide range of business contacts and then sent droves to London following the line of the Great North Road: in 1560 such a drove was on its way South with Bartholomew Fox and William Johnson comprising 56 cattle valued at £78 10s 0d. The destination of many of these unfortunate creatures were the butchers of St Nicholas' Shambles, London, who were amongst Wymoke's best customers.[38] But many people stood in debt to him, not just for cattle, sheep and horses, but also money lent 'by his bill obligatory'. When he died he was owed almost £500, some of it in the form of credit transactions being paid off by instalment.[39] Many of Wymoke's business contacts have been traced along the line of the Great North Road from Doncaster and Brotherton in the North, through Colsterworth in Lincolnshire, to Biggleswade and Baldock near London. He made a fortune out of exploiting two of the town's greatest assets — its tradition of producing good livestock and its fortuitous location adjacent to the main arterial route of the kingdom.

The cloth trade rested on the wool of sheep and also on the extensive local cultivation of flax and hemp. The *Valor Ecclesiasticus*, which provides one of the earliest opportunities to undertake a survey of the parochial economy, reveals that almost all parishes in the Retford Deanery grew flax, but that its production was centred to the North of the town and particularly in parishes such as Misson, Everton, Sturton-le-Steeple and Sutton-cum-Lound where it was a prominent feature of the local economy.[40] Flax and wool were brought to Retford to be spun and then woven into fabric or, alternatively, the processes were carried out in the surrounding villages and the cloth brought to the town for sale. Indeed, the only people released from the all embracing monopoly of the town companies, outside of fair trading, were those who made woollen and linen cloth themselves and brought it to Retford to be sold. Moreover, the regulations of 1600 conceded that many of these manufacturers would be women, and this poses a problem since women working on a domestic basis tend not to figure very prominently in the surviving records.[41] What is clear is that the term 'spinster' really did mean 'one who spun' in Retford, because two cases of married spinsters have been encountered: Emmot Hodgson in 1541 and Gertrude Cobb in 1631.[42] Only four inventories have survived for the town, but all provide evidence of the trade, suggesting it was once commonplace. Nicholas Pettinger II (1578) had two spinning wheels and a linen wheel: he had lin in the yard (presumably unsoaked) valued at 33s 4d, and undressed lin worth 6s 8d. In his 'Outer Parlour' he had eighteen yards of harden cloth, eighteen yards of hempen cloth, and, 'of linen 42 yards at the weaver' valued at 43s 4d.[43] George Turvin (1617) had two wool wheels and two little wheels, rough hemp and lin worth 13s 4d, and fine lin, coarse lin and hemp valued at 24s.[44] Richard Elsam (1628) owned a spinning wheel, a wool wheel and a linen wheel, and had in his house six and a half yards of woollen cloth.[45] Finally, John Watt (1640) possessed in his modest household three linen wheels and a wool wheel.[46] Wills are a more speculative source, but nevertheless they provide considerable evidence for the trade. In 1550 Joan Thompson left to her daughter 'all my hemp, giving Anne Halton half a stone of the same', and in 1558 Elizabeth Backhouse gave to Alice Blighton:

> six score lin of this year growth...To every poor woman within the parish of West Retford, being a householder, five score of unbroken lin...To Margaret my maid 3s and six score of lin and a peck of linseed.[47]

In 1632 John Carberton, yeoman, gave his servant, Ann Otter, all the flax and hemp in his house spun and unspun, and in 1639 Elizabeth Parnell gave her son-in-law 'all my lin standing and being in my said son William, his yard'.[48]

Some interesting points emerge from these statements. Firstly, out of four testators who mentioned lin in their wills three were women, suggesting that its preparation and spinning was a largely female activity. Secondly, all of the men, or at least members of their households, pursued spinning and weaving as a secondary occupation, and John Carberton's bequest to Ann Otter raises the possibility of servants specifically employed to undertake spinning, taking the industry away from simply a family orientated pursuit. Thirdly, spinning was clearly an activity thought to be appropriate for the poor, since it was a skill easily assimilated and did not require substantial capital investment to get started. The only problem with linen production was that it was likely to become contentious. The slow moving river Idle and the pools of the Cars and Commons might have been ideal for the spinners to soak their flax, but the retting process created an offensive smell, poisoned the water and blocked up the river. In 1611 Anne Childers of Moorgate was called before the Quarter Sessions accused of trespass and riot. Evidently she had been washing hemp in the river accompanied by William Bing, labourer, and Dorothy Shersy, spinster, when things got out of hand in some unspecified way. Anne was fined 6d as the leader of the group, the implication being that Bing and Shersy were her servants, further evidence of the production of linen on a semi-industrial basis.[49] Similarly, in 1619 John Watt was prosecuted for soaking his flax in the Idle, a simple breach of the statute of 1541/2 without trespass for tumult involved.[50] Much of our information about the pre-industrial linen industry comes from Gervase Markham's book *A Way to get Wealth* published in 1611. It is no coincidence that Markham came from Nottinghamshire and may have been a resident of the town.[51]

Of our four inventories, two of the clerics, in particular, indicate a special interest in wool. Nicholas Pettinger II had in 'The Store Chamber' twelve stones of wool valued at £4 13s 4d, and George Turvin owned 18lb of fine wool and 30lb of lamb's wool worth 24s.[52] This was hardly surprising, since Pettinger owned a flock of 134 sheep and Turvin one of 129. Both men, it should be remembered, had spinning equipment on the premises. Looking at wills, the giving of wool is fairly common, though the suspicion must be that the majority of testators merely took it for granted: in 1558, for example,

Elizabeth Backhouse bequeathed a stone of it and in 1600 Brian Eaton half a stone.[53] The town had a succession of professional weavers such as Thomas Carr, Nicholas Bend and James Lees who in their wills made reference to their 'workhouses' containing looms and other equipment, and in 1593 Richard Merebeck, shereman, made his will leaving his tenters and shop furniture to his son.[54] More interesting than these 'professionals', perhaps, is the gift by Jane Braithwaite, widow, to Peter Whitfield of 'my weaving loom with all gere belonging to the same' in 1558.[55] This, of course, suggests that weaving was carried out on a domestic basis by people other than those who might describe themselves as 'weavers', another example of the confusing diversification already alluded to. The evidence suggests that the spinning and weaving of linen and woollen fabric was a considerable industry in Retford, largely concealed from formal record because it was conducted by women, by the poor, and by those whose primary occupational description might be quite different. As Nesta Evans states for East Anglia:

> For many families the preparation of linen yarn and its weaving into cloth was a normal activity which called for no comment.[56]

The people who creamed off the greatest profits from the fabric and leather trades were the mercers and tanners, and these men always played a prominent part in civic government.[57] An investigation of the wills of eight mercers between 1516 and 1631 indicates that all of them had invested heavily in property in and out of the town, often as far afield as Lincolnshire and Derbyshire. William Dawson, for example, owned tenements in East Retford and had a share in the lease of the Idle mills, raising the question, of course, that they might have been used for fulling or bunching rather than the production of wheat.[58] In addition he owned lands in Barnby, tenements in Bawtry and land in Lincolnshire called 'Lawnys and Carres': finally, he had a lease of more Lincolnshire property at Upton.[59] The tanners, in general, had invested less heavily in property and had narrower horizons, but they were nevertheless prosperous, William Rossell II being in a position to give his daughter a dowery of 100 marks in 1578.[60]

The wealthiest of the tanners encountered in a sample of eight between 1520 and 1627 was John Coulbie who died in 1613 leaving an extraordinarily lengthy will. Apart from his tan yard in the town, he owned at least six houses there, most of them rented out to local people: in addition to this, he owned land at Sutton-cum-Lound and had taken copyholds there and at Askham. His numerous cash legacies came to over £200.[61] Not included in this survey, but nevertheless related to the leather and fabric trades, are the drover John Wymoke and the draper William Spivy whose wills reveal them to be possibly the wealthiest citizens of the town during the period under review. Other operatives in these areas were by no means so successful. Shoemakers, despite their numerical strength in the town and influence in civic government, rarely showed much sign of prosperity or inclination to invest heavily in property.

It is difficult to gauge the overall wealth of the town, but the best impression can be gained by reading the wills of its inhabitants. Many of them left short and simple testimonies, but occasionally luxury items appear, generally connected with high status tradesmen or the landowning gentry and yeomanry. William Rossell I owned 'a towney gown furred with white lamb': Agnes Lane 'a powder box of silver': William Bolivant a 'jacket edged with fur of fomiard': and Margaret Marre silver brooches and 'a gold ring with a precious stone'.[62] The land market too seems to have been buoyant, with many people mentioning 'takes and leases in the town' rented from the more prosperous burgesses. They in their turn followed the example of the mercers and tanners and invested in property as opportunities arose. Miles Townson, yeoman, referred to 'that house and land I lately purchased of Thomas Golland' in 1607, and in 1624 John Rogers, haberdasher, mentioned 'all that my messuages and tenements...in East Retford which I lately purchased'.[63] This property, either purchased or leased from the town estate, was quite commonly in surrounding villages, and one of the threats voiced by the Countess of Devonshire in the 1624 election campaign was that if any townsman had undertaken enclosures in areas where the Cavendish influence was strong, notably in Clarborough and Ordsall:

that they shall be thrown open, and actions brought for every trespass, and thus they fright those burgesses that have closes or lands there.[64]

But litigation such as this was inevitable once burgesses became involved with the purchase and sale of land, and though this sometimes got as far as the Chancery and Exchequer courts in London these cases have not generally been followed up.[65]

From our sample of 107 wills between 1600 and 1642 an analysis of the nature of property bestowed by testators was made and the results are presented in Table 2.[66] It is important to remember that in a will a person mentions what he or she values most, a choice which does not necessarily reflect the overall nature of the estate. Thus, the fact that husbandmen do not make bequests of farming equipment does not mean that they did not have any, but simply that they took it for granted and did not think it worth recording. This syndrome is most clearly seen in the case of the gentry who did not feel it worthwhile to make bequests of items such as furniture, household goods or clothing, but invariably mentioned much higher than average amounts of landed property. Many of the conclusions were predictable — the interest of women in linen, for example, and of craftsmen in their trade tools — but some observations can be made which confirm earlier statements, particularly with regard to the numerous but shadowy yeomen, who show a low level of interest in livestock but a notable preoccupation with property. By contrast, the involvement of craftsmen with livestock is notable, as indeed is the interest shown by women in raw materials. These observations confirm the view of 'status' yeomen, often divorced from the land, and of craftsmen and women obliged to diversify to guarantee a reasonable standard of living. In terms of cash legacies, which were the subject of a separate study, it was discovered that the social group with most cash to dispense was the gentry, followed by widows and yeomen: they commonly bestowed cash legacies in excess of £50, and sometimes considerably more than that. Table 3,[67] which represents an analysis of 93 cash legacies, shows that they tend to be grouped at the two extremes of the scale, 30% over £50 and 31% less than £5. All of the clues we have, therefore, seem to indicate that the town enjoyed a moderate prosperity, at least amongst the minority of its citizens who chose to make wills.[68]

The availability of capital was essential to any commercial community, and we have already seen in the case of John Wymoke that wealthy townsmen were prepared to extend loans and make sales on credit. Apart from Wymoke, a number of people have been identified who were prepared to lend money on mortgage or on bond. Nicholas Pettinger II had several debts outstanding on bond in 1578 and he had taken from Robert Lily, rector of Babworth, a gold ring as a security; William Rossell II lent £100 to Thomas Tye, a Clarborough gentleman, the bond being in the name of his brother-in-law, John Alton; Robert Browne, the town clerk, held lands in mortgage from Henry Barthrop and Richard Parnell in 1620 and William Spivy held mortgages on the lands of two of his brothers-in-law, John Sloswicke and an unidentified member of the Otter family.[69] William Billiald was able to lend Paul Gresham £36 13s 4d prior to 1582, but he had need to write to him in 1590 complaining that the debt had not been paid and that in the circumstances he did not think that a repayment of £40 was unreasonable.[70] The question of interest was indeed a contentious one, as Grace Scott found to her cost in 1592. William Spivy was able to speak of a 5% interest rate on loans as a matter of course, but when Scott lent a noble to Richard Barley's wife, she found herself before the Archdeacon's court 'suspected and defamed as a usurer' when she asked for 11d 'for the use thereof' for a week. An acrimonious case followed, which ended only when she claimed the general pardon in 1593.[71] Most loans, it seems, were small affairs between neighbours and members of the same family rather than the larger transactions arranged by the likes of Browne and Rossell. Edward Hodgson, for example, had lent his brother-in-law £3 6s 8d, William Senior had lent his father £3 on a bill, and Robert Parnell owed £4 'which I am in bond for my son Daniel'.[72]

The only attempt to formalise the structure of borrowing, and take it away from such casual representations made to wealthier relations or neighbours, came in 1602 when William Spivy created an endowment of £30 to be put into the hands

21: A woman spins flax outside her cottage door while huntsmen traverse the fields near her house.

22: Inside a grocer's shop: delicacies were available in market towns which were difficult to obtain in villages.

of the corporation to provide loans 'to fifteen or twenty of the most poorest tradesmen in the said town'. Each beneficiary of this fund was to:

> put in good securities...to bring in the said money within one year and shall pay every pound so to them lent twelve pence and after that rate for so much or so little as shall be lent to them.[73]

In May 1603 the corporation agreed to speak to Sir Edmund Bussy, Spivy's executor, about the legacy, which it was agreed should be paid out at the Moothall during the Easter court leet.[74] But since the gift was only to last until Spivy's son, Edmund, achieved the age of 21, and the corporation was to enter into a bond to guarantee repayment of the money, it is by no means clear how many citizens of the town actually benefitted from the scheme. Spivy's specific request in his will that:

> I do most earnestly intreat the bailiffs and burgesses for the time being to see these my bequests to be given and bestowed according to my true meaning[75]

underlines the lack of trust which existed in the town at this time, particularly, perhaps, where money was concerned. It is a significant point that in setting up a similar scheme to operate in Grantham Spivy did not feel it necessary to 'earnestly intreat' the town fathers in quite the same tones. Nevertheless, it was a positive attempt to stimulate trade amongst a group in society who might otherwise have found it extremely difficult to raise a loan by more conventional means and it came at a time when poverty was perceived as a particular problem nationally as well as locally.

Merchants of all complexions quite frequently left their 'debt books' as legacies, which provides further evidence of a widespread network of credit sales within the town. William Spivy, who as a successful businessman had many of these, was realistic enough to remind his wife that 'many debts will be slack and long in coming in' and that she would be well advised to take her share of his estate 'in some reasonable time'.[76] When debts were written down like this or formalised in a bond, there could be little dispute since repayment could in the last analysis be enforced by the law courts. What caused disagreement, and bad feeling amongst neighbours, was the informal arrangements which appear to have been struck from time to time. When he wrote his will in 1605 Edward Hellaby, an ex-bailiff, remembered with obvious resentment the four quarters of malt he had lent to William Flint three years ago 'whereof Humphrey Ratcliffe is a witness', and in 1558 Thomas Bowringe, blacksmith, stated with equal chagrin 'John Hardy of Laxton doth owe me a certain sum of money, what it is I refer it to his conscience'.[77] But the most complicated case involved Francis Grenall, a Retford yeoman, who had a series of complex dealings with his brother-in-law John Todd, rector of Waltham, Lincolnshire, and one of the 'masters' of the close of Southwell. Greenall, whose will in 1585 was a tirade against the imagined injustices of Mr Todd, claimed that he had lent Todd £40 and other money:

> also I did serve him three years as a servant having nothing for the whole time but only two pair of harvest gloves which I refer to his own conscience.[78]

Greenall had a 'chamber' at Waltham and some small items of property in the parsonage house, and he certainly felt aggrieved, though it is clear that there had been loans and favours extended by both sides in the past. These complicated networks of unsecured loans, coupled with the custom of bestowing some of the smaller properties of the town 'by promise' rather than by formal lease, must have led to a good deal of dissention.[79]

Having said this, debt does not figure that significantly in the sample of wills referred to above.[80] The highest proportions of debts owed and owing are noted in the wills of tradesmen and women, with gentlemen and husbandmen/labourers, the richest and poorest sections of the will making community, being the least likely to obtain or extend credit. Overall, debts are mentioned in 39% of wills, the balance between those owed and owing being fairly even. If well over half of the will-making population of Retford lived outside the network of credit, there were a few for whom indebtedness was a major problem and one which looked likely to decimate their estates when they died. Nicholas Wharton, mercer, Walter Day, maltster, and Richard Parnell, chandler and alderman, were all in the position of requiring their executors to sell all or a portion of their estates to satisfy their creditors.[81]   This may well have been the result of unwise speculation or economic forces over which they had no control. They might have envied the humble weaver, Thomas Carr, who stated on his death bed in 1558 that:

> being in good and perfect remembrance and lying at the mercy of God [he] did take it upon his death that he did not owe to all the whole world not the value of 4d to his knowledge.[82]

By some, particularly the poor, thrift was regarded as a virtue, and so the credit economy was by no means universal, restricted to the dissolute or to the ambitious and upwardly mobile.

Although Retford provided commodities and credit for its hinterland, it was dependent on the country districts for supplies of food and manpower to service the town's industries during periods of prosperity. The ebb and flow of people in and out of the town was very considerable, and in the family reconstitution project it was found that many families could not be successfully resurrected because of the temporary nature of their sojourn: many more presumably stayed for even shorter periods and did not figure in the parish register at all, young people whose temporary presence in Retford is totally forgotten to history. Many of the names of the 'temporary' residents who could be traced seemed to originate from elsewhere in the Bassetlaw Hundred, suggesting that migration and movement was not over a very great area. Many migrants were probably absorbed into the spinning and weaving of linen and wool, but the textile trade was notoriously volatile and when a depression set in Retford was likely to suffer along with other production centres. The vicissitudes of the town's population are traced in Chapter 1, and it is important to note that the demographic problems of the late 1580s are to be linked with a depression in the cloth trade in 1586/7.[83]   More important was the major slump which occurred nationally after 1614 when Alderman Cockayne of London persuaded James 1 to prohibit the export of 'white' cloth to the Low Countries in the belief that he could develop dyeing and finishing processes in England. The scheme was a disaster because Cockayne's promises failed to materialise and the Dutch retaliated by developing a 'white' cloth industry of their own. The exports of the Merchant Adventurers were cut by half, and throughout the country cloth producing centres suffered profound depressions which endured until the 1620s, made worse by serious shortages of food and foreign war in the middle years of the decade. It is notable that Retford's most startling population collapse came in the wake of the Cockayne project, and it did not begin to recover until the late 1620s. This in itself lends considerable weight to the argument presented above about the extensive nature of fabric production in the town, and, by implication, an export trade to the Low Countries which was probably based on Gainsborough. There was a serious mortality in the town in 1616, but the prolonged depression was caused by people moving away rather than by sudden trauma. The migrant population of Retford, suffering under the financial ineptitude of the first Stuart King, had either to find pastures new or hang around in the town seeking what sustenance could be gained from the operation of the poor laws.

There was an awareness of a problem of poverty in Retford throughout the sixteenth and seventeenth centuries, but it was worst during the post-1614 depression. In 1617 William Billiald, described as gentleman but also an alderman, put himself at the head of a gang of sixteen men and one woman 'riotously culling the grain of Charles Oxenforth'. At the Quarter Sessions the rioters denied the charge and placed themselves 'on the country', being represented by the town clerk and under sheriff for that year, Robert Browne. Although William Ashton, who was included amongst the number of the rioters, was bound in £10 to prosecute the matter at the next Sessions the case was not heard again.[84] The court record is frustratingly terse, but some clues can be derived from other sources. Charles Oxenforth came from a Clarborough family and had married Janet Ashton, widow, at Clarborough in 1608: he may well have been related to William Ashton, the rioter who turned King's evidence. The

Oxenforths, moreover, had malting interests in Moorgate, represented by Alexander Oxenforth who was probably a brother of Charles.[85] Was the disturbance caused by a load of barley going to feed the family maltings while the poor stood in need of bread? By 1622 the justices of Bassetlaw were showing serious concern about shortages of food, and the Commissioners for Musters wrote to the Privy Council from Retford informing them that the trained bands were standing by ready to suppress riots, if any occurred.[86] In the next year the justices were following a stringent policy of suppressing alehouses and maltsters, but food was still in short supply and work for the poor was lacking. The bailiffs stated that there were 915 quarters of corn in the town and that this was being released into the market at a rate of 48 quarters a week, with an order that it should be sold first to the poor: twelve maltsters and ten alehouses had been suppressed.[87] In 1624 there was still an awareness of a problem since, during the disputed Parliamentary election of that year, the question of the poor loomed large. The Countess of Devonshire made 'great promises' that if her candidate was elected she would purchase land in the town 'and build a house and lay a stock to it for the poor to be set on work'. If that failed to convince the burgesses of the need to uphold the Cavendish interest, she raised the spectre of the sort of whirlwind she was able to raise if her desires were thwarted:

> For all the poor in general that they shall never be suffered to strive out of our own town. That the fetching of ling on their backs from of the forest, which in charity they have been suffered to do, shall be restrained. And that they shall not be suffered to glean in any of these towns adjoining in the time of harvest. By this means a great mutiny and outcry raised by them...amongst the poor and commons of the town, that if the Countess have not her will the town will be utterly undone.[88]

With threats such as these in the air it is not surprising that John Watt was able to raise a discontented mob to demonstrate in the market place in favour of the Devonshire candidate, and the corporation was expressing alarm that they were likely to be 'carried away by the feet against the head'.

Retford had reached a flashpoint by the mid-1620s, but it failed to erupt entirely and a gradual recovery characterised the next decade, though the Quarter Sessions continued to show concern about engrossers of grain who were likely to disrupt the supply of food to the market.[89] As late as 1652 the town was described as 'very populous and full of poor people'.[90]

Concern for the poor rested on a combination of individual benevolence, sometimes linked with the church, and state responsibility, eventually formalised in the Elizabethan Poor Law of 1601. Out of the income from the rectories of East Retford and Clarborough the lessees were bound to pay £4 13s 4d to the poor of the parishes on Maundy Thursday, a regular payment which ameliorated, in some small degree, the fact that so much 'spiritual' revenue was diverted into secular hands.[91] Bequests by individuals in wills span the entire period from 1520 to 1642, though it is plain that only a minority ever gave to the poor. In the 1600-42 sample only 44% of testators gave anything: 78% of gentlemen contributed in this way, but only 37% of tradesmen and 33% of husbandmen/labourers, suggesting that a willingness to give was directly linked to the prosperity of the testator and the expectations the community had of him.[92] The aristocratic families, who were attempting to flex their muscles in the political and economic life of the town, proved that they were capable of magnanimous gestures towards the poor as well as threatening to damage them if they failed to get their own way. In 1638 Elizabeth, dowager Countess of Devonshire, perhaps making good her earlier promise, gave £40 to the town 'until it might be disbursed for lands which should remain for ever', and her sister-in-law, Lady Frances Pierrepont, created a further annuity of £10 for the poorest and most aged inhabitants.[93] Amongst the burgesses Nicholas Dickons made a generous bequest of £12 in 1597, but that was rare and a formalised legacy of about 5s characterised the sixteenth century, rising to about 30s in the seventeenth.[94] Sometimes testators preferred to give commodities rather than cash. Agnes Ward in 1521 gave 'a land of rye...when it is ripe': after leaving his best clothing to his son in 1542 Richard Marre requested that his wife 'dispose my workday raiment to poor folk': Edmund Sampson gave the poor of Moorgate two loads of wood to be delivered three years after his death in 1558: and in 1582 John Wilson provided gowns of 3s 4d per yard for three poor women and requested 'meat for the poor' at the funeral feast which he organised.[95] Retford's proto-Protestant, Thomas Marshall, was notably generous to his less fortunate neighbours in his will of 1542. In all he bestowed 13s 4d in legacies 'to the poor and needy people' of the town, and provided the poor of Moorgate with two cows to be managed by the freeburrows 'by the advice of the most honest persons therein inhabiting'.[96] Protestantism brought new concepts of social concern, and in 1547 'the common box for poor folk' made its first appearance at West Retford, soon to be followed in other parts of the town.[97] Moreover, a new terminology begins to creep into some wills. The poor now are sometimes described as 'poor neighbours', and legacies are often directed to 'poor households' rather than simply the poor in general.[98] John Morland attempted an even more discriminating approach in 1563: he gave 2d to every poor household in West Retford 'and whereas great need standeth, 4d'.[99] The poor man's box became a feature of all of the churches of the town and those who refused to contribute to it, by paying fines imposed by the churchwardens, were prosecuted.[100]

Alongside the church the corporation also expressed some responsibility for the poor, and there is a reference to collectors for the poor in operation in 1597.[101] Sometimes testators specified that legacies were to be dispensed at the discretion of the bailiffs, and when Simon Pettinger created a small endowment for the poor in 1597 it was to be administered first by his family and then by the bailiffs and burgesses 'for ever to this use abovesaid and no other'.[102] The main stake which the corporation had in local poor relief was the ownership of a range of almshouses, probably located in Carolgate. During the problems which followed the 1528 fire some of the chantry income was diverted to the 'poor almsmen' of the town, but whether or not this was a lasting arrangement is not clear.[103] A few testators directed legacies 'to the poor folk in the almshouse row', particularly John Wymoke who endowed the almshouses with a house and tenement in Churchgate 'for ever' and William Spivy who left 8s *per annum*, but these were relatively uncommon and during the Archbishop's Visitation of 1636 it was stated that the almshouses were in decay and that the judge would visit them to carry out an inspection.[104] It was the general inadequacy of the corporation provision on the eve of the Civil War which persuaded Richard Sloswicke to establish Sloswicke's Hospital for six poor old men in East Retford in 1658, and John Darrell to set up Holy Trinity Hospital in West Retford for sixteen similar paupers in 1664.[105] An element of competition can perhaps be seen in two benefactions so close to one another, one the creation of *nouveau-riche* gentry and the other of a more established family, but they brought benefit to the poor of the town so long as they were aged, impotent and male.

The problem, of course, was that many paupers did not fit into these categories, especially in a town beset by the vagaries of the textile trade where young people, many of them female, were likely to come in search of work. The Poor Law of 1601, supplemented by Spivy's local initiative, was designed to tackle problems such as these and provide a measure of support for the deserving poor and punishment for the idle vagrant: it was administered by overseers of the poor appointed in each parish and funded by a poor rate imposed on local inhabitants.[106] Constables were expected to keep a look out for vagrants and for those who attempted to make a quick profit by harbouring them in rooms and outhouses. A steady stream of Retford people appeared before the Quarter Sessions accused of this offence, sometimes alehouse keepers, but most surprisingly George Turvin, the town vicar, who was 'harbouring inmates' in 1609.[107] Vagrants, when apprehended, might be whipped and placed in the House of Correction, but for the deserving poor, the old and the sick, often widows, the problem was to see that they received their entitlement in the face of parsimonious parish officials who attempted to keep the poor rates low by denying it to them. In 1621, for example, the overseers of West Retford were ordered to provide a convenient 'houseroom' for Margaret Clark, a poor widow with children, where she might obtain a living, and in 1613 Robert Aneley, labourer, was obliged to complain against the same overseers because they had not paid him fully for looking after Anne, the daughter of Thomas

23: A poor family on the move: migration was a crucial factor in the demographic profile of the town.

24: A watchman on patrol with his dog, keeping a wary eye open for night walkers and other deviants.

Reason.[108] These cases indicate that it was clearly the policy of the West Retford overseers to lodge paupers in the town and subsidise their rents from the poor rate: in their 'houserooms' they could then be set to work spinning or undertaking some other useful task. When work was available this was an excellent embodiment of how the Elizabethan legislation was conceived to work: the problem, of course, came when the bottom fell out of the textile trade in the 1620s just when the volume of paupers was on the increase. How the overseers coped with this problem we do not know, but it is probable that East Retford used its legal and coercive powers to expel paupers from the borough, thus driving them towards the suburban areas of West Retford and Moorgate. Substance is given to this theory by the local pattern of bastardy and by the fact that on the eve of the Civil War Clarborough needed three overseers and East Retford only one, despite a much larger population in the latter parish.[109]

The last means which a poor person had at his or her disposal to redress the injustices of society was, of course, crime. It was also the means whereby unscrupulous townsmen could enrich themselves at the expense of their neighbours or settle feuds by recourse to violence. The means of resisting crime was the parish constable, a part-time official similar to the churchwarden, who functioned under a chief constable for the Hundred, a post sometimes held by a Retford man.[110] Constables were drawn from a similar level of society as churchwardens, indeed the same names crop up in both lists, though we are much more knowledgeable about the latter than the former. In 1642 East Retford supported three constables and Clarborough and West Retford one each, yet the incompetence of these officers had become a joke even on the popular stage and the Quarter Sessions and town bailiffs had their work cut out in attempting to achieve a modicum of application.[111] In 1631 Brian Smith, thirdbarrow of Clarborough, was fined 5s for failing to execute a warrant against Childers Keyworth when he stood accused of recusancy, breach of the peace and failure to pay levies, and in 1637 Richard Fairbank, constable of West Retford, was fined 10s for allowing William Hall, charged with stealing linen sheets, to escape from his custody.[112] In theory constables were expected to be able to fall back on the local community for support by enroling men as watchmen to look out for 'night walkers' and other deviants and ultimately to raise the 'hue and cry' against offenders: certainly in 1666 the bailiffs were expected to provide lanterns and candles for the borough watch out of the income appertaining to their office.[113] But the records show an irritating tendency on the part of the townsmen not to support the constables in their work, failing to watch or to carry out the hue and cry.[114] Indeed, on occasion they deliberately pitted their efforts against the forces of law and order.   In 1603 an East Retford constable had been assaulted by a 'stranger' who was sheltered subsequently in the house of one of the burgesses, George Ford. Ford, however, refused to hand over the offender to the bailiffs for punishment and, in consequence, lost his freedom; a reflection of how seriously such unneighbourly actions were viewed by the corporation.[115] Given the problems of laziness, incompetence and non-co-operation the likelihood of apprehending offenders was fairly remote.

A major attempt to tackle the inefficiency of local law enforcement was made at Clarborough in 1615. Traditionally there had been only one constable, or thirdbarrow, for Clarborough and he had been expected to serve the hamlets of Little Gringley, Welham and Bolham as well as the 'urban' areas of Moorgate and Spital Hill. Needless to say this had resulted in:

> the delay of the King's service, the annoyance of the constable and the neglect of other villages within the said parish in which the constable does not live.

In the January Quarter Sessions it was decided therefore that the outlying areas of the parish should have their own constable, and Robert Parnell of Moorgate was duly appointed to serve for a year. However, in the April Sessions it became evident that objections has been raised to the decision and:

> great inconvenience is like to be increased thereby, and a quarrel to be set up by many inhabitants in the said hamlets.

Each hamlet, it was now revealed, had a 'freeburrow' who was able to serve as a constable, and the justices, afraid of overturning 'ancient custom', reversed their earlier decision and stated that any innovation would have to be referred to the Assize judges when they made their next circuit. Not to be defeated the upholders of the earlier plan appeared before the judges at Nottingham and procured an order for the election of two constables, one to serve Clarborough and the hamlets adjacent to it and the other to serve the remainder of the parish (i.e. the suburbs of Moorgate and Spital Hill) 'and to continue hereafter two distinct or several constablewicks'.[116] The problem with the earlier plan was that it had not differentiated between the hamlets and had coupled the Retford suburbs with fairly distant rural spots such as Little Gringley. Robert Parnell would not have relished the task of taking responsibility for these areas, and for their part the villagers might have resented a Moorgate man overlooking their affairs — hence the animosity. The judges took the best decision open to them by separating out Moorgate and Spital Hill and leaving the other hamlets under the traditional jurisdiction of Clarborough.

If the corporation court books had survived we would have known more about the nature and extent of crime in Retford. As it is we are restricted to a few miscellaneous references for the sixteenth century and what appeared before the Quarter Sessions after 1603. The Coroner's Inquests for Nottinghamshire give a graphic picture of a murder which took place in the town in 1541:

> About 10 pm on November 23 Christopher Hodgson late of East Retford, barber, assaulted Richard Westby of East Retford and feloniously and treasonably struck him in the right side with a thrust to the heart with a sword worth 2s which he held in his right hand, giving him a wound of which he immediately died. Thus Christopher feloniously murdered him.[117]

Hodgson was outlawed in 1543, but incidents like this could be expected in a society in which men, of all social ranks, carried swords and daggers as a matter of course. Many chose to bestow these in their wills as prized possessions, and towards the end of the sixteenth century guns began to make an appearance.[118] In 1634 John Pye of Moorgate, codder, was indicted before the Quarter Sessions for the murder of an unknown woman, but the charge does not appear to have been pursued and he might be identified with Robert Pye, 'a poor simple man', against whom Martin Squire, a Moorgate tailor, was making frivolous allegations in 1632.[119] The Quarter Sessions' clerks did not have a good track record of accuracy with names and other descriptions, and malicious accusation was a feature of any system which rested heavily on presentment by neighbours to bring offenders to justice. No other reference to homicide has appeared in the court records, though the parish register of Clarborough alleges that William Carter was 'slain' in 1587 and that of East Retford states that William Smith was 'slain by William Thornton' in 1635.[120] Interestingly, Thornton had been party to another suspicious happening seven years earlier when he and John Butler were accused of burying by night in the churchyard one Denman, 'who was supposed to cut his own throat whereof he died'.[121] Lesser crimes of violence were more commonplace and were not restricted to the poorer sections of the community. Marmaduke Wharton, mercer, was found guilty of assault and affray in 1607 and fined 5s, and John Rogers, gentleman, was accused of wounding in 1625.[122] A more persistent offender was John Dawson, shoemaker, accused of assault, affray, bloodshed and bad language: having broken an undertaking to be of good behaviour, he was committed to Nottingham gaol in 1605. Dawson was evidently a notorious character, since he had already been called before the Archdeacon's court in 1597 for having carnal knowledge of Joan Riche and then again in 1601 'for striving to enforce Alexander Johnson's wife and also John Deeping's wife'.[123]

The most trivial crimes of violence, 'frays' and 'blood wyppes', were dealt with by the town court and in 1554 attracted minimal fines of 2d or 4d.[124] The most common form of felony, viewed more seriously than casual violence, was theft, which varied in scale of severity according to when and where it was undertaken and what the value of the stolen goods was. In 1573 Guy Farley was part of a gang who entered the house of Richard Foster at Flaxton, Yorkshire, and stole goods valued at £7: two years later Richard Lasenby, yeoman, broke into the property of Ellis Markham at Dunham and stole two geldings. Normally both of these would have been capital crimes, tried at the Assizes, but both Farley and Lasenby managed to purchase pardons, indicating that their crimes can hardly have been motivated by poverty.[125] The Quarter Sessions cases are rather more poignant. In 1629 William Gilby of Mansfield was in custody having stolen from Hugh Cressey, gentleman, a ruff band, seven silver spoons, a salt cellar and various linen cloths, a failed attempt at burglary by a man from outside the area.[126]   But local people were just as likely to offend, Henry Buxton, husbandman, being charged with sheep stealing, and Richard Shaw, shoemaker, and Anne Jenkinson, spinster, with petty larceny.[127] If the charge was proved, as it was against George Murfin of Moorgate, carpenter, in 1625, the offender was likely 'to be stripped and whipped'. As the townsmen watched Murfin receive his punishment, they knew that here was a man who was frequently absent from church and was more often than not to be found drunk in the alehouse.[128] Just as some citizens saw themselves as of the elect, others, like Murfin and Dawson, were just as clearly regarded as living embodiments of reprobation. Theft was to be seen in its most trivial form in trespass and poaching, and there was a constant procession of townsmen before the Quarter Sessions for hunting rabbits and hares with greyhounds, snares, nets and guns, a reminder of Retford's semi-rural aspect. Often these offenders were treated leniently, but in 1620 Henry Howson, labourer, was ordered to pay 20s to Sir Percival Willoughby as compensation for rabbits taken in his free warren with nets.[129] Henry Turner, labourer, having once been accused of killing hares with snares (1632) was for his second offence (1635) sent to the House of Correction to be set to work for his living until he was lawfully discharged.[130]

Second offences were rare, but at least one Retford recidivist crops up in the person of Morgan Watson. His origins are obscure, but he appears in the will of Nicholas Watson, woollen draper, a leading burgess who served as bailiff on more than one occasion. In it he received a legacy of 20s and was released from all debts, but no relationship between the two men was spelt out.[131] By the time he received this legacy in 1623, Morgan Watson was already a seasoned offender. In

1613 he was ordered to keep the peace with Edmund Robson and was discharged on the production of sureties.[132] However, in the following year he was in court for assault and affray and in 1618 for robbery and affray, in the latter case being fined ls.[133] In 1628 came a more serious matter when he was bound over to appear at the Assizes on a charge of desertion, having been pressed as a soldier to serve the King in the wars: one Edward Robson of West Retford, possibly his adversary from 1613, was to give evidence against him.[134] How he fared in this matter we know not, but in 1633 he was again before the Quarter Sessions apparently accused of a confidence trick. He had attempted to obtain 6s 8d from John Dickenson of Misterton under colour of a warrant from Nicholas Whitmoor, when Whitmoor had ordered him specifically to the contrary. Clearly, by this time, the justices' patience with Watson was wearing thin because, having failed to produce sureties, he was committed to prison where he remained for the next two months.[135] His final appearance came in 1635 when he was bound in a surety of £60 to prosecute Isabel Harby, wife of an East Retford tinker, who was in prison for felony.[136] Watson then disappears from the record after over twenty years of intermittent court appearances for wholly petty crimes: in his earlier court appearances he is described invariably as yeoman, but by 1633 that had changed to labourer, a typical confusion for a man who perhaps never really found his way in the world.

Retford's economy rested on a subtle interdependence with the surrounding countryside. The country districts produced cattle, barley, wool and flax which were vital raw materials for the artisans of the town because, once converted into leather, malt and fabrics, they could be redirected back into the countryside from whence they came. Clothing, indeed, appears to have been an important key to the town's prosperity, since suits of 'Sunday best' were required by all seventeenth-century countrymen and the wherewithal of fashionable production was beyond the capabilities of a cottage seamstress or a village craftsman; this is where the shoemakers, tailors and haberdashers of the market town came into their own. This was a very flexible form of 'specialised' economy, since it could contract to serve the hinterland or expand to furnish a wider market if needs required, sending shoes to London or taking on board military contracts during the boom years of the Civil War.[137] In circumstances such as these people were the most important, and potentially most troublesome, part of the equation because just as Retford depended on the countryside for agricultural produce so it depended on the same areas for labour when times were good. However, when the urban economy needed to contract (as it did in the 1620s) its casual workers became an embarrassment, a drain on the poor rates and a potential source of crime and disorder. This never seems to have got badly out of hand in Retford which was, basically, a law abiding town, but it was nevertheless a constant consideration in the minds of the corporation.

That corporation was dominated by 'specialist' operatives such as tanners, mercers and drapers — who had it in their power to profit from periods of prosperity — while the rank-and-file burgesses were more often the middling tradesmen whose entrepreneurial horizons were more limited and orientated towards the 'general' marketing role of the town rather than the particular. On close examination the cohesion of the local economy is remarkable, its interdependence and lack of extraneous flab being notable features. Kilns, primarily conceived for malting, could also be used for drying hemp or brick making, using local deposits of clay: water mills, primarily conceived for grinding corn, could also be used for fulling, bunching or crushing linseed to make oil. Tallow, a necessary by-product of butchery and tanning, supported a flourishing candle making industry, and linseed oil could be turned back to the tanners because of its much valued role in the softening of leather. This was an economic profile in which very little went to waste, and it served the town well over a long period of time, except, perhaps, for the extensive hazard of fire which it brought in its wake. The unanswerable question is the extent to which Retford was able to export its major produce — shoes and fabrics — during periods of prosperity; circumstantial evidence would seem to suggest that trade links were open with centres such as Gainsborough, Boston and London (and beyond them with the Low Countries), but the extent of that trade must remain a matter of speculation. So too must the aspirations of the vast majority of townsmen who lived comfortable lives but, with one or two exceptions, rarely aspired to great wealth.

FOOTNOTES AND REFERENCES

1. Piercy, p.32.
2. NAO, QSMI/3.
3. *Ibid.*, Wills (Brian Thornton, 1604).
4. RM, Ordinances, 1600. For Anderson's contribution to sorting out the town's problems, see Chapter 2, p.48.
5. *Ibid.*, Orders and Constitutions, 1599 and 1639.
6. The concern may have been over cheap, lightweight draperies produced, or retailed, by non-apprenticed operatives. See Chapter 2, pp.42-3.
7. Broken down between the parishes, status descriptions (i.e. gentleman, yeoman, husbandman, labourer etc.) accounted for the following proportions — East Retford (62%): West Retford (68%): Clarborough (79%). As might be expected, status descriptions were more common in the semi-rural parish of Clarborough, where there were fewer tradesmen.
8. NAO, QSMI/1-12.
9. *Ibid.*
10. BI, PR 23 ff.90,104, NAO, QSMI/10,11. The surgeon in 1585 was Richard Burrell and in 1637 Thomas Golland: Golland was possibly the same man who kept an alehouse in West Retford and was fined for permitting disorder in 1621. QSMI/5.
11. *Ibid.*, 15A f.145, NAO, Wills (William Smyth, 1603).
12. See, for example, NAO, Wills (Rosamund Fletcher, 1632).
13. *Ibid.*, (Jonie Oxenforth, 1605), BI, PR 11 f.666. Marshall typified the diversified economy: in his will he made reference to animals, cultivated land, gloving equipment and malt.
14. *Ibid.*, Chancery Wills (1578), P(robate) D(ocuments), (1617, George Turvin).
15. See Chapter 9, pp.251-2.
16. JA, RB 2 ff.6/7. The penalty for a bailiff engaging in this activity was a fine of £50 (half of which went to the poor), only mitigated if his estate was worth less than £100.
17. NAO, Wills (Dorothy Watson, 1620: Henry Atkinson, 1636), BI, PR 25 f.1135.
18. PRO, PROB 11/101.

19. *Ibid.*, QSMI/10. Several prosecutions were brought by the Quarter Sessions for this offence in 1638/9 and this probably prompted the corporation to reissue the apprenticeship regulations in 1639.
20. For example, NAO, Wills (Francis Parnell, 1634: Gertrude Cobb, 1631).
21. BI, PR 9 f.287, 24, f.269, 25 f.1025.
22. NAO, Wills (William Dunstan, 1642).
23. BI, PR 18 f.3.
24. *Ibid.*, 22 f.188a.
25. *Ibid.*, 23 f.104.
26. NAO, Wills (John Earle, 1632).
27. In 1592, for example, Anthony Leake's daughter, Mary, was a servant with Henry Taylor of Eaton, BI, PR 25 f.1025.
28. *Ibid.*, QSMI/10.
29. *Ibid.*, 11.
30. Piercy, pp.10, 235.
31. BI, CP 1043.
32. JA, RB 2 f.91.
33. RM, Orders and Constitutions, 1599.
34. JA, RB 2 ff.85-99.
35. *Ibid.*, f.89. It is likely that animals were slaughtered in this area adjacent to the market place: the tanneries, however, were probably to the North of Bridgegate (often at the base of Moorgate burgages running down to the river) so as to minimise the offensive effluvia running through the town.
36. *Ibid.*, ff.85-99.
37. *Ibid.*, f.86, BI, PR 16 ff.144/5, RM, Ancient Deeds, 1535. The source of the following observations on Wymoke is his will in BI, PR 16.
38. For example, Thomas Bagshawe, John Brodbury, John Skull and Mrs Underwood.
39. Hugh Jackson, for example, owed £4 for a horse of which he had paid off 19s 4d 'as appeareth on the backside of his bill'. I have calculated the money owing to Wymoke at £487 11s 2d and the money owed by him at £169 12s 0d.
40. Caley (ed.), *Valor Ecclesiasticus*, 5, pp.181-85. At Misson the hemp and linen tithe was 26s 8d out of a total of £6 4s 4d: at Sutton-cum-Lound 26s 8d out of £10; and at Sturton-le-Steeple 26s 8d out of £5 6s 8d. For a regional study of this underrated aspect of the pre-industrial economy, see N. Evans, *The East Anglian Linen Industry, 1500-1850* (1985).
41. RM, Orders and Constitutions, 1599.

42. R. F. Hunnisett (ed.), *Calendar of Nottinghamshire Coroner's Inquests, 1485-1558*, Thoroton Society, Record Series, 25, 1969, p.207, NAO, Wills (Gertrude Cobb, 1631). The term 'singlewoman' applied to one who was unmarried.

43. BI, Chancery Wills, 1578.

44. *Ibid.*, PD (1617, George Turvin).

45. NAO, Wills (Richard Elsam, 1628).

46. BI, PD (1642, John Watt).

47. BI, PR 13, f.647, 15C ff.429/30.

48. NAO, Wills (John Carberton, 1632: Elizabeth Parnell, 1639).

49. *Ibid.*, QSM1/3.

50. Copnall, p.61.

51. The element of doubt is caused by the fact that there were two Gervase Markham's, Gervase the poet and author (1568-1637) and 'the other' Gervase (1557-1637). Since the author spent much of his time in London, it is perhaps more likely that 'the other' Gervase, whose seat was at Dunham-on-Trent, was the one who also had interests in Retford. C. Markham, *Markham Memorials* (1913), 1, pp.64-70, 138-42.

52. BI, Chancery Wills 1578, PD (1617, George Turvin).

53. *Ibid.*, PR 15C ff.429/30, NAO, Wills (Brian Eaton, 1600).

54. BI, PR 15C f.421, 23 f.735, 25 f.1467, NAO, Wills (Thomas Deeping, 1588: William Field, 1637: James Leese, 1627). A dyer appears in an indenture of 1532. RM, Ancient Deeds, 1532.

55. BI, PR 15B f.246.

56. Evans, p.3.

57. For the important role played by tanners in the municipal government of Nottingham, see C.E.L. Williams, 'The Tanners of Nottingham and their household Inventories, 1679-1749', Certificate in Local History dissertation, University of Nottingham, 1983.

58. Bunching was the beating of hemp fibre prior to spinning. Evans, pp.24-6.

59. BI, PR 15C f.431. Other mercer wills are George Smyth (9, ff.37/8): Richard Cock (15A f.321): Nicholas Wharton (15A f.177): Thomas Stockham (22 f.690): Thomas Bate, 1628: John Jepson, 1617: John Wharton, 1631. The last three are NAO wills.

60. BI, PR 21 f.295.

61. NAO, Wills (John Coulbie, 1613). His Inquisition Post Mortem (1615) stated five houses in the town, a bovate of land in West Retford, five acres in Welham and Little Gringley, and twelve

acres and a messuage at Sutton-cum-Lound. DP 47/1. Other tanner wills are Thomas Barker (BI, PR 9, f.122): John Marshall (13 f.81): Henry Mason (23 f.851): Thomas Salmon (23 f.734): John Mason, 1607: Richard Childers, 1627. The last two are NAO wills.

62. BI, PR 9 ff.80, 287, 13 f.977, 15C ff.429/30.

63. NAO, Wills (Miles Townson, 1607: John Rogers, 1624).

64. NUMD, Cl. LP 52.

65. See, for example, John Proctor v. John Fox of Retford: refusal to complete demise of property in Sturton. PRO L(ists and) I(ndexes) 55, File 1461, 69-70. Thomas Stockham v. Robert and Jane Roger: plaintiffs purchase of reversion of house in Moorgate. *Ibid.*, File 1469, 74.

66. See Appendix, Table 2.

67. See Appendix, Table 3.

68. On average the extended town might have seen about 40 burials *per annum*, compared with about ten wills each year. Allowing for married women and children, perhaps 50% of eligible males made wills.

69. BI, A(rchbishop's) R(egister) 31 f.84, 21 f.295, NAO, Wills (Robert Browne, 1620), PRO, PROB 11/101.

70. *CSP Dom, 1566-79*, p.646.

71. NAO, DDTS 3 ff.179, 213, 4 ff.5, 40, 200. Grace Scott was again before the archdeacon on unspecified charges in 1596/7 and 1600: she was excommunicated and never sought absolution. 6 ff.55, 67, 69, 248.

72. BI, PR 17B f.458, 27 f.658, NAO, Wills (Robert Parnell, 1632).

73. PRO, PROB 11/101.

74. JA, RB 2 f.163. The corporation record speaks of a legacy of £20 from Spivy, not £30 as stated in his will.

75. PRO, PROB 11/101. Edmund Spivy was only four when his father made his will; therefore, on the death of the elder Spivy in 1603 the scheme would have had sixteen years to run.

76. For example, BI, PR 22 ff.423/4, NAO, Wills (George Wharton, 1637).

77. *Ibid.*, (Edward Hellabye, 1605), BI, PR 15C f.423.

78. *Ibid.*, 23 f.90.

79. *Ibid.*, f.104.

80. See Appendix, Table 3.

81. BI, PR 15A f.177, 28 f.490, NAO, Wills (Richard Parnell, 1626).

82. *Ibid.*, 15C f.421.

83. Barry, p.131.

84. NAO, QSMI/5, JA, RB 2 f.4. Browne's duties as under sheriff

prevented him from attending the election of the bailiffs in 1617.

85. *Ibid.*, NUCLH, FRF.

86. *CSP Dom, 1619-23*, p.427.

87. *Ibid.*, p.532.

88. NUMD, Cl. LP, 52.

89. NAO, QSMI/9-11. The campaign against engrossers was widespread in the county but many Retford men, generally described as yeomen, were involved.

90. A. D. Grounds, *A History of King Edward VI Grammar School, Retford* (1970), pp.55/6.

91. *CPR, 1560-63*, p.284, 1575-78, p.210.

92. See Appendix, Table 3. In 1619 Richard White, labourer, gave 13s 4d to the poor of the town, a generous gesture by a poor man, strengthening the suggestion about the Whites made in Chapter 9, pp.258, 263. NAO, Wills (Richard White, 1619).

93. JA, RB 2 f.5, Kidson, pp.114/5. Elizabeth was the widow of William Cavendish, 2nd Earl of Devonshire: Frances was the widow of Sir Henry Pierrepont of Holme Pierrepont and sister of the 1st Earl of Devonshire.

94. BI, PR 26 f.582. Because of the contacts mentioned in his will, Dickons must be suspected of being an advanced Protestant.

95. *Ibid.*, 9 f.287, 11 f.664, 15C f.275, 22 ff.423/4.

96. *Ibid.*, 11 f.666.

97. *Ibid.*, 13 ff.438, 779.

98. For example, 13 ff.732, 852, 1022.

99. *Ibid.*, 17 f.295.

100. NAO, DDTS 2 f.51.

101. BI, PR 26 f.582.

102. *Ibid.*, 9 f.287, 26 f.582.

103. PRO, LI 51, File 972, 65-66.

104. BI, PR 13 f.81, 16 ff.144/5, V 1636, CB f.444, PRO, PROB 11/101. Piercy noted that the corporation almshouses in Carolgate were taken down in 1823, because they were in a 'dilapidated condition'. Piercy, p.137.

105. *Ibid.*, pp.135-7, 187-92. The emphasis on men is interesting and is possibly explained by the fact that the corporation almshouses came to concentrate on women. NAO, DD 461, Piercy p.138.

106. Evidence about overseers in the town is scarce. However in 1642 East Retford had one, West Retford one, and Clarborough three. *Protestation Returns*, pp.6, 10, 33.

107. NAO, QSMI/2.

108. *Ibid.*, 4, 6.
109. *Protestation Returns*, pp.6, 10. It is possible that the church rates' issue in the 1620s and 1630s was linked to the rising demands of the poor rate. For the debate about bastardy, see Chapter 5, pp.140-2.
110. Hugh Hill in 1603, for example. Copnall, p.16.
111. *Protestation Returns*, pp.6, 10/11, 33.
112. NAO, QSMI/9, 10.
113. JA, RB 2 ff.20/22.
114. For example, Robert Golland refusing to follow the hue and cry in 1629 and Robert Swift refusing to night watch in 1638. NAO, QSMI/8, 10.
115. JA, RB 2 f.163.
116. NAO, QSMI/4.
117. *Coroner's Inquests*, p.207.
118. BI, PR 17 ff.294, 473, 22 f.383, 23 f.9l, 24 f.269, 27 f.658.
119. NAO, QSMI/9.
120. *Ibid.*, CPR (1587), ERPR (1635).
121. NUMD, Arch. PB 339 (1628).
122. NAO, QSMI/2, 7.
123. *Ibid.*, 1, DDTS, 6 f.121, 7 f.40. In 1597 Dawson was described as 'lodger'.
124. JA, RB 2 ff.89, 97. These crimes of violence are comparatively rare on the 1554 court roll.
125. *CPR, 1572-75*, pp.257, 313, 556.
126. NAO, QSMI/8.
127. *Ibid.*, 2, 4, 5.
128. *Ibid.*, 7, NUMD, Arch. PB. 339.
129. NAO, QSMI/6.
130. *Ibid.*, 9.
131. *Ibid.*, Wills (Nicholas Watson, 1623).
132. *Ibid.*, QSMI/3.
133. *Ibid.*, 4, 5.
134. *Ibid.*, 8.
135. *Ibid.*, 9.
136. *Ibid.*
137. Hoskins, of course, suggested that pre-industrial urban economy was 'unspecialised'. See, Barry, p.64. The supply of the Newark garrison would have been an obvious outlet for the Retford craftsmen in the 1640s.

Chapter 5

FAMILY LIFE

I give and bequeth unto Martha Cooper, my wife, and to my children all my goods and chattels ... for and towards the education of my said children ... and I make Martha Cooper my sole executrix, of this my last will and testament.[1]

The area of family life is perhaps the classic example of an historical theme which was of critical importance to the people involved yet is largely impenetrable to historians because of the nature of the sources on which they depend. Piercy chose not to consider this question at all within the orbit of urban history as he saw it, yet modern studies, notably by Ralph Houlbrooke, have explored the family as an important and self-contained theme in early modern history. For Retford no family letters have survived, enabling us to re-create the sort of vivid picture which emerges for the Norfolk Pastons in the fifteenth century, but a considerable amount of information is thrown up in passing by probate records and the archives of the church courts. The problem is that in both of these sources we see the family group in a situation of crisis, or near crisis, and what is missing is any sort of flavour of the normality of life related to everyday questions such as diet, relationships, domestic arrangements or dress. Although these were important, and perhaps overriding priorities, for the men and women of Retford before the Civil War they must remain shrouded in obscurity or extrapolated from data available elsewhere. What we are able to speak of with some degree of certainty are the circumstances surrounding sexuality and marriage, in which the Archdeacon's court showed a particular interest, and the picture of family relationships when that minority of citizens who actually made wills put pen to paper, generally a very short period before they died. It is on these sources that this chapter tends to concentrate, not because of their intrinsic importance but because, by being generally available, they shed what little light there is on this important socio-historical theme.[2]

Retford, like all small towns and villages, was in many ways an inward looking, and to some extent voyeuristic, community. The churchwardens took sexual malpractice seriously enough to cause it to figure consistently at or near the top of the list of prosecutions in the Archdeacon's court, and there is evidence to suggest that other townspeople, and visiting apparitors, were prepared to pass on gossip or to act on their own volition to initiate cases against neighbours. They did this for two reasons. Firstly, because fornication and other sexual crimes were offences against the law of God and if they were allowed to flourish unchecked they were likely to bring down divine wrath on the whole community in the form of plague, famine, and, during the later years of Elizabeth's reign, the possibility of a Spanish invasion. Secondly, sexual crime was likely to cause problems in the community itself. Adultery, for example, created disharmony between neighbours, and the sexual coupling of unmarried young people was likely to give rise to bastards which might become a drain on the town's poor rate. Thus, in order to pacify God and maintain social stability, sexuality had to be confined strictly to the limits laid down by Christian matrimony. It could not be suggested that the churchwardens were notably successful or even consistent in this task, but nevertheless they worked along generally agreed guidelines enforced by the courts and countenanced by the community by way of presentment.

The power of rumour is underlined by several cases of 'suspected incontinence', or people who by their actions hinted at an 'evil life'. At its most harmless this was to be seen in sexual suggestiveness, Anthony Bett going into the house of one Stirrup and saying to the owner's wife 'I have come here to tuckle your dobbe'.[3] More seriously, men were alleged to have pestered women by 'striving to enforce' them, sometimes with physical actions which verged on indecent assault. In 1605, for example, George Lidiard was accused of attempting the chastity of Joan Ubie when 'he reared her against a peas stack'.[4] The complicity, or paranoia, of some women in these matters is implied by the prosecution of Hercy Hurst and Robert Bird later in the year for alleged offences with the same woman.[5] Often these allegations could not be proven one way or the other — Hurst was dismissed because he had not been presented by the churchwardens — but it is clear that some individuals evoked continuing suspicion, Hercy Hurst and Thomas Horsefole being cases in point.[6] An individual determined to prove his or her innocence in face of such innuendo might commence a civil action for defamation before the Archdeacon's court. In 1583 Elizabeth Morton sued Elizabeth Wordes because she called her 'whore', and in the same year Thomas Kirkman proceeded against Edward Mason because Mason was spreading it around the town that Kirkman's wife was 'jeped' in the church porch, apparently after a lively wedding feast.[7] Given the frequency of this sort of litigation elsewhere in Nottinghamshire and in the diocese of York it is surprising that Retford saw so little of it, only nine cases being recorded for the three parishes between 1565 and 1610.[8] None of these lasted very long and most faded out without a conclusion, it perhaps being considered sufficient that the action was brought, and honour salved, rather than that the matter was pursued to a long, and costly, conclusion.[9] The low incidence of defamation litigation might owe something to the long distance separating Retford from the seat of the Archdeacon's jurisdiction at Nottingham where instance cases were invariably heard; proctors would need to be engaged, and the possibility of recourse before the court of the bailiffs and burgesses in the town may have dampened the enthusiasm of would-be litigants.

In many instances, of course, incontinence was either freely admitted by the defendant or assumed to be proven by his or her inability to produce compurgators who would come to court and swear to the untruth of the 'common fame'. The system was invidious because it placed the burden of proof on the defendant, and a popular local personality could easily arrange for a group of friends to turn up at court and swear to his innocence. Accused of fornication in 1589 Anne Watson named Charles Hyde as the father of her child: subsequently Hyde produced four compurgators and was dismissed, while Watson was judged to be guilty by her own confession.[10] The spread of prosecutions is very even amongst the families of the town, and prominent burgess names such as Mason,

Parnell, Wharton, Jepson and Stockham figure regularly amongst the ranks of the accused.[11]   Lack of depositions prevent us from filling out the bald records of the cases as presented in the Act Books, though we do know that in 1597 John Howes and Frances Wilson committed the crime of fornication 'in the kilnhouse and chamber of John Twels of Retford'.[12]   It sounds like a relationship between two servants, a common enough occurrence in a crowded town where accommodation was often shared between young people of opposite sexes.[13]   Where offenders have been traced on Family Reconstitution Forms, it becomes plain that very often the marriage partner is not the person with whom the illicit sexual experience was gained. In 1606, for example, John Strongitharme and Elizabeth Mason were married at East Retford.[14]   It was not the marriage of virgins formally approved by the church, because four years earlier both parties had pleaded guilty to fornication with different partners.[15]   George Turvin must have heaved a sigh of relief as he tied the knot, testing the forgiveness of the community to its limit. West Retford's much lower rate of presented sexual crime than East Retford or Clarborough, might have something to do with the fact that it was a 'semi-close' community with a resident rector and generally recognised 'gentry', people prepared to take on a role of correction and reconciliation before a matter like this ever got to court. The explanation is speculative, but the low rate of prosecution is notable, particularly for a comparatively poor community where marriage might have been delayed through lack of economic advancement.

Arguably the chief motive for pursuing moral offenders was to enforce their marriage, and the number of truly wanton characters, who engaged in promiscuity or prostitution, was very low indeed. In 1574 Margaret Duckes, who was pregnant, was cited for fornication with Thomas Calton who had fled and could not be found: on hearing that one Shacklock was prepared to marry her, Archdeacon Louth stated that she would not be punished if they were married before the next court.[16]   Jane Walleys, pleading guilty to fornication with John Fisher in 1583, said in her defence that he had promised to marry her, and in the following year John Plomber and Anne Cawood went so far as to make their contract in open court before the judge, promising to marry on the Monday after Trinity Sunday.[17]   However, there is a suspicion that such ploys were sometimes used by defendants to obtain lenient treatment. Edward Slater was prepared to plead guilty to fornication before marriage with Janet Ratcliffe in 1595, a charge which was viewed with less seriousness than fornication. However, there is no evidence that he ever married her since the name of his wife in 1616 was Anne.[18]   The most tangled case involving fornication, and possible marriage, concerned the once-important Smyth family, which had fallen from grace somewhat by the Elizabethan period. In 1583 William Smyth Jnr was accused of fornication with Anne Johnson, a case which was adjourned in hope of their marriage.[19] William Smyth Snr, shoemaker and prominent local oligarch, then intervened to 'put away' his son in an attempt to exonerate him from the support of his illegitimate child, which Anne had given birth to, and to avoid further punishment.[20]   Both Smyths were sentenced to do penance and excommunicated, though the bailiffs took the unusual step of intervening with the official to ask for lenience, no doubt to prevent the public humiliation of a man within the 'inner ring' of town government. Eventually the elder Smyth's punishment was commuted to a modest fine of 5s and the younger Smyth was said to have fled, with no evidence of his marriage in the East Retford register.[21]

However, the family's problems were by no means over. In 1595 William Smyth Snr again found himself before the Archdeacon's court, this time on the promotion of his wayward son. William's mother, Alice, had died in 1585, soon after the earlier traumas, but by the summer of 1594 his father had become involved with a woman called Isabel Shepston with whom he was accused of committing fornication.[22] The younger Smyth took the unusual step of appointing a proctor, John Hacker, to prosecute the case against his father, and the official was warned not to issue a marriage licence since Isabel was alleged to be precontracted to a John Woodesdale of Chester. Why the younger Smyth resisted his father's remarriage so strongly is not clear, but the fornication was taken to be proven and the old man and his paramour were sentenced to do penance. The case had eleven hearings over three months, and an indecisive ending. Neither defendant performed penance and both were excommunicated, though father and son were stated to be reconciled in April 1595. Subsequently William Smyth Snr married Isabel Shepston, or at least cohabited with her as his 'wife', and in his will of 1604 he showed a decided, and understandable, preference for his other son, Francis, who was made sole executor and, along with Isabel, came in for the bulk of the estate: William received a few small legacies and forgiveness of 'all debts he oweth me in lieu and full satisfaction of his filial and child's portion'.[23] The incident not only shows the heated passions which could be unleashed over sexual malpractice and marriage within a family group but, also, the limitations of the court in dealing with it. There is no evidence that penances were performed, excommunications observed or even that the main protagonists were married to one another. It underlines the point that the Archdeacon's jurisdiction was effective only to the extent to which people saw that it was relevant and were prepared to co-operate with it. Beyond that its authority stood in grave doubt in Retford, as elsewhere.

The punishment for incontinence and other serious moral crimes was penance. In August 1567 at the Archbishop's Visitation court meeting in York Minster before Richard Barnes, suffragan Bishop of Nottingham, Isabel Martin of West Retford was sentenced as follows for fornication with Robert Gillope:

> That she shall be ready on Saturday next come a seven night, being the 30th of August instant, in the market place of Retford about eleven of the clock before noon in the presence of all the people then and there congregated with the apparitor of the Deanery of Retford, bare legged with a white sheet about her and a white rod in her hand, where and when she shall openly confess and say as shall be contained in a schedule to be directed to the Dean of Retford and the like she shall do in the parish church of West Retford aforesaid upon Sunday then next following. And to certify under the hand and seal of the Dean of Retford the Wednesday after Michaelmas Day.[24]

The standard form of 'declaration' in the deanery comprised a confession of the 'filthy sin of fornication' with a named co-respondent and a request that both God and the community should offer forgiveness of the offence caused thereby, 'and to take example by my punishment to lead a chaste and godly life'.[25] In a case regarded as serious, such as that of Katherine Steadman in 1573, penance could be repeated up to three times in the market place and parish church, but in less dire circumstances (and fornication before marriage generally fitted into this category) a defendant might be asked 'to acknowledge the offence before the curate and five honest neighbours', as was the case with William Holt and Elizabeth Rye in 1593.[26] But even this could be a traumatic experience, and the court, realising this, offered money commutations to those who were able to pay. In 1603 Henry Mason and Setha Childers were charged £5 to purge their sin, but other commutations were bought for 40s, 20s, 10s or as little as 6s 8d. The sum rested entirely on the defendant's ability to pay.[27] Money raised in this way was often diverted to local good causes, such as the support of the church, the poor, or other 'pious uses' at the discretion of the bailiffs. Indeed, in one instance in 1602 the bailiffs, vicar and churchwardens of East Retford were invited to impose a commutation of their own, but, since nothing was done in four weeks, the judge took the matter back into his own hands and the experiment was not repeated.[28]

Table 4 provides an analysis of 76 penances imposed for sexual transgressions in the three parishes between 1565 and 1610.[29] East Retford gave rise to 44, Clarborough to 22 and West Retford to only ten. Of the total, 37% were certified as lawfully performed under the hands of the minister and churchwardens, 46% were not certified and 17% were commuted for cash payments. In other words, faced with the possibility of humiliation before their neighbours, a clear majority of townspeople chose to defy the authority of the court rather than obey. In this case they were faced with excommunication, and if they stood excommunicated for more than 40 days a writ of *pro captione* could be obtained authorising their arrest by the sheriff. In 1592 such a writ was applied for against William Mawer Jnr who had failed to certify his penance for incontinence with Isabel Merriweather, but it was a rare occurrence and hardly ever effective in its declared objective.[30] On a gender based analysis, 47% of people sentenced to penance were male, compared with 53% female. Compared with the figures quoted in Chapter 7, showing men to outnumber women

25: Maypole dancing was a popular pastime but it was frowned upon by puritanical clergy.

26: Making hay while the sun shines: illicit sex was one of the dangers of the long hot days of summer.

in all church court actions, the figure would seem to show a certain severity directed against women when public contrition was the order of the day. Once sentenced women also succumbed more readily to penance than did men (40% certified as opposed to 33%), but the rate of non-certification was also higher (53% as opposed to 39%). This is explained by the much greater ability of men to buy commutations to prevent the legal disabilities implicit in excommunication. In short, if there was a prejudice against women, it came in the management of the penance system rather than in the presentments of the churchwardens: it was institutionally, not communally, based.

One of the consequences of fornication, feared by responsible townsmen, was the begetting of bastards, and the parish registers provide an opportunity to trace the ebb and flow of bastardy in the town. The East Retford register notes only eight illegitimate children between 1573 and 1640, all of them coming in the post-1600 period.[31] The small number, and the general sketchiness of the East Retford register, might cause us to question seriously whether or not this is a complete record.[32] Clarborough, by contrast, records 26 bastards between 1567 and 1640, with a distinct tailing off of numbers after 1600, the antithesis of the pattern noted at East Retford.[33] The terminology 'bastard' or 'base' child is only generally applied at Clarborough after 1580, suggesting that a more severe attitude might have entered the parish with the incumbency of the Protestant vicar, Nicholas Watkins, who arrived in 1577.[34] A correlation was made between known cases of illegitimacy at Clarborough between 1567 and 1610 and prosecutions for fornication and incontinence in the Archdeacon's court. During these years twenty bastards were born in the parish and in nine cases the mother and, when he could be found, the father, was prosecuted.[35] When that period is subdivided into two subsections based on the archidiaconates of Louth and King (i.e. 1567–1590 and 1590–1610), it appears that each section produced ten bastards. The remarkable feature is that all of the prosecutions are placed in the second phase, which saw a 90% prosecution rate of mothers. Why this was so is not easy to determine. King certainly took a more 'legalistic' approach to the workings of his jurisdiction than did Louth, with much less emphasis on forgiveness and reconciliation, but the presentments stemmed from the community, not from the archdeacon, and the phenomenon suggests strongly that Clarborough people were more worried about bastardy after 1590.[36] Watkins, as vicar, had tolerated a policy of non-prosecution in the 1580s, despite his dislike of bastardy, so the only remaining explanation would seem to lie in the economic difficulties of the decade, augmented by the ever increasing demands of the poor rate and the possibility of the parish serving as a haven for pregnant single women driven out of East Retford. Unfortunately, a comparative study for the borough area is not possible because of the vagueness of the information and the general non-correlation between the births of bastards and the prosecution of their parents.

The other side to this argument, of course, is that many of the people prosecuted for immorality, some of whom were said to have given birth to children, do not appear as the parents of bastards in the registers, a phenomenon particularly true at East Retford, with a high level of fornication and a low level of registered bastardy. The explanation of this may lie in poor record keeping, as already suggested, or in non-conception, abortion, stillbirth or infant mortality through natural or unnatural causes. Another explanation lies in the 'conveying away' of offenders, or in their concealment to avoid detection or punishment, which might have been greater in East Retford because of the powers of the borough court. Indeed, it is likely that the corporation used its powers to attempt to keep the corporate town clear of bastards, a policy which may also have been pursued against paupers with equal vehemence. In 1600 John Drayton sent his servant to Worksop after he had had an adulterous relationship with her, and in 1608 Henry Parnell had allowed a servant to go to Sturton in an attempt to escape prosecution.[37] On the other hand, Retford, and particularly the suburbs, was an obvious base for offenders from elsewhere to come to to try to seek anonymity and shelter. William Ross in 1581 was a harbourer of suspicious persons who had lately had a child, and three years later Robert Rogers was 'keeping a bastard unknown', evidently hired for the purpose by one Greaves of Treswell.[38] The fact that often money was involved in these covert transactions is confirmed by the case of Oliver Burton, a

Clarborough alehouse keeper, accused of harbouring a fornicatrix 'whose name the churchwardens cannot get' in 1595. When questioned Burton said that one Wimprey of Gate Burton, Lincolnshire, brought to him a pregnant woman by the name of Anne Hudson:

> where he keeping an alehouse gave her entertainment for one fortnight, and then Wimprey fetched her away and she paid for her keeping herself 5s and no more as he thinketh.[39]

Many illegitimate children might, therefore, never have been registered at all, or, if they were, far away from their place of origin with spurious 'parentage' alleged to deceive local churchwardens who would generally have known no better.

From an offender's point of view, it was well worth moving out of the area, if at all possible, to avoid the humiliation of penance and the imposition of bastardy orders by the Quarter Sessions. Established townsmen with property and other obligations, might find this sort of movement difficult and over the long term would probably make financial arrangement for a bastard if marriage to the mother was impossible for one reason or another. Richard Marshall of Moorgate was such a person, who accepted and supported his illegitimate daughter, Janet, alongside his wife and legitimate child, Joan.[40] But when the father was not a person of property or was unwilling to face up to his responsibilities, the parish authorities had to take action to indemnify the poor rate from the need to support the child. In 1628 Francis Ridley, labourer, was ordered by the Quarter Sessions to support the child of Joan Staniland: he was obliged to produce four sureties who forfeited a bond of £10 if Ridley reneged on his obligation.[41] Five years later Daniel Padley, labourer, was not so fortunate, because failing to find sureties for the support of the child of Elizabeth Roper he was committed to prison.[42] Bastardy was, therefore, a problem which was regarded with some seriousness, particularly after the passing of the Poor Law of 1601.

One of the major problems in the area of sexual control in Retford, as elsewhere, was the fact that sexual intercourse was generally accepted after a couple had been contracted or betrothed and before their canonical marriage in church. Some people, for reasons best known to themselves, decided never to progress beyond the contractual stage or were debarred from lawful marriage by one of a range of impediments, for example, being under age, excommunicated or married to someone else. One solution was to cohabit without marriage as some Retford people, such as William Woodrough and Thomas Holland, appear to have done. Woodrough's arrangement was dashed in 1573 by the intervention of a relation of his co-habitee, Elizabeth Somerbye, and the judge ordered them not to consort with one another except in public places or before six honest men 'and not to lay down in her house under pain of the law'.[43] Another solution was to contract a clandestine marriage performed by a priest in some out-of-the-way spot with no questions asked: this form of marriage was canonically sound and indissoluble but if it was discovered it lay the parties open to an *ipso facto* excommunication and other penalties. Nevertheless, it was a service that some Retford people took advantage of. Henry Wright married in the chamber of Alexander Oxenforth in East Retford: John Addye 'married as is supposed in a lawless church in Derbyshire' and John Staniland married at night in a barn in Warsop by candlelight.[44] Once the statutory forms had been adhered to the court was generally prepared to treat the parties with lenience, marriage being the social cement of the community whether it was performed in church or some other less conventional spot.

Lawful marriage was performed in the parish church during a non-prohibited period after the reading of banns or the issue of a licence by the archdeacon.[45] Its declared purpose, according to the 1559 Prayer Book, was for the avoidance of lechery and the procreation of children. In an attempt to find out more about the nature of marriage in Retford, Family Reconstitution Forms were completed for 60 selected families using evidence drawn from parish registers, wills and miscellaneous sources. Due to the shortness of the period for which registers are available, and the rapid movement of many families in and out of the town, the exercise was not as successful as had been hoped but, nevertheless, many families were reconstructed over two or three generations, and occasionally more.[46] In the cases in which age at a first marriage was detectable, the average was calculated at 27 for males and 25.5 for females. The average family size was four to five children, with a maximum of nine and a minimum of one. These children were spaced by an average of 35 months between births; in other words, a mother could expect to become pregnant again 26 months after the birth of her previous child. In the reconstructed families, generally the more established and less mobile groups in the town, pre-marital pregnancy was rare and it was encountered only in the case of Margaret Blythman (married four months before the baptism of her eldest child) and Dorothy Bailey (married only five weeks before the baptism of her eldest child), both in 1609. In the latter case John Bailey of Moorgate, the father, was summoned before the Archdeacon's court on an unspecified charge, doubtless connected with his wife's pregnancy, but Thomas Blythman appears to have got away scot free.[47]

Except during visitations of plague, infant mortality was not a major problem, though some families seem to have been prone to it, all of them in Clarborough.[48] Of William Baxter's eight recorded children, five were lost in infancy; of William Colley's eight, from two wives, four were lost in infancy and, of Thomas Oxenforth's seven, three perished. All of these families appear to have been poor — Oxenforth is clearly identified as a labourer — and the mortalities might have been the result of deprived living conditions as much as genetic problems in the families involved. By contrast George Earle, a solid East Retford tradesman, produced nine children none of which died in infancy.[49] There was not sufficient data to allow a meaningful average to be worked out for the life expectancy of male and female adults. William Baxter, father of the family noted above, died 'old and blind' in 1619, a man of at least 70 years of age, and this sort of life expectancy was far from unusual for both men and women.[50] On the other hand, some families do demonstrate a tendency towards early demise. Of the sons of Avery Keyworth and Anne Childers, a substantial Moorgate yeoman family, Avery died at 40, Thomas at 42 and Childers at 47.[51] This might have been viewed as unusual in seventeenth century Retford just as it would be today.

Inter-relationship between the settled and property owning families of the town was very considerable indeed. Many people were related to their neighbours and were, doubtless, well aware of it. Denmans, Masons, Whartons, Spivys, Cobbs, Gollands and Parnells were drawn together in a complex and ever expanding network of marriage. An awareness of any sense of ancestry is more difficult to determine. None of the families of the town, with the exception of the West Retford Denmans and Darrells, were gentry in the true sense of the word, though some, especially members of the aldermanic bench affected the title of 'gentleman' as the seventeenth century progressed.[52] After the death of Sir John Hercy, without heirs, in 1572, the descendants of his sister Anne and Nicholas Denman began to disperse the old gentle blood of Grove around some of the more prominent families of the town. In this way a successful tradesman, such as William Spivy, could rub shoulders with the gentry and speak of 'my worshipful cousin and friend Mr Edmund Bussy Esq'; the same Edmund Bussy who hailed from the ancient Bussys of Hougham and Haydor, Lincolnshire, and who was knighted by James I at Belvoir in April 1603.[53] The Whartons, in particular, liked to show off their connections with the *élite* and had a tradition of 'gentry' christian names such as Stoughton, Markham and Saville.[54] In general, though, the *real* gentry of the hinterland — the Hercys, Wastneys and Thornhaughs — kept themselves separate from the burgess families of Retford, though George Smyth, mercer, did note in 1516 that his mother was now called Katherine Hercy, and in 1524 William Rossell I enjoyed an unspecified relationship by marriage to Lord Saville.[55]

Family burial areas and, later, pews, were devices by which some feeling of group identity, status, or kinship with the past might be expressed. In his will in 1578 William Rossell II requested to be buried in the church of East Retford 'in the place where my ancestors do lie, the next stone but one to the stall', and on his seal he used the rose and escallop device derived from the ancient arms of the Rossells of Radcliffe-on-Trent.[56] But such an awareness of history was unusual. A more common feature was a request that a particular symbolic item, generally a gold ring, should descend by a preordained route within the family. Richard Cock, mercer, passed on to his eldest son a ring of gold 'being

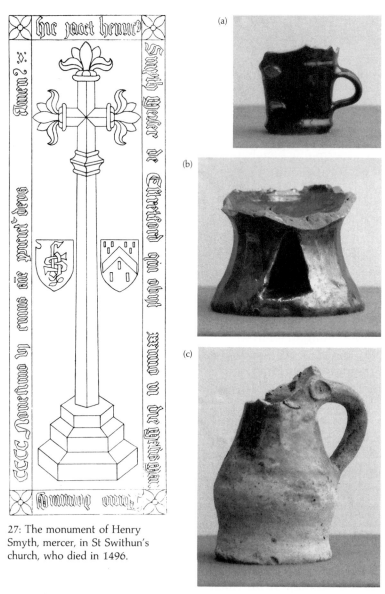

27: The monument of Henry Smyth, mercer, in St Swithun's church, who died in 1496.

28: A selection of domestic pottery recovered from the river Idle in the vicinity of the town bridge in 1988: (a) A tyg or three handled drinking cup: sixteenth century, Midland ware; (b) A chafing dish base: sixteenth century, Midland ware. Chafing dishes were used to keep food warm at table; the triangular hole in the base was for the insertion of hot charcoal; (c) A 'green glaze' jug: fourteenth or fifteenth century, probably locally produced.

my signet' with the instruction that if he died it was to pass to his second son, and Thomas Bate, another mercer, gave to his son 'a gold ring which was my father's'.[57] An unusual case was that of the draper William Spivy who ordered that:

> my best gown, my best cloak, my best jerkin, my best dublet, two pair of my best breeches shall be locked up in a chest and kept safe unto my son's use by Emme Spivy, my wife, until he come to the age of one and twenty years, putting in sufficient security to my supervisors in her widowhood for the safe keeping and faithful delivery of the said clothes to him at his age aforesaid.[58]

Spivy was a character whose relationships and interests linked him with the past as well as the future and his preoccupation with clothing might reflect as much his interest in draperies as his desire to produce an heir, literally, in his own image. But, with the odd exception, Retford families looked to the possibility of new dynasties rather than to the ghosts of old ones, hardly surprising since the origins of most burgesses were middling to say the least. Typical of this new town 'gentry' were the Sloswickes who married successfully into the Wharton and Spivy clans in the sixteenth century, thus opening up links with the Denmans and Darrells. In 1633 Richard Sloswicke, gentleman, was involved in a series of controversies over seating in East Retford church, possibly an attempt to obtain for this up and coming family the respect which he felt was due to it.[59]

For most people marriage provided a stable and long-term environment for the bringing up of children in which women were expected to participate in activities other than those involving the home. Their role in the workforce is examined in Chapter 4, and the detailed account of the 1624 election shows how, even without a vote, women could break through into the political life of the town. Agents attempting to procure the election of Sir Edward Wortley thought it worthwhile to treat the wives of certain burgesses in the taverns 'to make their husbands faster', and on polling day Amy Welch reciprocated by assisting the vicar, John Watt, to stir up the mob in support of their candidate.[60] Amy is, in fact, an interesting and relatively well documented character. Daughter of Walter Day, a bankrupt maltster, she married Richard Welch in 1592 and bore him at least six children between 1603 and 1613.[61] The reason for her delayed conception could have been that the parties were unusually young at the time of the marriage: Richard was eighteen and Amy probably as young as fifteen, so they may well have decided not to have had children before Richard's apprenticeship as a butcher was completed and he had set himself up in business. This was not achieved without some difficulties since he became embroiled in disputes with the corporation, and possibly because of that Amy was called before the Archdeacon's court for scolding with her neighbours in 1600.[62] Richard travelled to Nottingham and spoke to the official on her behalf and the case was dismissed through want of evidence. The family troubles with the corporation help to explain Amy's role in the 1624 election, by which time she was a woman in middle life. She died in 1632 leaving her husband to carry on his business as a widower.[63] We cannot know of the quality of relationship enjoyed by Richard and Amy Welch, but due to similar bondings of work and shared experience some testators certainly spoke affectionately of their spouses. Robert Browne, town clerk and an opponent of the Welches in the 1624 election, used a well worn *cliché* when he spoke of 'my loving wife' in 1620, but in giving her virtually all of his property in token 'of all the dear love that hath been betwixt us', he voiced the view of a man for whom conventional matrimony had worked.[64]

Sadly, that was not always the case, and the incidence of adultery and separation in Retford prove that the bonds of marriage were fragile, even in an age in which divorce was extremely difficult. Adultery does not figure so frequently as fornication in the records of the Archdeacon's court because, even if it gave rise to a child, there was generally a marriage into which it could be absorbed, thus relieving any burden on the community. There were also considerable social pressures against aggrieved spouses making an issue of a partner's adultery, with men fearful of being ridiculed as cuckolds and women open to blame for driving off their husbands as scolds.[65] However, cases *were* brought and when they were proved they were dealt with in a similar fashion to cases of incontinence, Thomas Rodwell and Mary Welbye being sentenced to penance in 1592.[66] In 1600 William Bradshaw's wife,

Joanna, was having casual sex with a 'paver' by the name of Richard 'that cometh to Retford now and then', laying the slabs of the market square as well as the occasional matron of the town.[67] Similarly, one wonders what lay behind Jane Denman's suspected adultery with Godfrey Crowder in 1601, a woman of about 50 years of age who had borne her husband, Alexander Denman, no fewer than eleven children.[68] Nefarious and casual sexual gratification was no doubt often the motive, but when partners did decide to go their own ways the court was quick to try to reinstate the marriage in the absence of a legal divorce.[69] Cases of 'living apart' are fairly common, particularly in East Retford, and it is plain that the reasons for these marital ruptures were very mixed. Anne Barker blamed her husband, saying that he 'went unlawfully away from her about a year past': John Jackson blamed his wife, saying 'she departed unlawfully from him and liveth and continueth with her father': Joan Saundbey said that 'a crime committed seven years ago was the cause': Katherine Borrell claimed financial distress, saying that her husband had been forced to move away to earn money, and a similar defence was put up by Edward Jackson when he said of his wife 'that although he do live from her yet he relieveth her to his ability'.[70] Sometimes the circumstances were bizarre. Elizabeth Williams:

> confesseth that she was married with the same [John] Williams for the space of 23 years and another wife came and challenged him with whom he presently departed.[71]

Thomas Stephenson explained:

> that he is from his wife upon no other cause but fear of suit and trouble for her children, and so soon as he can take order in these causes will gladly return to her and live with her.[72]

Most of these cases were dismissed or referred to the vicar for 'social reports' but, here, we may well be seeing only the tip of an iceberg. For people without ties of property, it was extraordinarily easy to desert a disliked spouse and move on to find pastures new elsewhere, leaving the abandoned wife and children for the community to support. In the Quarter Sessions of 1623 the justices found themselves in something of a quandary. About ten years previously Thomas Chapman had deserted his wife and children and vanished. Subsequently the wife had married William Wither who had taken over Chapman's goods, but now she had died and there was a danger of the children becoming vagrants. The best that could be suggested was that the overseers should impound Wither's goods, on the understanding they were really Chapman's goods, and try to raise enough money from them for the support of the children.[73] As ever in these so-called 'moral' issues the bottom line came down to money, the law of God steadfastly upholding the law of man.

As death approached townspeople considered the possibility of making a will, though this was only relevant for those with some estate to dispose of and a risk of disagreement amongst their family as to who got what. It is, therefore, important to remember that in assessing wills we are exploring the aspirations and attitudes of only a minority of the population, influential though that minority might have been. In 1542 Thomas Upton of West Retford made an interesting and unique statement exploring the psychology of the will maker:

> remembering that death is duty by the ordinance of God to every man and woman living which must of necessity depart from this wretched world, considering also the hour of death uncertain by divers causes the perfect use of reason may be withdrawn at the article of death, considering that a gracious end and a blessed passing from this life is depending of a virtuous order of a will made by the time that we have before our death, for these causes and avoiding of all other casualties that which might be detrimental to my soul at the hour of death.[74]

Despite the fact that Upton's will was duly proved and enrolled in the probate register of the Archbishop of York, other town wills seem to have been dealt with informally by the executors without recourse to the church courts. Two references have been found in registered wills to wills of which no record can be found, an unusual occurrence given the thoroughness of the York archives.[75] The assumption must be that many small estates were passed on by word of mouth agreements or by written memoranda which the executors felt duty bound to implement, without going to the expense of obtaining a formal grant of probate.

The 'avoiding of casualties', which Upton referred to, generally meant dividing one's estate 'according to the law', or, more specifically, 'according to the custom of the province of York'.[76] This meant that a man with a family, the most common sort of testator, should divide his goods into three parts, one for his widow; one for his children; and one — the so-called Dead's Part — for the payment of his debts and funeral expenses.[77] Most wives received at least this legal third, 'clear to herself', as well as any other items she might have brought to the marriage, or income subject to a special agreement with her husband.[78] Wives were also commonly permitted to enjoy family houses and lands during their widowhood, the arrangement being that they should then pass to a named child.[79] This arrangement invariably lasted only so long as a widow remained unmarried and was occasionally subject to the payment of pensions, or other compensation, to the eventual heir.[80] Child's portions were a matter of greater disagreement, since there was often a number of competing forces to be considered and dispute as to what portion of its legal entitlement a child might have consumed during the life of a parent. Robert Witton was well aware of the latter problem:

> I give to Jane, my daughter, 40s to the helping of her living, for I did give her a sufficient child's part at her marriage. I will she have the cow which is in her possession...I give to Elizabeth Jackson, my daughter, in full contentation and last payment of her child's part...40s, for she and her husband hath had of me over and besides this my reward, £7.[81]

To prevent disputes, child's portions were sometimes itemised in considerable detail and the will of Joan Thompson (1550), who left three daughters, is a classic in this respect.[82] However, more commonly child's portions were to be assessed 'according to the rate and value of my goods' and executors, supervisors and 'impartial neighbours' were left with the unenviable task of division.[83] In the early sixteenth century child's portions were sometimes given in 'penny and pennyworth' (i.e. half money, half goods), but this custom and phraseology had died out by 1560.[84] Not so the custom of being 'cut off with a shilling'. Throughout the period a succession of unfortunate siblings received this token legacy 'in satisfaction of his portion', a reflection of deep family rifts or of considerable help extended to a child during the life of the testator.[85]

This standard package, of course, was subject to considerable variation and a degree of wheeling and dealing, on occasion, between the dead man and his living widow. William Spivy, wealthier than many of his neighbours, had entered into a detailed contract when he married Emme Browne and before the marriage had assigned to her tenements in Retford and Grantham for life. Moreover, he promised:

> that I shall leave her worth £300 over and besides certain plate and bedding set down and mentioned in a certain bond...which I sealed before marriage to her father Mr John Browne and Mr John Chirme...for that it was truly meant by her and her friends, at the conclusion of her marriage, that leaving her worth £300 I should have the benefit of the sale of her goods.[86]

The details of agreements such as these might have caused controversy after a testator's death, but marriage contracts had the effect of moving the question of inheritance out of the exclusive control of the ecclesiastical jurisdiction and involving the courts of common law in the complex question of who received what. John Wymoke gave his wife a series of legacies, 'so long as she doth keep her widow', but added that if she refused them 'then I will she shall have her full third' and the legacies were to be void.[87] Similarly, Nicholas Pettinger II appointed his wife as executrix on condition:

> she shall not challenge nor have any part of my goods by reason of her third part or other means, but only to hold her contented with her executorship or else not to stand nor be any executrix.[88]

Only rarely were women unfairly treated, but this seems to have been the case in the will of Richard Cock (1557). His wife received no third and no legacy except for 'my great silver spoon' which she was to enjoy only so long as she lived: moreover, she was not named as an executor and it was Cock's supervisors who were 'to see my children brought up as they shall think best'.[89] Perhaps there were forces at work we are not aware of. Cock's wife, who was pregnant at the time he made his will, was possibly unwilling or unable to administer his estate, or maybe she had been bought off with unseen gifts during her husband's life. Without one of these circumstances she would certainly have been within her rights to contest the will before the Archbishop's courts. But, in general terms, fairness is very much a feature of Retford wills, and that was a fairness which extended to *all* children of the family and not just the first born.[90] When a testator owned landed property he tried to distribute it around a number of sons, though there was often one who was obliged to accept cash in lieu: similarly, daughters were provided with cash sums payable on marriage or on achieving the age of 21.[91] This rejection of primogeniture, and tendency to spread property around the family group, helps to explain why the burgess 'dynasties' of Retford did not last for very long. When children were not in evidence property was dispersed to a wider range of relations including parents, brothers and nephews.[92] The will of John Wilson (1582) is a good example of the wide ranging generosity which was open to the childless testator.[93]

An analysis of 107 wills between 1600 and 1642 was undertaken to ascertain patterns of inheritance within the family group, particularly *vis-a-vis* members of the immediate and extended circles of relatives. The results are presented in Table 5.[94] Several problems were encountered here. Firstly, the division of testators into occupational groups (i.e. yeoman, tradesman, etc.) provided an unrealistic picture of what they actually did, since reading wills quickly drives home the point that in Retford farming and trade activities were very fluid and often overlapped: many 'yeomen' were tradesmen, many traders had an involvement with the land, and a 'gentleman' could be a tailor. Secondly, it proved to be impossible to quantify the somewhat vague information provided by wills, so what was done was to count up the numbers of bequests made by testators to individuals within the different social groupings, i.e. immediate family; extended family; and non-family. Each group had to be assessed on its own to avoid the misleading comparison between a widow receiving one (large) bequest and servants receiving three (minimal) ones. However, with those caveats, it became plain that within the immediate family all social groups made about 30% of bequests to widows and about 50% to sons and daughters, with grandchildren and sons-in-law and daughters-in-law taking up smaller portions of the estate.

In most cases a very large portion of the estate was involved in these immediate family bequests, except where a testator was unmarried or left no children. Within the extended family brothers and sisters and nephews and nieces were the major recipients, with parents figuring unusually high (21%) in the wills of tradesmen: aunts and uncles, interestingly, received nothing in any of the wills. The portion of the estate involved here was generally medium to small, except in the case of childless or unmarried testators, when extended family legacies took up a major share of the whole. Finally, in the small non-family category, there was a fairly even spread between friends, servants and godchildren, executors and supervisors being generally included amongst 'others'. Notable features here were the high premium placed on friends by husbandmen and labourers, and the high level of legacies bestowed on servants by tradesmen, hardly surprising, though, in view of the less nucleated lifestyle of the former and the dependence on workmen and apprentices amongst the latter. If the results of the survey were somewhat predictable, confirming an emphasis on the immediate family as dictated by the custom of the province — common to all social classes — women come over as very much a category of their own. Without a spouse to provide for, they could afford to be more generous to in-laws and to grandchildren, and they maintained closer links with cousins and with their servants. These women, of course, were widows generally, and the survey helps to paint a picture of the social priorities which dominated their salad days. Rose Fletcher, a spinster, left the bulk of her property to her nieces Mary and Elizabeth Mason, but requested that her grandmother, Joan Wharton, be allowed to have the South chamber over the shop during her life with free access 'at all times convenient'.[95] Sentiments such as these, and a general preoccupation with small and very personal legacies, prove the point that women's wills are worthy of study as a subject in their own right.[96]

A widow would generally be named as her husband's executrix, often jointly in the sixteenth century with the children who were residual legatees. Most testators appear to have had little doubt about a woman's ability to manage things in their absence, and phrases such as 'my wife...in whom is all my trust' are not uncommon.[97] Indeed some

29: A family group shares a meal around a table: the younger children were clearly expected to stand.

30: West Retford Hall, home of the Denmans and Darrells, was built during the reign of Elizabeth: the projecting wings were added in 1795.

women were so confident they jumped the gun and began to 'intermeddle' with their husband's estate before a grant of probate had been made and they were excommunicated by the Archdeacon's court for their 'presumption'.[98] To keep an eye on problems such as this, and to assist the executor in the management of the estate, supervisors were frequently appointed. Up to 1572 Sir John Hercy was a popular choice, his virtues summed up amply by Edward Hodgson in 1565:

> the right worshipful and my singular good master Sir John Hercy, knight, to take upon him as he hath been accustomed ever to do good.[99]

Good Sir John was bombarded with small gifts by the grateful people of the town—sums of money, 'my best horse', even a rent charge of 20d *per annum* for ever — and it seems likely that his judgement in difficult cases was beyond dispute.[100] Following his death there was no obvious replacement, and supervisors tended to be drawn from amongst the most respected families of the town — Denmans, Thorntons, Eatons, for example, and, of course, the clergy.[101] Between them the executors and supervisors were to undertake the complicated, and sometimes controversial, business of dividing up the estate according to the wishes of the testator expressed in the will.

There were two major problems likely to be faced in this task. Firstly, the intransigence of sons and daughters who felt they had been badly done to, and secondly the shock waves which were likely to reverberate through the family group if a widow remarried. The second possibility was highly likely in times of plague, notably in the late 1550s, when young widows with an inheritance in their pockets were suddenly turned loose on the marriage market to be snapped up by ambitious suitors. Often testators had foreseen problems such as these, and in their wills had left instructions designed to sidestep the worst pitfalls. Christopher Atkinson stated that:

> if any of my children be obstinate or sturdy and will not be ruled or ordered...that they so being have neither part or parcel of any of my goods.[102]

Similarly, Elizabeth Parnell said specifically of her son William:

> if he shall not rest satisfied and contented...but shall...question, sue, molest or trouble my executors...[her legacies to him

were to be void]...and in that case I do only give and bequeath to my said son William and Dorothy his wife twelve pence a piece in full payment and satisfaction.[103]

Armed with a clause such as this, which disinherited troublesome children 'labouring or striving' against the will, executors were on much stronger ground.

But the remarriage problem was potentially more troublesome. Generally speaking, while a widow remained unmarried she was trusted with the bringing up of her children and the management of their portions. William Spivy even extended the former privilege to a stepmother, his second wife Emme:

> reposing my trust next under God...that she will have that motherly care of my dear and only son and of his welfare and good education as if he were her own; and thereupon I freely give him unto her as sithence the time of our marriage she hath always used him and the rest of my children exceedingly well.[104]

But even having made this outstanding statement of confidence in his wife's maternal virtues, Spivy was circumspect enough to place his son's child's portion of £100 in the hands of his 'cousin', Christopher Bussy, requesting him to pay to Emme £3 *per annum* towards the boy's education. This might have been prompted by personal experience, since Spivy himself had a stepson (the son of his first wife Elizabeth Russell) and after his mother's death the property of that child had become the subject of an acrimonious suit in Chancery.[105] The main danger came if a widow (or a widower, in Spivy's case) decided to remarry, thus raising the prospect of the interests of the child of the former marriage becoming submerged in the new relationship—indeed, a young widow might well start a new family and completely reject the old one. During the plague year of 1557 John Upton stated that if his wife remarried before his children came of age:

> she shall be bound with sufficient surety unto my friends that my children shall have no loss or hinderance by her marriage.[106]

William Bryan went further, saying that in the event of remarriage a 'sure bond' was to be made with his supervisors 'for the performance of my children's parts', or the children were to be handed over to the supervisors 'my trusty and well beloved friends'.[107] Fears such as these persuaded some testators to nominate guardians, who could step in and have the 'ordering' of their children and their legacies if a widow remarried or died.[108] Guardians might also be appointed if there was no surviving parent to care for the children. Nicholas Wharton, mercer, whose wife had predeceased him by 1556, hoped that his friends would care for his children 'for very friendship without having or taking any profit or advantage', and in 1558 Janet Braithwaite, acutely conscious of mortality, desired that her daughter:

> shall be at the rule of John Madyn ... and if anything but good come at him I will she remain with Robert Atkinson.[109]

When a number of children was involved in a situation such as this the burden might be considered too great for a single parent or guardian to bear and the family group split up. Of the three children of William Spivy, by his first marriage, only his son Edmund was to remain with his stepmother, while his daughters, Elizabeth and Susanne, were farmed out amongst his Bussy relatives.[110] In general, children had no choice as to who these adult protectors should be, and in the will of Alice Atkinson (1636) they lost their legacies if they refused to accept them.[111] Only Nicholas Bird, weaver, showed a modicum of enlightenment when he stated in 1588 that in the event of his wife's death his children were to be at liberty to select their own guardians.[112] It was a statement of trust in the inherent commonsense of young people that had very few echoes in Tudor and Stuart Retford.

The fact that Retford people tended to marry in their mid to late twenties was dictated by the economic life of the town, principally the rules of apprenticeship and the problems of 'setting up', but it had a profound effect on family and society in all sorts of ways. Firstly, it limited family size by curtailing the period of a woman's fertility, and there is some evidence that a form of contraception may have been used to reinforce this trend.[113] Secondly, it meant that considerable numbers of young and sexually active people were living and working in the town, a situation which might possibly lead to acts of incontinence and the birth of bastards. However, since the parents of these were by definition unmarried, marriage, hopefully, could be enforced by legal agencies to indemnify the community against possible expense. Yet, for some, marriage proved to be a fragile bond, particularly if lack of property enabled one or other party to move away and seek a new relationship elsewhere. For those who remained in a state of Christian wedlock, emphasis rested firmly on the immediate family group, with an extended kinship network providing little more than fellowship and moral support. Within these groups women played an important and, no doubt, sometimes dominant role, and when they were left as widows they enjoyed virtually the same authority as men to conduct businesses and even to assume authority over apprentices. In most cases inheritance was governed by fairmindedness and a rejection of primogeniture, and boundaries of acceptable behaviour, based on precepts of church and state, were endorsed by the community at large as the only means whereby they could be made workable measures of social control. When consensus broke down, so did the ability of central or local government to enforce its demands by any other means. Little of this represented innovation in the Tudor or Stuart period. So far as family life is concerned, it is likely that the inhabitants of Retford on the eve of the Civil War enjoyed much in common with townsmen of the distant past.

FOOTNOTES AND REFERENCES

1. NAO, Wills (Thomas Cooper, 1626).
2. For general discussions of family life, see L. Stone, *The Family Sex and Marriage in England, 1500-1800* (1979), R. A. Houlbrooke, *The English Family, 1450-1700* (1984). For marriage, in particular, see M. Ingram, *The Church Courts, Sex and Marriage in England* (1987), and N. J. Pike, 'Marriage Formation and Breakdown in Nottinghamshire, 1570-1610', University of Nottingham MA dissertation, 1989.
3. NAO, DDTS 7 f.68.
4. *Ibid.*, 10 ff.99, 106.
5. *Ibid.*, ff.99, 101, 106, 111, 119.
6. *Ibid.*, 7 ff.48, 167, 10 ff.99, 176, 11 ff.103, 110, 151, 155/6.
7. *Ibid.*, 23 ff.137, 142, 150/1, 158, 164.
8. Of these, eight were from East Retford and one from West Retford. For a general discussion of defamation in the diocese of York, see J. A. Sharpe, *Defamation and Sexual Slander in early modern England: the Church Courts at York*, Borthwick Paper, 58, 1980.

9.   Johnson v Dawson, Retford's longest running defamation case, had eight hearings between July and November 1601, but was not brought to a conclusion. This case involved the notorious John Dawson who was accused of defaming Margaret Johnson. For Dawson, see Chapter 4, p.122, NAO, DDTS, 8 ff.128, 130/1, 133, 136/7, 139, 141.
10.   *Ibid.*, 3 ff.86, 88, 89.
11.   *Ibid.*, 7 f.148, 9 f.33, 10 ff.20, 32, 157.
12.   *Ibid.*, ff.99, 106, 111.
13.   See, for example, 6 ff.99, 106, 111.
14.   *Ibid.*, ERPR (1606).
15.   *Ibid.*, DDTS, 7 ff.142, 151, 155.
16.   *Ibid.*, 1 ff.215, 220, 224.
17.   *Ibid.*, 23 f.143, 24 ff.9,30.
18.   *Ibid.*, 5 ff.179, 181, 185, 188, Wills (Edward Slater, 1616).
19.   *Ibid.*, DDTS 23 ff.51, 129.
20.   Smyth was one of the signatories of the letter to the Earl of Rutland in 1586, probably as bailiff. *HMC, Rutland*, 1, p.208.
21.   NAO, DDTS 24 ff.177/9, 185, 190, 197.
22.   *Ibid.*, ERPR (1585).
23.   *Ibid.*, DDTS 5 ff.177, 180/1, 187, 199, 202, 208, 216, 218/9, 230, Wills (William Smyth, 1604).
24.   BI, V 1567/8, CB f.4.
25.   NUMD, Arch. PN 352.
26.   NAO, DDTS 1 ff. 153, 163, 168, 172, 175/6, 4 f.244, 5 f.5.
27.   *Ibid.*, 9 ff.33, 38, 6 f.124, 7 ff.94, 141, 146, 148, 151, 155, 177.
28.   *Ibid.*, ff.141, 146.
29.   See Appendix, Table 4.
30.   NAO, DDTS 3, ff.113, 116, 125, 127, 168, 189, 202, 4 f.39.
31.   NUCLH, A(ggregative A(nalysis) F(orms) (East Retford).
32.   Bastards have been identified by obvious descriptions (e.g. 'base son') or when the name of the mother only is recorded in the baptismal entry.
33.   NUCLH, AAF (Clarborough).
34.   'Filius populi' is used in 1613 and 1614.
35.   Fathers were identified in eight instances and were prosecuted when this information came to light. Three cases of bastards baptised at Clarborough are noted under East Retford for the purposes of litigation: these have been taken as parcel of the Clarborough statistics.
36.   Looked at another way, and ignoring the question of prosecution, bastardy in Clarborough could be seen as a ten year cycle i.e. 1577-81, four bastards: 1589-93, five bastards: 1601-04, five bastards. In other words, there is a clear

tendency towards the 'bunching' of illegitimate births into narrower periods, suggesting that social forces, such as example and emulation, might have been at work.

37. BI, V 1600, CB 2 f.39, NAO, DDTS, 11 f.54. Parnall was deposed as an alderman at about this time, which might imply a more severe attitude to sexual malpractice on the part of the corporation. See Chapter 2, pp.53-4.

38. NAO, DDTS 22 f.144, 23 ff.192, 204.

39. *Ibid.*, 6 f.36.

40. BI, PR 13 f.82, 11 f.666.

41. NAO, QSMI/7.

42. *Ibid.*

43. *Ibid.*, DDTS 1 f.163, 12 ff.151, 160, 163. In Woodrough's case the informant was Simon Somerbye of South Wheatley: the incident did not damage Woodrough's civic career, since he became bailiff in 1600/01.

44. *Ibid.*, 5 ff.60, 64, 81, 89, 94, 100, 121, 124, 7 f.40, BI, V 1600, CB 2 f.40.

45. People were cited for breaking all of these regulations. See, for example, NAO, DDTS 7 f.69, 11 f.112, BI, V 1600, CB 2 f.33.

46. NUCLH, FRF.

47. NAO, DDTS 12 f.27.

48. During the plague of 1557/8 several children were left legacies 'if it please God to give them life to come to lawful age', but this was unusual. See, for example, BI, PR 19 f.264.

49. NUCLH, FRF. Earle was an alderman and bailiff in 1623/4 and 1632/3.

50. NAO, CPR (1619).

51. NUCLH, FRF.

52. *The Visitation of Nottinghamshire*, pp.90/1. In 1623 Edward Darrell of West Retford Esq left cash legacies in excess of £1,000. NAO, Wills (Edward Darrell, 1623). For the property transactions of this family see NAO, *Catalogue of Mee Mss.*

53. PRO, PROB 11/101, *Lincolnshire Pedigrees, 1*, Harleian Society, 50 (1892) pp.215-19.

54. BI, PR 22 ff.423/4, NAO, Wills (Edith Himlock, 1617: Saville Wharton, 1637). The confusing name 'Ducke', is in fact, a contraction of Marmaduke.

55. BI, PR 9 ff.37/8, 287, *The Visitation of Nottinghamshire*, pp.14/15, 67/9, 69/70. In the seventeenth century an Anne Smith of East Retford married Parke Cressy of Owlcotes. *The Visitation of Nottinghamshire, 1662/4*, Harleian Society, New Series, 5 (1986), p.108.

56. RM, Ancient Deeds, 1562, BI, PR 21 f.295, *The Visitation of*

Nottinghamshire, pp.119/20. Other Retford burgess families probably enjoyed colateral links with the gentry, for example, the Salmons, Eyres and Tongs. *Ibid.,* pp.35, 43, 84/5.

57. BI, PR 15A f.231, NAO, Wills (Thomas Bate, 1628).
58. PRO, PROB 11/101.
59. NUMD, A 39 f.242, NAO, Wills (Isabel Sloswicke, 1614).
60. NUMD, Cl. LP. 52.
61. NAO, Wills (Walter Day, 1601), ERPR, NUCLH, FRF.
62. NAO, DDTS 6 f.268. See Chapter 2, pp.33-4.
63. *Ibid.,* ERPR (1632). Richard Welch appeared twice before the Quarter Sessions, for failure to pay taxes (1617) and for unlawful trading in sheep (1633). QSMI/5, 9.
64. *Ibid.,* Wills (Robert Browne, 1620).
65. Edward Arnall of Clarborough promoted a case against Robert Colley in 1585 claiming that he had had carnal dealing with his wife, Elizabeth. DDTS, 25 ff.6, 9.
66. Rodwell's penance was later commuted to a payment of £4, plus fees and 'presents' to the officers of the court: the money was directed towards the paving of the market place of East Retford. Welbye failed to perform her penance and was excommunicated. DDTS, 4 ff.27/8, 88, 99, 100/1, 129, 142.
67. BI, V 1600, CB f.31.
68. NAO, DDTS, 11 ff.11, 16.
69. *Ibid.,* 7 f.103, for example.
70. *Ibid.,* 2 ff.30, 33, 47, 104, 198, 202, 204, 3 f.103, 23 f.16.
71. *Ibid.,* 22 f.141.
72. *Ibid.,* 3 f.174.
73. *Ibid.,* QSMI/6.
74. BI, PR 11 ff.663/4.
75. For example, the will of Nicholas Holme, vicar of East Retford, referred to in the will of Nicholas Wilson (1558) but nowhere to be found. PR 15C, f.407.
76. *Ibid.,* PR 15B f.242, 19 f.420.
77. NAO, Wills (William Field, 1637).
78. BI, PR 9 f.287, 11 ff.664, 772, 13 f.309.
79. *Ibid.,* 11 f.233, 666, 13 f.1022.
80. *Ibid.,* 11 f.233.
81. *Ibid.,* f.259.
82. *Ibid.,* 13 f.647. See also, 13 ff.733, 1022.
83. *Ibid.,* 22 f.690.
84. *Ibid.,* 9 f.287, 15A f.231.
85. NAO, Wills (Richard Parnell, 1626: Henry Tong, 1640).
86. PRO, PROB 11/101
87. BI, PR 16 ff.144/5.

88. *Ibid.*, AR 31, f.84.
89. *Ibid.*, PR 15A f.231.
90. This sense of fairness is seen in an extreme case in the will of William Smyth (1604): in bestowing six silver spoons around the family he noted that one was damaged and that the recipient of the damaged spoon should receive 1s as compensation! NAO, Wills (William Smyth, 1604).
91. BI, PR 22 f.690, NAO, Wills (John Spivy, 1622).
92. BI, PR 16 f.170, 23 f.507, 26 f.284, 27 f.197, NAO, Wills (Nicholas Watson, 1614: William Wharton, 1614).
93. BI, PR 22 ff.423/4. Wilson was an ex-alderman of Lincoln and a cousin of the Whartons. He may have originally come from Retford since a family of that name was settled in the town in the early sixteenth century.
94. See Appendix, Table 5.
95. NAO, Wills (Rose Fletcher, 1632).
96. For an assessment of widows' wills in Nottingham, see Sandra Dunster, 'An Independent Life? Nottingham Widows, 1594-1650', *Transactions of the Thoroton Society*, 95, 1991.
97. BI, PR 9 f.111. William Carter (1607), for example, appointed his wife guardian of their children during their 'nonage and minority, according to the trust I repose in her'. NAO, Wills (William Carter, 1607).
98. NAO, DDTS, 5 f.144.
99. BI, PR 17B f.458.
100. *Ibid.*, 13 ff.160, 163, 15B f.357.
101. *Ibid.*, 11 f.233, 19 f.382, 25 f.1022, 26 f.582.
102. *Ibid.*, 15B f.242.
103. NAO, Wills (Elizabeth Parnell, 1639).
104. PRO, PROB 11/101.
105. *Ibid.* Spivy's caution was well founded. He was buried on February 7 1603 and on May 23 of the same year his widow married Mr Francis Longlands. C.W. Foster (ed), *The Parish Registers of Grantham, 1, 1562-1632*, Lincoln Record Society, Parish Register Section, 4, 1916, pp.139,142.
106. BI, PR 15B f.246.
107. *Ibid.*, 15C f.421.
108. *Ibid.*, 13 f.733, 23 f.851.
109. *Ibid.*, 15A f.177, 15B f.246.
110. PRO, PROB 11/101.
111. NAO, Wills (Alice Atkinson, 1636).
112. BI, PR 23 f.735.
113. See Chapter 6, pp.177-8.

Chapter 6

PRIESTS AND PREACHERS

Queen Elizabeth restored me to my flock and I thereupon worked that Retford should reap the fruits of my labours.[1]

The clergy of Retford were potentially among the most influential men in the community, particularly during the period of rapid and unprecedented religious change between the reigns of Henry VIII and Elizabeth I. Yet despite this their economic position in the town was weak, a situation which had its origins long before the Reformation. In the twelfth century Archbishop Roger of York had established the collegiate church of St Mary and the Holy Angels, commonly known as St Sepulchre's, adjacent to York Minster. It was endowed with extensive spiritual possessions in North Nottinghamshire, including the tithes of Clarborough and East Retford, and the sacrist of St Sepulchre was made responsible for the nomination of the clergy to these and other livings. Kidson suggests that the vicar of East Retford was always a prebendary of St Sepulchre, but if that had been the case the custom had certainly lapsed by 1535.[2] In that year the tithe corn of Clarborough, Welham and Bolham brought the York church an income of £21 and the personal and mill tithes of East Retford accounted for a further £6 6s 8d.[3] Out of these the sacrist was expected to pay a salary of £5 to the vicar of East Retford along with payments to the poor of Clarborough and East Retford, the latter being provided from the mill tithes.[4] The vicar of Clarborough received the lesser tithes of his parish, deemed to be worth £9 15s 4d, giving him almost double the income of his counterpart at East Retford for the cure of many fewer souls.[5]

When the chapel of St Mary and the Holy Angels was dissolved in 1547 its property passed to the crown which presented clergy to East Retford and Clarborough for the next

50 years, despite a grant of the Clarborough advowson, amongst others, to Nicholas Heath, Archbishop of York, by Queen Mary seventeen days before her death in 1558.[6] In 1562 the new Queen leased the entire property of St Sepulchre's for 31 years to George Webster, her servant, and in 1577 the same lease was made to Sir Thomas Manners: in line with the conservatism with which these transactions were invariably underpinned both lessees were bound to make the traditional payments to the poor 'as accustomed'.[7] Interestingly, the lease to Sir Thomas Manners is the only clear record of a member of the high steward's family using his influence to obtain a financial stake in the town.[8] The rectory of Clarborough was eventually sold by the crown to John Harwood of Edensor, Derbyshire, in 1599, and from him it appears to have passed quickly to the Cavendish family who also obtained East Retford at about the same time.[9] As the eventual successors of the sacrist of St Sepulchre, the Cavendishes were the last of the Protestant families to benefit from the Henrician Reformation, and their attempts to exert influence in the town were to be seen increasingly in the seventeenth century.

These changes disrupted long established traditions in the two parishes and a case at Clarborough in the early seventeenth century illustrates the tensions which could be unleashed. The first hint of a problem came in 1606 when George Spivy, a West Retford yeoman, was prosecuted in the Archdeacon's court for his failure to contribute to the Clarborough church rate. Spivy's descent has not been traced with any certainty, but he was possibly a brother of William Spivy of East Retford and therefore closely related to the Sloswickes and the corporation dissidents of the 1590s. Spivy said in his defence that he held no land in the parish except that which belonged to the parsonage, of which he was farmer, presumably under the Cavendishes, and that because of this he was not bound in law to pay any rate to the church. The judge accepted his defence and the case against him was dismissed.[10] Evidently Nicholas Watkins, vicar of Clarborough, did not share the judge's view because, in the following year, Spivy was obliged by the Quarter Sessions to put up sureties of £20 to keep the peace with the vicar.[11] Local ill will eventually erupted in 1611 in an acrimonious case before the Archbishop's Consistory Court at York.[12] In it Thomas Tye of

Clarborough, gentleman, proceeded against Spivy for the alleged usurpation of his stall in the chancel of Clarborough church.[13] The Tye family had sat, traditionally, in the chancel ever since the vicar of Clarborough, John Thackwray, had lodged with them prior to 1550 and had granted the privilege.[14] However, Spivy, as farmer of the tithes, now proposed to exercise what he saw as his rectoral right of sitting in the chancel stall. What the Tyes had enjoyed for half a century by virtue of local status and absentee management, Spivy — a newcomer with little backing in the community — sought to usurp by the force of law.[15] The tension between the two men snapped on Christmas Day 1610 when Thomas Tye and his brother arrived late for morning prayers and found Spivy 'and some others, servants and boys' already seated in their stall. When Spivy confronted the angry Tye with the words 'Mr Tye you shall not sit here...here is no place for you', a struggle ensued in which both men were thrown to the ground and the disputed stall was broken. Nicholas Watkins, who heard a distant commotion in the chancel, refused to become involved and continued with the Christmas service 'till the same was ended'. Witnesses were examined at St Swithun's in August 1611, but the conclusion of the case is not clear. However, when Spivy made his will in 1613 he requested to be buried 'in the chancel in the parish church of Clarborough aforesaid near unto the place where Elizabeth my late wife were buried', and when he died later in the same year it was proclaimed in the parish register that he was 'farmer of the rectory and tithes', evidently a role in which he took some pride.[16]

No such dissentions and uncertainties troubled the Spivy heartlands in West Retford. Here the living was a rectory under the paternalistic control of the Hercys of Grove since the thirteenth century.[17] On the death of Sir John Hercy in 1572, without issue, patronage passed to his Denman relatives until it devolved on Edward Darrell by virtue of his marriage to Barbara Denman in about 1600.[18] Despite its rectoral status West Retford was not a good living according to the *Valor Ecclesiasticus* which gave the rector an income of £9 13s 4d, slightly less than his neighbour at Clarborough.[19] However, the rector of West Retford had increased room for manoeuvre because of his possession of glebe land, and the greater moral authority which he possessed in his parish, because of the close link between the rectory and the manor house, showed itself in a distinctive sociological profile of that part of the town, especially where presentments to the ecclesiastical courts were concerned. At East Retford and Clarborough 400 years of management from York had created vacuums of authority which it was not easy to fill, problems which were likely to be considerable since the Protestant reformers of the sixteenth century saw leadership from the pulpit as essential in their fight against the dark forces of popery.

Lack of consistent clerical leadership showed itself most markedly before the accession of Elizabeth, which might be expected with property changing hands between a dissolved religious institution and the crown. The transitional incumbent was John Thackwray, presented to the vicarage of Clarborough in 1508 and that of East Retford in 1521 by Thomas Magnus, sacrist of St Sepulchre.[20] However, there is little evidence that Thackwray had much active involvement with the town, and his role at Clarborough seems to have been far from dynamic.[21] In both parishes a series of curates or parish priests occur, sometimes termed 'vicar', three being traced at East Retford and five at Clarborough prior to Thackwray's death in 1550.[22] These men seem to be quite separate from the guild and chantry priests who worked in the town before 1547, though it is sometimes difficult to be certain because of the vagueness of the descriptions employed.[23] Whether they were deputies of the vicar or unofficial replacements for him is impossible to say, though he did acknowledge William Carr as his curate at Clarborough in 1550 leaving him 'my worsted tippett'.[24] Thackwray had family ties in East Retford, even though his hold on the vicarage is doubtful by the time of his death.[25] He never married, and his use of a 'Catholic' preamble to his will as late as January 1550 indicates a man of a strongly conservative disposition. Moreover, the fact that he became a virtual pensioner of the Tyes of Clarborough and that he valued 'my bow, my quiver [and] my shafts' sufficiently to bestow them as a legacy, hint at an individual for whom the pursuits of the gentry weighed as heavily as the priestly vocation. Thackwray was a man who in all likelihood disapproved strongly of the Protestant Reformation but, not made of the stuff of martyrs, took refuge in the life of the countryside and delegated his clerical responsibilities to others. This can be the only explanation of why he remained such an ineffectual force in the spiritual life of the town at such a critical period in its history.

On his death Robert Armstede, curate of East Retford, was appointed vicar of Clarborough, though at East Retford curates continued to serve for the next four years until the presentation of Thomas Wilkin by the crown in 1554.[26] Wilkin was probably the same man who was a chantry priest or curate in the town in 1546,[27] but his appointment as vicar did not last long because in 1556 he was replaced by Nicholas Holme, the ex-vicar of Sturton, who had been deprived for marriage in 1554 but had recanted.[28] Holme spent a busy year in the town, but he was dead by the end of 1557 and the living was held vacant for a further four years, served by curates, until the appointment of Edward Hodgson in 1561.[29] Hodgson died in 1565 and was replaced by Avery Tempest, another probable conservative, who died eight years later in 1573.[30] Compared with this rapid turnover of personnel, West Retford, where the advowson and tithes did not change hands, fared much better. Here Thomas Elton was rector until c1530[31] when he was replaced by Nicholas Pettinger I who remained in office until succeeded by his nephew, Nicholas Pettinger II, in 1559.[32] West Retford had its share of curates over these years,[33] but there was at least a stability at the head of the parish which was lacking at Clarborough before 1550 and at East Retford before 1561. The abiding impression of the populace of the town must have been of clergy who passed through the place rapidly because of the poor career prospects there, with only the shadowy figure of Thackwray offering any sense of continuity. The conservative nature of all of the clergy prior to the accession of Elizabeth, with the exception of Robert Reveley at East Retford during the reign of Edward VI, helps to explain why Protestantism was so slow to take root.[34] The town, which should have been seen as a beacon of light for the reformed faith within the Bassetlaw Hundred, stumbled along with footloose and mediocre clergy, the victim of financial transactions pursued in the distant past.

To obtain a living in the town an aspiring clergyman needed to catch the eye of the lay patron of West Retford or of the more distant Lord Keeper who managed clerical appointments on behalf of the crown. As might be expected, the advowson of West Retford was used from time to time in a semi-nepotistic fashion. Sir John Hercy presented two Nicholas Pettingers in succession to one another — evidently he liked the family — and William Denman, the Protestant rector of Ordsall, presented his brother, Francis, to the living in 1578.[35] Francis Denman, the classic 'squarson', was as often referred to as 'gentleman' as minister, and he resigned from his living in 1596 in order to concentrate on the management of his estates.[36] But there was nothing illegal about any of these transactions. In each case they appear to have put a sound, if privileged and well-connected, local man into the living. Indeed, some clergy did not like to stray far from home and their obtaining of a posting in the area might be seen as highly desirable. James Colley, vicar of East Retford (1617-18) was possibly related to a family of that name in the town, and the same could be said of Robert Hurst, vicar of Clarborough (1630-43).[37] Certainly there was a long standing tradition in the Middle Ages of local priests serving the town chantries. In a slightly different category was Christopher Say, who became ordained in 1573 to take on the vicarage of East Retford: he was already master of the grammar school, possibly since its refoundation in 1551.[38] But the majority of clerics after 1559 were younger men who were also newcomers to the area, career clergy who were prepared to travel to obtain the best prospect available.[39] Some had had previous careers. Zachary Jenkinson came to West Retford in 1596 after fifteen years as vicar of Stapleford in Leicestershire: Nathaniel Hunte had been ten years as an assistant to a Doctor of Law at York before arriving at Clarborough in 1620.[40] But such experience was unusual. The most typical pattern, as with the masters of the grammar school, was for a young man to take on one of these cures directly from University or possibly after two or three years serving as a curate elsewhere. This, at least, seems to have been the case for three particularly long serving incumbents — Nicholas Watkins at Clarborough (1577-1617); Thomas Bishop at West Retford (1600-1642), and John Watt at East Retford (1618-1640).[41] We must assume that, in cases like this, patrons judged applicants on their merits or had personal information which enabled them to make an informed choice. Sir

John Hercy, for one, probably carried considerable weight with the Lord Keeper, and Edward Hodgson certainly regarded him as 'my singular good master':[42] successive Archdeacons of Nottingham were another potential source of recommendation.

A striking point about the clergy of the area is the general quality of their academic backgrounds. This was not always parallelled in other parts of the country at a time when widespread concern was being expressed about the educational abilities of the ministry. Between 1520 and 1642 twenty beneficed clergy served in the three parishes and of these half had University degrees: indeed, after about 1580 degrees were virtually universal, the non-degree men tending to be placed in the earlier period. Out of the ten clergy with degrees, it is notable that seven graduated from Cambridge: only Zachary Jenkinson was an out-and-out Oxford man, and Henry Bate matriculated at Cambridge though his degrees were awarded at Oxford.[43] Most of the clergy graduated with BA or MA degrees, though Henry Bate was a BD and Christopher Say a graduate in law. The marked favour shown to Cambridge men — and particularly graduates of colleges such as Trinity, Christ's, St John's and Emmanuel — begins to underline the clear Protestant sympathies expressed by the patrons of this part of North Nottinghamshire after 1559. Many of these institutions were well known for their puritan dons or had been set up specifically to augment the supply of godly ministers in the country at large. Despite the educational improvement evident amongst the beneficed clergy, curates remained an under-privileged sub-culture. Out of about 25 curates and chantry priests traced over the period 1520-1640, twenty served in the troubled times prior to 1560 and only two appear to have had degrees.[44] Thus, the unmistakeable trend initiated by the Reformation was towards fewer clergy in the town and better qualified men, in an academic sense at least, taking direct personal responsibility for their cures.

Since new incumbents were appointed at West Retford in 1559 and East Retford in 1561 there was little danger of the 'hangover' caused by reactionary clergy which was a problem in so many parts of the diocese: only at Clarborough did Robert Armstede linger on until his death in 1577.[45] His will contained a neutral preamble, but his nomination of William

Denman, the Protestant rector of Ordsall, as one of his super-visors indicates that he cannot have been too far out of sorts with the new regime.[46] As early as 1565 Edward Hodgson, vicar of East Retford, left no doubt about his enthusiasm for the Elizabethan settlement when, in a fit of patriotic fervour, he left to the Queen and her successors the sum of 40s. Neither was his own spiritual welfare neglected:

> First, and above all things, I commit my soul unto God Almighty, through the merits of Jesus Christ my only saviour and redeemer by the mightly operation of the Holy Ghost three persons and one God to whom be praise for ever and ever, Amen. And my body to be buried within the parish where I die, wherein I trust my body shall rise again at the last day of judgement with the faithful and elect to everlasting salvation.[47]

Protestant belief was spelt out even more emphatically by Nicholas Pettinger II, rector of West Retford, in his will in 1578:

> First, and principally, I yield and commit my soul into the hands and tuition of the Holy Trinity, God Almighty in persons three in substance one: to God the father that made it: to God the son which redeemed it: and to God the Holy Ghost which sanctified it. Believing faithfully and hoping assuredly that God of his mercy, and for Christ's merits, will embrace it with the arms of his mercy and shall rest in Abraham's bosom, and at the last day at the general resurrection, together with the body, shall from thenceforth continually and for ever remain amongst the number of God's elect and chosen people in joys perpetual and glory everlasting.[48]

Such was Pettinger's veneration for his Geneva Bible and copy of Calvin's *Institutions* that he separated them out of the general body of his books to be passed on, with other selected heirlooms, to his only daughter, Elizabeth. This was a form of Calvinist orthodoxy which was to prevail amongst the clergy of Retford, with only minor hiccups, up to the Civil War.

What is perhaps even more remarkable than the general ability and orthodoxy of the clergy after 1559, is the question of how such men were attracted to the area given the compara-

tively poor endowments on offer there. The *Valor Ecclesiasticus*
valuations have already been dealt with, but by the second
half of the sixteenth century they already represented a
significant under-valuation of the livings involved. Com-
parisons with valuations made in the early seventeenth
century, elsewhere in the province of York, suggest that the
Valor figure should at least be multiplied by three in order to
obtain a realistic sum for the later sixteenth century when
prices were more stable.[49] This sort of adjustment would put
West Retford and Clarborough up to about £30 and East
Retford to about £15. But even with these increases, none of
the town livings represented a secure investment for a young
clergyman who had that supreme, and much in demand, gift
— an education, and possibly a family to support too. West
Retford and Clarborough were borderline prospects, and
East Retford's emoluments would have condemned a man to
a definite life of hardship. When the Nottinghamshire justices attempted to set wage rates for manual workers in 1627
carpenters, plumbers and bricklayers were deemed to be
worth 10d per day in summer and 9d during the shorter
working hours of winter.[50] Translated into an annual sum
this comes to about £12, which would have put them on an
approximate par — economically, if not educationally —
with the vicar of East Retford. Not only were the clergy
poorly paid, they also suffered the additional complication of
having to collect their income from a wide assortment of tithe
payments and customary dues which their parishioners were
obliged to offer them. Although this must have been time
consuming, it does not appear to have been as contentious an
issue as it might have been, and this implies that the town
clergy had succeeded in winning the broad respect of their
parishioners. In 1603 Thomas Bishop, rector of West Retford,
proceeded against Robert Bend in the Archdeacon's court for
tithe of fourteen sheep and five lambs, but the matter seems
to have been settled amicably.[51] No litigation at all has come
to light for Clarborough and East Retford, though when
George Turvin died in 1617 he was still owed £2 in mortuaries
by the widows of four of his East Retford parishioners, one of
them being John Jepson, alderman, who had been dead for
almost two years.[52]

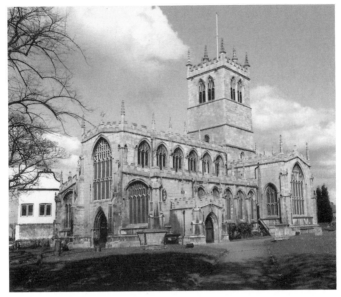

31: St Swithun's church, East Retford, still dominates an extensive churchyard near the centre of the town.

32: Thomas Magnus, archdeacon of the East Riding: a noted diplomat and educationalist and one-time patron of the livings of East Retford and Clarborough.

Of the town clergy only the rector of West Retford had a right to glebe land, and this was a valuable asset since it enabled him to keep pace with inflation and other market forces by direct farming. Nicholas Pettinger II appears to have taken advantage of his glebe, and in August 1578, soon before harvest, he had on the ground six acres of barley, seven acres of 'fallowes for rye' and three acres of oats, as well as hay and rye in store 'with peas of the last year'. To work this land he had an impressive array of farming equipment and six oxen and five horses to provide transport. He owned a bull and nine cows, pigs, poultry and 134 sheep and lambs.[53] Farming on this scale, it is tempting to assume that Pettinger occupied property other than his glebe, but if he did it is not stated in his will. The rectory house must have been a hive of activity with brewing, malting, spinning and dairying all going on within the immediate vicinity. With 'a flitch of beef and another of bacon' hanging in the milk house, Pettinger and his family clearly ate well, and the valuation of his goods at £236 7s 4d gave his widow a measure of financial security after his death. George Turvin too was farming on a moderate scale at the time of his death in 1617, though here he was utilising the glebe lands of Babworth, and some rented closes, rather than properties appurtaining to his vicarage of East Retford.[54]

Pluralism was a traditional answer to the economic problems of the clergy, and though there were scandalous examples of this practice within the neighbourhood of Retford — the case of Edmund Mason, rector of Ordsall, for example[55] — there was an argument that pluralism could bring real benefits to the church by providing rewards for deserving clergy who might otherwise be underpaid. Much depended on the distance between livings held in plurality, and whether or not a man could be expected to combine them with a fair degree of efficiency. Many pluralities probably represented sensible working arrangements. John Thackwray united East Retford and Clarborough before 1550, and nearby Babworth was held by Thomas Bishop, rector of West Retford, after 1617.[56] Between 1605 and 1617 the rector of Babworth was George Turvin, but his acceptance of the post brought to a head another traditional plurality of the vicar of East Retford, the mastership of the town grammar school. In 1573, probably because of the general shortage of clergy early in Elizabeth's reign, the master of the grammar school, Christopher Say, was persuaded to take orders late in life and assume the additional responsibility of vicar. The mastership carried a salary of £10, plus accommodation and perquisites and, combined with the vicarage, it brought in an income of over £25 *per annum*, putting East Retford on a par with its immediate neighbours.[57] Despite the inevitable difficulties in doing the two jobs satisfactorily, the arrangement was repeated for George Turvin in 1588, though the townsmen must have had some serious misgivings during the period he doubled-up as vicar of Radford between 1588 and 1595.[58] Turvin's resignation from Radford was probably the result of problems such as this, because in 1605, when the rectory of Babworth fell vacant, he was asked to make a choice between the rectory and the mastership.[59] By this stage of his career Turvin clearly preferred the life of a country parson to the cut-and-thrust of a town schoolroom, and thereafter — at least until the Civil War — the vicarage and mastership were separated, though subsequent schoolmasters were permitted to hold less demanding curacies at Ordsall, Babworth and West Retford from time to time and presumably helped out with services in the parish church, if required. In the seventeenth century it was not deemed possible to do both jobs to the required standard. In any case there was a better choice of potential employees to take on the work. Pluralities were, therefore, tolerated as temporary working arrangements to overcome specific problems and provide just rewards for worthy men; they were not tolerated when they sought to cultivate self interest rather than virtue.

But there were other ways in which the clergy could augment their incomes without undermining their basic *raison d'etre*. John Thackwray owned a tenement and garden in Pottergate, Worksop, which brought in some rent;[60] Nicholas Pettinger II was a money lender and had several debts owing to him on bond,[61] and George Turvin and John Watt were involved in the spinning of linen and wool.[62] Between 1609 and 1617 Turvin sat as a surrogate in the Archdeacon's court, and an analysis of handwriting indicates that both Nicholas Watkins and John Watt made a small business out of writing wills for their parishioners.[63] And, as death looked them in the face, those parishioners would often remember the clergy favourably in their wills, either by giving them small cash legacies or by providing payment for special services.[64] The will of Sir John Hercy in 1570 contained the following bequest:

> to the preachers for making of three sermons at the day of my burial and two days after of one hours long, 30s.[65]

Similarly, in 1625 George Malin, yeoman and apparitor for the Retford Deanery, gave to John Watt, Thomas Bishop or William Saxton, vicar of Gringley 10s, 'which of them so ever shall preach my final sermon',[66] but bequests such as this are surprisingly rare in a town which became noted for its Protestantism. Thomas Bishop, in particular, seems to have won a reputation as a preacher, and when he died in 1642 the parish clerk remembered him as 'sermonist and parson'.[67] Indeed, it was tasks such as these that made up the stock-in-trade of a clergyman's life — performing services: conducting rites and ceremonies: preaching: teaching the catechism: visiting the sick: and attempting to maintain the fabric of the church. Much of this work went on without the generation of records, but occasional glimpses break through the silence — Christopher Say turning up at the Archdeacon's court to give evidence in support of one of his parishioners; or Edward Hodgson dispensing legacies to the poor, to his parish clerk and 'to the poor cobbler of East Retford'.[68] More often than not records are created when things go wrong, and the general silence of the sources in this case would seem to imply a high degree of conformity and general satisfaction with the role of the local clergy. Many of them enjoyed very long incumbencies and must have known their people well — Robert Armstede, 27 years at Clarborough; George Turvin, 29 years at East Retford; Thomas Bishop, 42 years at West Retford.

It is clear that the clergy of the town did not make this sort of commitment for the remuneration they were likely to receive, because, with the exception of Nicholas Pettinger II, they were not wealthy men. The sixteenth-century wills of John Thackwray (1550), Edward Hodgson (1565) and Robert Armstede (1577) imply a level of prosperity certainly no greater than that of the middling burgesses of the town[69] and, by the seventeenth century, things had not improved since the probate valuation for the goods of Nathaniel Hunte (1630) was in the region of only £40.[70] The inventory of George Turvin, his goods swollen by the assets of the rectory of Babworth, begins to look impressive with a total of £222 1s 1d, until it becomes plain that he was in debt to the tune of £104 11s 8d, which cut back his assets very considerably indeed. His largest creditor was Hamlet Jackson to whom he owed over £60. He had also failed to pay his servants' wages and there were bills outstanding from threshers and maltsters.[71] Turvin's problems are likely to have been the result of bad management rather than out-and-out poverty, a situation not shared with the purely urban cleric, John Watt, who died in 1640 leaving goods valued at only £25 8s 10d. With no involvement in husbandry and a minimal income from parochial sources, Watt illustrates well the economic problems which were likely to be faced by the urban cleric who was unable, or unwilling, to enter the world of the pluralist.[72]

The wives of the clergy were important since it was their duty to supervise households and augment the family budget by spinning or producing food items for domestic consumption or sale. Most of the clergy of the town after 1559 were married, including Robert Armstede whose ordination dated back to the days of celibacy.[73] Wives in general did not share the educational attainments of their husbands, and of the five clergy wives who attested administration bonds in the seventeenth century Dorothy Colley, Grace Watt, Elizabeth Watkins and Elizabeth Hunte subscribed with marks.[74] Only Anne Turvin was able to sign her name, and since her maiden name was Say (she was married to George Turvin in the town in 1596) it is likely that she was a daughter or relation of the schoolmaster/vicar, Christopher Say, who may well have been responsible for her education.[75] In general, families were small. There is no record of Nathaniel Hunte, James Colley or John Watt having fathered any children. Robert Armstede, Nicholas Pettinger II and William Howe each had one child and Nicholas Watkins, Robert Hurst and George Turvin two, all of whom survived to adulthood. In addition to this Howe, Hurst and Turvin each lost one child in infancy and the fact that Elizabeth Watkins and Anne Turvin both ceased bearing children when they had long periods of fertility in front of them might imply some deliberate attempt at family planning.[76] This was undertaken probably because of the difficult financial circumstances in which the clergy found themselves. As major exponents of education they no doubt wanted to do as well as they could for their offspring, and numbers were likely to be critical in that consideration. Mary Hodgson, the wife of Edward Hodgson, clearly perceived for herself a role outside the walls of the vicarage. She was the sister of a rector of Babworth (probably Robert Lily), and when her husband made his will he gave her £3 to be distributed amongst:

> succourless children...as she shall think most meet and convenient...at her being better and more able to do it.[77]

To help run their households these women invariably had the support of servants, both male and female. George Turvin had two to whom he owed wages: Nicholas Pettinger II left 2s 6d 'to every servant in my house': and Edward Hodgson, with characteristic generosity, left 6s 8d to his four servants 'if they diligently serve their dame and be faithful to her'.[78]

There are few details of the houses in which the clergy families lived since glebe terriers are, in general, too late to be of much use. However, the inventory of Nicholas Pettinger II provides a picture of the rectory house at West Retford in 1578. It comprised a hall, two parlours, a kitchen and buttery on the ground floor: and upstairs three chambers and a servants' chamber. In addition to this, possibly as outhouses, there was a store, a corn chamber, a milk house, a kiln house and a stable. Within the house floors were carpeted, windows were glazed, and the walls were hung with painted cloths. The hall was deliberately set out to impress visitors, with a hall cupboard and an array of silver including a basin, a ewer, a covered goblet and a covered salt.[79] By any standards it was a substantial household, comfortable and well furnished. At the other end of the scale stood the vicarage house at East Retford, located adjacent to the church, comprising a hall, parlour, kitchen, buttery, three upstairs chambers and a stable. On paper this house does not seem too far removed from the West Retford rectory, but the standards of furnishing and comfort that appurtained within it were very different. Its occupier in 1640, John Watt, possessed little of any value, and it is significant that the most highly appraised item was 'all the books in his library', valued at £6 13s 4d.[80] Here, indeed, was the successor of Chaucer's poor town parson, and an indication of contrasting clerical lifestyles separated only by the width of the river Idle.

The accession of Elizabeth in 1558 brought back to the area Protestant incumbents such as William Denman, rector of Ordsall, who had been deprived of his living by Mary in 1556. It also opened the door to new enthusiasts such as Edward Hodgson, Nicholas Pettinger II, and William Denman's brother, Francis, all of whom were linked together by family ties. Another member of this remarkable puritan cousinage was Robert Lily, rector of Babworth, who appears to have been Hodgson's brother-in-law and was possibly a relative of the famous grammarian, William Lily.[81] But, as time went on, it became plain that the Queen's interpretation of Protestantism did not always correspond with that of her subjects, particularly those who had been educated at the puritanical Cambridge colleges. Up to a point non-conformity was shielded in the 1570s and 1580s by a succession of sympathetic Archbishops of York — notably Grindal and Sandys —and the puritanical Archdeacon of Nottingham, John Louth. William Denman was also an important local protector. A graduate and fellow of St John's College, Cambridge, during the reign of Edward VI, and therefore an associate of such individuals as James Pilkington and Thomas Lever, Denman's zeal for the reformed faith was never in doubt. Having lain low during Mary's reign, the involvement of William Denman with the cause of radical Protestantism was underlined afresh by the marriage of his nephew, John, to the sister of the leading puritan divine and controversialist, Walter Travers, perhaps the most prominent critic of the Elizabethan church settlement. To complete a truly remarkable web of relationships, Walter Travers' brother, John, erstwhile fellow of Magdalen College, Oxford, and rector of Farringdon in Devon, was married to a sister of the Anglican apologist, Richard Hooker, who engaged Travers in a series of formidable preaching duels in London during the 1580s.[82] Denman's connections with the top flight of Protestant thinkers of his day was supplemented by his position at the very apex of the social

33: St Michael's church, West Retford: its most remarkable feature is its impressive Medieval spire.

34: The stump of a Medieval preaching cross in the churchyard of West Retford.

pyramid of the town. As nephew and heir of the influential and highly respected Sir John Hercy, succeeding him as lord of the manor of West Retford in 1572, Denman possessed considerable practical and moral authority in the community. His epitaph, inscribed on a vanished brass plate in Ordsall church, summarised his position well:

> I was a squire's son, my mother was
>   heiress of a knight.
> My name is Denman, I was a Master of Arts,
> Rector of Ordsall in Mary's reign removed,
> Queen Elizabeth restored me to my flock
> And I thereupon worked that Retford
>   should reap the fruits of my labours.
> If any are zealous to make progress in religion
> Ordsall knows that I built houses for the poor.[83]

Denman died, leaving this slightly cryptic statement to posterity, in 1588, two years after Walter Travers' suspension from preaching in London and at a critical juncture for local Protestants. Nationally, the Queen was becoming increasingly concerned about the problem of puritanism, and Archbishop Whitgift was inviting criticism because of the nature of the methods used to combat it. The new Archbishop of York, John Piers, and the Archdeacon of Nottingham, John King, wished to establish a greater degree of conformity in line with national policy, and unorthodox parish clergy provided an obvious target. In many areas — and this seems to have been the case in the puritan enclaves of North Nottinghamshire—minor deviations from the Prayer Book rite had been tolerated in the past, such as clergy not wearing the proper vestments or leaving out portions of the services they disapproved of. But this was no longer to be the case. Retford felt the impact of this general onslaught more keenly, perhaps, because of the presence at Babworth after 1586 of one of the leading non-conformists, Richard Clifton, who did much to influence the attitudes of the local clergy. It would not be difficult to conceive of a brotherhood of godly ministers around the town, comprising such men as Clifton, Francis Denman at West Retford, George Turvin at East Retford and Nicholas Watkins at Clarborough. This concentration was no doubt viewed by William Denman as one of the 'fruits' of his labour, though some of it was to fall beneath the pruning hook of the bishops.[84]

The first direct evidence of non-conformity in the town came in 1592 when George Turvin was summoned before the Archdeacon of Nottingham for not wearing the surplice; permitting others to officiate without the surplice in his absence (this was his period as vicar of Radford), and not carrying out the Rogation Week perambulations according to the Prayer Book.[85] He admitted all of the charges and promised to conform in the future, though he did not rationalise his failure to perambulate as an objection to a popish ceremony (a point which many puritans would have made) but because there were no fields to traverse, 'nor can have company for that purpose'.[86] Clearly he saw no point in it, and neither did the parishioners if his defence is to be believed. The accusation of permitting non-conforming clergy to officiate in his absence is interesting and may relate to Thomas Hancock, recently employed as curate of West Retford by the rector, Francis Denman. By taking on Hancock Denman was engaging a known and controversial commodity. A Cambridge graduate, Hancock had served as curate of Scrooby where he had officiated at a much publicised clandestine marriage between the radical preacher Robert Southworth, curate of Headon, and Jane Wastneys: this was a union between two notable families of puritan gentry, but it was irregular because of Jane's previous marriage to one William Riggs.[87] If Hancock did not have enough trouble on his hands already, he further jeopardised his position by being prosecuted for not wearing the surplice and not using the sign of the cross during baptisms at West Retford in 1593.[88] Although he stated that he was willing to conform he failed to attend court and was excommunicated, though this must have been lifted since Hancock was still in the town in 1597 and in 1608 was representing a defendant in the Archdeacon's court as a proctor.[89] However, Turvin's problems continued unabated. Despite his promise to conform, he was again presented on the perambulation issue in 1593 and on the surplice issue in 1595.[90] Indeed, as late as 1601 it was stated that he did not always wear the surplice for ordinary services, though he did for the ministration of the sacraments, a concession which was probably less objectionable to him than wearing the cope.[91]

These difficulties were reflected in a very disturbed period in the life of the parish and were, of course, being fought out against the background of the divisions in the corporation between the supporters of Symcock and Watson which possibly also had a religious edge to them. There is no clear evidence that the two disputes were closely linked, but their coincidence must have made for a particularly tense atmosphere. In 1592 while the town was agog with the first rumblings of dissent, George Kirkby and Oliver Foster were presented to the Archdeacon's court for 'talking and whispering together at the time of common prayer'. Ralph Welch made his feelings felt in another way:

> The minister and people at evening prayer were singing of a psalm and he coming in did sing aloud a song of ribaldry in a higher tune than the rest, to the great offence of the people.[92]

When he was confronted for his behaviour by Thomas Wharton, one of the churchwardens, Welch compounded his offence by turning on the warden and saying:

> Almightiful God knows my righteousness and that thou bald pate...hast abused me.[93]

Edward Houldon, the surrogate who heard these cases, viewed them with some seriousness. Of the defendants Foster had vanished, but Kirkby and Welch were sentenced to do penance though in neither case was it performed, Kirkby being excommunicated for failure to certify and Welch successfully claiming the Queen's general pardon granted in the Parliament of 1593. Both men, indeed, had proved tough opponents of the court. Kirkby had initially refused to be sworn and Welch stood excommunicate for eighteen months before he discovered the bolt hole of the royal pardon. More heated passions were aroused in 1602 when fights broke out in church involving Jane Billiald and Francis Smyth and James Horsefole.[94]

Then, in May 1605, nine parishioners from East Retford and four from Moorgate absented themselves from church on Sunday to attend a sermon by John Robinson 'a strange preacher, whether he was sufficiently licenced or not'. Robinson, who came from Sturton-le-Steeple and had been a fellow of Corpus Christi College, Cambridge, was more than

just 'strange'; to the church authorities he was acutely dangerous. In 1602 he had entered into a covenant with like minded
puritans:

> to walk with God and one another in the enjoyment of God's
> ordinances according to the primitive pattern whatever it
> might cost them.[95]

Although his sermons look like a blatant attempt to drum up
support for the separatist cause the defendants were dealt
with leniently, shilling payments to the poor being the order
of the day. But the incident was a significant one, particularly
in terms of its timing, because 1605 was the year of Richard
Clifton's deprivation from Babworth for non-conformity and
Clifton and Robinson were soon to become leading lights in
the separatist congregation about to be established at Scrooby.
The defendants in this action, which included Robert Parnell,
John Denman and John Sloswicke, along with their wives,
were amongst the leading puritans of the town (Sloswicke
had been one of the bailiffs for the previous year), and it
illustrates a widening gulf separating them from their own
vicar, George Turvin. We do not know whether John Denman
and his friends attended the Scrooby conventicle but they
may well have done so, paying only lip service to their parish
church. Finally, on Easter Sunday 1606 a further disturbance
occurred in church during which John Denman's wife, Anne,
the sister of Walter Travers, violently interrupted a baptism,
objecting to the vicar's use of the sign of the cross; once more
she found herself before the Archdeacon for her pains.[96] The
vicar of Everton, Peter Haworth, summed up well the tense
atmosphere of these years in a letter to Matthew Dodsworth,
the Archbishop's Chancellor, following the metropolitan Visitation held at Retford in 1607. Complaining of the disobedience of some of his churchwardens, especially John Clifton,
he stated:

> he would neither come before me nor any my Lord's officers,
> and whereas he had yielded to presentments before...if it
> were now to do again he would not do it, and that
> excommunication was a small matter, he cared not for that.
> The same words he also gave to Edward Rayne, one of the
> new churchwardens, who also seems to subscribe to his

opinions, for having appointed a day with the rest of his fellows he likewise held back and would not come, holding that they ought not to present these schismatical errors, though he see that they forbear to participate with our church in prayers or sacraments and use secretly to assemble themselves to hear those that be manifest enemies of Christ ...I pray you let me be directed from you what to do in the action, or rather I beseech you to take it wholly to yourself and reform it as you see cause, for if some order be not taken with Mr Clifton, their teacher, and John Clifton, his brother, I doubt a great many will be infected with their pestiferous opinions.[97]

Turvin knew better than most that 'pestiferous opinion' had indeed taken root in the area and that Richard Clifton, while rector of Babworth, had been a major instigator of it: Retford undoubtedly had its share of these schismatics, shielded from presentation by sympathetic bailiffs, church-wardens and clergy. It is likely that for many years local Protestant families, such as the Denmans and Sloswickes, had become used to a form of ministration which did not include those aspects of the Prayer Book rite to which puritans took exception: for his part Turvin had probably been only too happy to oblige them during the early years of his incumbency. However, the prosecutions of the 1590s had begun to test his loyalties, and the demand for subscription from the clergy following the Hampton Court Conference had presented the stark choice of conformity or suspension. Turvin, by now a married man with a young family suffering ongoing financial problems, had clearly chosen the former, so much so that he agreed to accept the rectory of Babworth following Richard Clifton's removal. The fact that he was presented to the living by Sir Gervase Helwisse, probably a relative of Thomas Helwisse, John Smith's companion in the separatist congregation of Se-baptists at Gainsborough, indicates that Turvin was just about as far to the edge of the Church of England as it was possible to go without suffering suspension.[98] To the Denmans, and other puritan families of the town, however, it must have looked like treason and betrayal, and hence Mrs Denman's outburst at this particularly sensitive time: she could point to her own brother, as she no doubt often did, as one of the principal 'martyrs' to the cause! Turvin, not made of such stalwart stuff, went on to complete his *volte-face* by becoming a surrogate to Archdeacon Hall after 1609, one of many clergy — Archbishop Whitgift amongst them — who assuaged a misspent youth with an old age of conformity.

But this was not quite the end of the non-conforming tradition amongst the clergy of the town. Turvin's successor, John Watt, found himself in trouble in 1623 on charges remarkably similar to those of 1592 — he had refused to wear the surplice; he had allowed strange ministers to preach without examining their authority; and he had failed to follow the Prayer Book rite in matters as trivial as Turvin's digressions, not meeting corpses at the church stile and not reading the first lesson on Sundays.[99] It is unlikely that the accusations against Hancock, Turvin and Watt represent a full catalogue of Protestant non-conformity as it effected the clergy of the town between 1559 and 1642. For the accusations to be made in the first place implies that there was someone in the parish — probably a churchwarden — who disapproved enough of what the vicar was doing to make an issue of it, with all of the risks and complications that that involved. Where a non-conforming Protestant concensus existed, as it appears to have done for much of the time at East Retford, no such charges would be brought. Such a conspiracy of silence is suspected at Clarborough during the long incumbency of Nicholas Watkins. As a minister Watkins had many similarities with men like Richard Clifton and Richard Bernard, the godly vicar of Worksop, yet his only appearances in court were for a failure to read out the register book in 1600 and for an undisclosed offence six years later.[100] Given the circumstances of the time, it seems reasonable to suppose that Watkins, a known member of Clifton's circle, had been summoned to give an account of himself in 1606 and guarantee his good behaviour in the future.

A clergyman's relationship with his parishioners, and especially the churchwardens was, therefore, of prime importance if he was to avoid unwelcome scrutiny at the eyes of the church hierarchy. Generally speaking the parish consensus appears to have held but, just occasionally, dissidence was expressed either by individuals or by groups. The former was less dangerous, because it could easily be dismissed as the

The Orthodox true Minifter,   the Seducer and falfe Prophet.

35: The 'orthodox true minister' competes against 'the seducer and false prophet'; a situation faced by George Turvin when the separatist preacher John Robinson visited the town.

36: Edwin Sandys, Archbishop of York, and his second wife: Sandys, by way of his puritanism and interests at Southwell and Scrooby, might be said to have encouraged the growth of Protestantism in the town before 1590.

venom of anti-clerical cranks. In 1585 Christopher Say was abused in the following vitriolic terms by William Rose — 'Thy preaching is naught, and thy doctrine is naught, and thy life is naught', a critical, and possibly astute, comment on the personality of the lawyer/schoolmaster who had come to his minister's vocation late in life.[101] A more sustained attack was launched against John Watt in the 1620s and 1630s, probably the least popular of the vicars to serve after 1550. The origin of Watt's unpopularity is difficult to determine but it no doubt encompassed his personal qualities along with more practical matters such as the attempt to enforce church rates and the high profile he sometimes adopted in political matters. During the disputed election of 1624 Watt initially came out in support of the candidate favoured by Sir Gervase Clifton and the majority of the corporation:

> John Watt, vicar of the town, being present at the delivery of the letters [nominating John Darcy as candidate for Parliament] seemed to be overcome with a sudden passion of joy, giving thanks to God, that it had pleased him to put Sir Gervase in mind to recommend so worthy a gentleman and how in that respect the town was blessed, commending the gentleman to be of extraordinary learning and qualities and every way complete.[102]

However, on receiving letters from his own patron, the Countess of Devonshire, nominating Sir Edward Wortley, Watt changed his tune completely, an act which hardly endeared him to his former allies:

> On Sunday Mr Watt showed himself plainly in the pulpit to be a mere Luisie Wolsie [*sic*] or rather a plain turncoat, for all the sermon was for this election with all persuations to carry it the other way, pleading all to be for conscience, religion and God's glory, naming the Countess divers times in his sermon, pressing what good her honour had done to him and intended to the town, wherein he showed so much folly as instead of thanks his own faction did both dislike and condemn him...And then again the vicar took upon him to make another speech, idle and full of folly, his strongest motive being that if my Lady had her desire he himself should be removed from us within a month...as that we should take it as a great favour to be rid of him.[103]

Such was Watt's determination to see the Countess's candidate returned that he placed himself at the head of a band of paupers in the market place on polling day, and when the events of the election were subsequently examined by the Committee of Privileges, the vicar was one of those censured for his behaviour. The revelations that even Watt's allies 'did both dislike and condemn him' and that the town 'should take it as a great favour to be rid of him', illustrate how fragile the position of a minister could be.[104] The vestiarian accusations against Watt have already been noted, but, in addition to this, he was called before the Quarter Sessions on unspecified charges in 1620, accused of pulling down the stalls and pulpit in 1623 and of being suspected of fornication with Catherine Sloswicke, widow, in 1624.[105] Thereafter, things calmed down somewhat, but as late as 1638 the unfortunate vicar was accused of not performing services on Wednesdays and Fridays, a strange indictment since his work was cut out enforcing attendance even on a Sunday.[106] It is clear that some of these complaints were rooted in malice, because in 1620 Watt was aquitted by a jury at the Quarter Sessions and awarded costs against the informer, Francis Smyth.[107] His own assessment of why the town would be glad to see the back of him was that 'he had behaved himself so well amongst us', implying, perhaps, that he saw himself as an exemplary incumbent whose high standards courted the oppostion of a libertine multitude.[108] When he died in 1640 his widow very soon moved away to live at Hiperholme in Yorkshire, doubtless relieved to have at last cast the dust of Retford from her feet.[109]

John Watt, indeed, epitomised many of the successes and failures of the post-Reformation clergy in the town. An educated man who valued his books above other worldly possessions, he reflected in this a succession of Protestant ministers to serve after 1559, two of them being also masters of the grammar school. This scholarly and evangelical achievement is, perhaps, all the more surprising in view of the generally weak financial foundations of the local livings, and the clergy of the town constantly had to devise shifts and contrivances in order to make ends meet. With the notable exception of the Denmans, the status of the clergy within the community was not high, a vindication of the complaints about secular ownership of tithe which went back to the earliest days of the Reformation and was amplified by Archbishop Laud in the 1630s. Another baneful consequence of the involvement of laymen in the running of the church was to be seen at East Retford and Clarborough in the growing, and controversial, influence of the Cavendish family after 1600, a web in which Watt, in particular, found himself entangled. Finally, considerable energies were dissipated into doctrinal squabbles as the clergy attempted to pick a path between their own convictions, the expectations of their parishioners and the demands of their ecclesiastical superiors. Faced as they were with financial, political and doctrinal difficulties, it is perhaps remarkable that they achieved what they did. Their success was to be seen in the solid Protestantism of the town, the ripening of Denman's 'fruits' through painful care and husbandry.

FOOTNOTES AND REFERENCES

1. Piercy, p.215.
2. Kidson, pp.91/2, *Valor*, 5, pp.18-20.
3. This was surely a considerable underestimate. *Valor*, 5, p.18.
4. *Ibid.*, pp.18, 183, Kidson p.93, £3 6s 8d at Clarborough and £1 6s 8d at East Retford.
5. *Valor*, 5, p.183.
6. *CPR, 1557-58*, p.420.
7. *Ibid., 1560-63*, p.284, *1575-78*, p.210. The rent payable was £137 19s 2½d.
8. But see Chapter 1, note 28.
9. *CSP Dom, 1598-1601*, p.278. The value of the Rectory of Clarborough was put at £86 2s 6d *per annum* and the purchase price was £2,734 12s 1¾d. The Cavendish family may have obtained an interest in East Retford sooner than this or were, at least, already farmers there. In 1586 George Cavendish Esq proceeded against George Saunderson of East Retford for non-payment of tithes in the Archdeacon's court. NAO, DDTS 25 f.100.
10. *Ibid.*, 10 f.185.
11. *Ibid.*, QSMI/2.
12. The details of the case are drawn from BI, CP, H660.
13. The social distinction between the two men was not so great as it might seem since as 'gentry' the Tyes were non-armorial

and Spivy had similar 'gentry' links in West Retford.

14. Thackwray's will (1550) confirms close contact with the Tyes or Tees. BI, AR 29 ff.92/3.

15. The disputed stall was not the only one in the chancel of the church. Thomas Dickinson of Moorgate testified that he also sat in the chancel 'near unto them'.

16. NAO, CPR (1613), Wills (George Spivy, 1613).

17. Piercy p.183.

18. White, p.676.

19. *Valor,* 5, p.181.

20. YML, Torre Mss (East Retford, Clarborough), Piercy pp.122, 238. Magnus was a noted diplomat who founded a grammar school at Newark. See N.G. Jackson, *Newark Magnus: the story of a gift* (1964), pp.17-36.

21. Thackwray witnessed no wills at East Retford and only three at Clarborough, all between 1537 and 1542. BI, PR 11 ff.259, 362, 704.

22. *Ibid.,* AR 29 ff.92/3. At East Retford there is a note of Robert Holme (1520/21): John Draper (1535): and Robert Armstede or Armitage (1540 and 1549/50). At Clarborough of John Draper (1535): Nicholas Nalson (1537): Thomas Stamondey (1540): Richard Sawer (1545): and William Carr (1549/50). *Valor,* 5p.183, BI, PR 9 ff.111, 183, 11 ff. 259, 514/5, 625, 13 ff. 82, 647, 648, 665.

23. For example, BI, PR 9 f.287, 13 f.325. For a more specific description see 9 ff.37/8.

24. *Ibid.,* AR 29 ff.92/3.

25. In the will of his sister, Alice Lincoln (1543), Thackwray received £10, four silver spoons (three with gilded knots), a maser with a gilded handle, a house in Worksop and the residue of the estate: he was also executor. BI, PR 11 f.704.

26. *CPR, 1550-53,* p.325, *1554-55,* p.214. The man who filled this gap for the most part was the Protestant Robert Reveley, for whom see Chapter 8, pp.223-5.

27. BI, PR 13 f.325.

28. *Ibid.,* AR 29 f.33, *CPR, 1555-57,* p.498, *TTS,* 20, p.174. There is no record of an institution for Wilkin in Archbishop Holgate's Register.

29. *CPR, 1560-63,* p.91. Robert Routhwood occurs in 1558 and Thomas Collinson in 1560/61. Collinson favoured fairly distinctive Protestant will preambles. BI, PR 15C ff.369, 434, 275, 407, 16 ff.84, 114, 144/5.

30. *CPR, 1563-66,* p.295, *1572-75,* p.136. Tempest was probably an 'old priest' because of his habitual use of the archaic title 'Sir' before his name. BI, PR 19, ff.223, 265, 382.

31.   *Ibid.,* 9 ff.249, 287, 320.
32.   *Valor,* 5, p.181, *TTS,* 20, p.160. Train seems to confuse these men. The distinction is only apparent in the will of Nicholas Pettinger II.
33.   For example, Richard Barneby (1547) and William Southwood (1556). BI, PR 13 f.163, 15A f.178.
34.   See Chapter 8, pp.223-5.
35.   BI, AR 31 f.84, Piercy p.186.
36.   BI, PR 23 f.507, 25 f.1022, 26 f.582. Another consideration may have been the increasing drive to enforce conformity, for which see below p.181.
37.   NUCLH, FRF, NAO, CPR, ERPR.
38.   *CPR, 1572-75,* p.136.
39.   For a discussion of the clerical profession at this time see R. O'Day, *The English Clergy: the emergence and consolidation of a profession* (1979).
40.   Train, pp.27, 160, J. and J. A. Venn, *Alumni Cantabrigienses* (1922-27), J. Foster, *Alumni Oxonienses* (1891).
41.   Train, pp.37, 155, 160, Venn, *Alumni.*
42.   BI, PR 17B f.458.
43.   Foster, Venn, *Alumni.* John Watt is described as MA but his University has not been traced.
44.   Charles West (1549) and Thomas Hancock (oc 1593-1608).
45.   NAO, CPR (1577).
46.   BI, PD (1577. Robert Armstede).
47.   *Ibid.,* PR 17B f.458.
48.   *Ibid.,* AR 3l f.84.
49.   D. Marcombe, 'The Dean and Chapter of Durham, 1558-1603', University of Durham PhD thesis, 1973, p.292.
50.   RM, Rates of Wages (1627).
51.   NAO, DDTS 9 f.74.
52.   NAO, ERPR (1616), BI, PD (1617 George Turvin), NCLH, FRF.
53.   BI, PD (1578 Nicholas Pettinger).
54.   *Ibid.,* (1617 George Turvin).
55.   *TTS,* 20, p.148. Venn, *Alumni.* Mason, a tutor to Prince Charles, held livings in Lincolnshire, Cambridgeshire and Huntingdonshire as well as the Nottinghamshire cures of Newark and Ordsall. He eventually became Dean of Salisbury in 1630 and was buried in Westminster Abbey in 1635. He may have been related to the East Retford Masons, but no link has been established.
56.   *TTS,* 20, p.160, Venn, *Alumni.*
57.   See Chapter 7, p.206.

58. *TTS*, 20, pp.4, 155.
59. JA, RB 1 (Grammar School).
60. BI, AR 29 ff.92/3.
61. *Ibid.*, 31 f.84.
62. *Ibid.*, PD (1617. George Turvin: 1642. John Watt).
63. Turvin sat on October 30 1609 at East Retford, for example. NAO, DDTS 12 f.18. Nicholas Watkins' use of a notary's symbol on the wills which he wrote indicates that he may have followed the profession of scribe prior to, and/or in the early stages of, his ordination.
64. These legacies were generally no more than tokens — 3s 4d was typical — and were far from universal. The tradition of a legacy for 'forgotten tithes' persisted amongst some testators up to the Civil War. BI, PR 20 f.6, 22 f.464, 23 f.734, 24 f.416, 26 f.582.
65. *Ibid.*, 19 f.482.
66. NAO, Wills (George Malin, 1625). Saxton was a Cambridge MA but had been presented in 1618 and 1619 for frequenting alehouses and being a 'gamester or player at tables and dice'. *TTS*, 20, p.80.
67. SML, West Retford BT (1642).
68. NAO, DDTS 2 f.33, BI, PR 17B f.458.
69. *Ibid.*, AR 29 ff.92/3, PR 17B f.458, Chancery Wills (Robert Armstede, 1577).
70. *Ibid.*, AR 32 f.52.
71. *Ibid.*, PD (1617 George Turvin). Turvin, a persistent debtor, also owed a shoemaker 9s 4d and a further 10s 'for things brought into the house'.
72. *Ibid.*, PD (1642 John Watt).
73. *Ibid.*, (1577 Robert Armstede).
74. *Ibid.*, (1618 James Colley and Nicholas Watkins: 1630 Nathaniel Hunte: 1642 John Watt).
75. *Ibid.*, (1617 George Turvin), NAO, ERPR (1596).
76. NUCLH, FRF.
77. BI, PR 17B f.458.
78. *Ibid.*, PD (1617 George Turvin), AR 31 f.84, PR 17B f.458.
79. *Ibid.*, PD (1578 Nicholas Pettinger). The silver in the hall alone was valued at £19.
80. *Ibid.*, (1642 John Watt).
81. *TTS*, 20, p.3, Venn, *Alumni*. Robert Lily was rector of Babworth from 1559 to 1586. He had been a fellow of Magdalen College, Oxford, and was usher of the College school between 1550 and 1553: he was presented for not wearing the surplice in 1581.
82. P. Collinson, *The Elizabethan Puritan Movement* (1967), pp.294/5. For the career of Walter Travers, see S.J. Knox, *Walter Travers:*

paragon of Elizabethan puritanism (1962).

83.   Piercy, p.215.
84.   For a general discussion of events in the diocese and in the Archdeaconry of Nottingham in particular, see R. Marchant, *The Church Under the Law* (1969). For a discussion of Louth and King, see M. Bonsall, 'John Lowth and John King, Archdeacons of Nottingham: a study of ambition and mediocrity in the Elizabethan church', *Bulletin of Local History East Midland Region*, 21, 1986, pp.17-27.
85.   NAO, DDTS 3 ff.173/4.
86.   *Ibid.*, 4 ff.241, 243.
87.   *Ibid.*, ff.199, 202, 244, 5 ff.6, 11; Venn, *Alumni.*
88.   NAO, DDTS 4 f.243.
89.   *Ibid.*, 10 ff.11, 12, 13: BI, PR 26 f.582.
90.   NAO, DDTS 4 ff.241, 243: Grounds p.48.
91.   *Ibid.*
92.   NAO, DDTS 4 f.32.
93.   *Ibid.*
94.   *Ibid.*, 7 ff.91, 151, 155.
95.   *Ibid.*, 10 ff.53, 55-7, 64, 71, B. Brook, *The Lives of the Puritans* (1813),2, p.334. The defendants were John Sloswicke and his wife; Peter Lanford and his wife; John Denman and his wife; and Simon Bullivant—all from East Retford. From Moorgate there was Robert Parnell and his wife; William Robinson; and William Keyworth. Bullivant was remarkable because having been ordered to pay 6d to the poor he certified payment of 1s! It is just possible that William Robinson was a brother of the preacher.
96.   *Ibid.*, 11 ff.33/4.
97.   BI, V 1607 (Misc correspondence).
98.   *TTS*, 20, p.4. For Helwisse, see Brook, pp.279-82.
99.   NUMD, PB 339 (1623).
100. NAO, DDTS 10 f.185, BI, V 1600, CB 2 f.31.
101. *Ibid.*, 25 f.26.
102. NUM, Cl. LP 52.
103. *Ibid.*
104. *Ibid.* For a full discussion of the 1624 election, see Chapter 3, pp.77-86.
105. NAO, QSMI/6, NUMD, PB 339 (1623, 24).
106. *Ibid.*, 341 (1638).
107. NAO, QSMI/6.
108. NUMD, Cl. LP. 52.
109. BI, PD (1642. John Watt).

Chapter 7

A GODLY EDUCATION

Because nothing is more needful than wisdom and understanding we therefore congregate in this place to learn...that we may have our whole affection upon wisdom in these years of our infancy.[1]

Education in Retford went back a long way, because as early as the fourteenth century there are references to a grammar school in the town.[2] However, this school does not appear to have had firm roots and in 1518 Thomas Gunthorpe, rector of Babworth, entered into a covenant with the corporation to put education on a more stable footing, it being emphasised in the endorsement on the deed of gift that Gunthorpe's donations were for 'the *re-edifying* of the school in East Retford', implying a continuation with the earlier foundation.[3] Gunthorpe agreed to build a new schoolhouse of 'timber workmanship' where a schoolmaster could live free of charge 'for his scholars to learn in his parlour chamber'. The schoolmaster could be a cleric or a layman, and the pupils were to be taught free of charge on condition they said each night *De Profundis* with a special collect for the soul of Thomas Gunthorpe and all Christian souls. The bailiffs and burgesses were given power to supervise the new school, along with the vicar and chantry priests, and during a vacancy they were to ensure that the property was well cared for and that a new schoolmaster was appointed 'in so short a time as conveniently can be'. The funding of the scheme is more difficult to penetrate since it was not set down in the surviving indenture. Gunthorpe lived on until 1536 and may well have supported the school personally: there were also funds available from the corporation and the religious foundations of the town, all of which were involved with the school to some extent or another.[4]

The fire of 1528 threw the chantry foundations into crisis and by 1535 it must have been evident that the life of Thomas Gunthorpe was not to last much longer. What the bailiffs and burgesses decided to do, as an emergency measure, was to take the decayed chantry property into their own hands and try to raise sufficient money to keep both school and chantries afloat on a curtailed basis. Accordingly, in 1535 the corporation set down conditions of employment for 'an honest discreet priest' to serve the chantries:

> and to keep a common school within the schoolhouse...for the bringing up of young children in virtue and godly learning and he to have yearly for his stipend £5 6s 8d.[5]

This reforming initiative did not meet with universal approval. In 1538 John Crowder of Haxey, heir of Henry Crowder, vicar of Clarborough, contested in Chancery the claim of the burgesses to utilise the chantry lands 'to the common uses and common profits of the town', especially 'toward the funding and sustentation of the schoolmaster',[6] but the claim was not upheld, or never reached judgment, because in the Chantry Certificate of 1549 the arrangement of 1535 was spelt out with Charles West 'priest and schoolmaster' made responsible for 'the bringing up of youth'.[7] West, who served both school and chantries, was a Cambridge graduate, but he does not seem to have stayed long in the town and witnessed only one will there in January 1549.[8] Doubtless, he was well aware of the uncertainties of his position, because the Chantries Act, already passed in 1547, stated that only schools mentioned in foundation charters would be immune from dissolution.[9] Since the Retford scheme was clearly the product of the last twenty years the schoolmaster was deprived of his income and the future looked very bleak indeed.

The situation was saved by the timely intervention of some influential local men, led, according to tradition, by Nicholas Denman. However, this may represent a confusion with his son, William, who was by then a fellow of St John's College, Cambridge, and in close association with some of the leading educationalists of the day. Roger Askham in *The Schoolmaster* commended the Edwardian fellows of St John's as amongst the most 'perfect scholars' of their generation, and Denman himself was possibly a product of the old grammar school which now stood in danger of collapse.[10] By a stroke of good fortune Sir John Hercy and Sir Anthony Nevell, the principal landowners of the area, were amongst the Chantry Commissioners for Nottinghamshire and they, along with the Denmans, doubtless used their influence with Robert Holgate, Archbishop of York. Holgate was a well known champion of education, having founded grammar schools at York and Malton, and he may well have visited Retford and the nearby priory of Mattersey in his role as master of the Order of St Gilbert of Sempringham in England prior to the Dissolution. But, despite his roots in the monkish past, Holgate had become an enthusiastic convert to Protestantism and his was an important voice in the petition which was addressed to Edward VI for the saving of the school. Hercy, too, had a genuine interest in education, because in his will he left 'to every parish clerk that teacheth children...12d, and to them that teach grammar 2s'.[11] Accordingly, on December 9 1551 Letters Patent were issued establishing:

> The Free Grammar School of King Edward VI for the education and instruction of youths in grammar, to be continued at all times hereafter for ever.[12]

By this time the old chantry lands in Retford had been sold, so the school was endowed with other chantry property in the locality which was put in the hands of the corporation for the 'sustentation' of the school.[13] The dissolved chantries involved were at Sutton-cum-Lound, Tuxford and Annesley, an accumulation of properties expected to bring in £15 5s 3¼d, rather less than the £20 which was standard for the Edward VI foundations. In view of this the town was empowered to receive or purchase additional lands to the value of £20 over and above the initial grant. The school was to be under the control of a schoolmaster and usher nominated by the bailiffs and burgesses, and statutes were to be drawn up for its governance with the advice of the Archbishop of York.

The school statutes were duly approved on April 30 1552, and they form a detailed insight into how an institution such as this was meant to function and what it was expected to achieve.[14] The masters, it seems, needed to be as tightly regulated almost as their pupils. The schoolmaster was given

37: Robert Holgate, Archbishop of York: the ex-Gilbertine canon who was instrumental in the refounding of the grammer school and moulded its statutes in 1552.

38: St John's College, Cambridge: the probable inspiration for the refoundation of the grammar school.

superiority over the usher, who was designated to teach the younger boys in the lower forms but, if controversy broke out between them, it was to be 'pacified and ordered' by the corporation. Neither master was permitted to be absent from the town for more than three days in every quarter without special permission, and he was only to be absent from school 'for honest, necessary and reasonable causes'. Even if this was the case, due to illness for example, he was to provide a deputy, presumably at his own cost. Both masters were to attend the parish church on Sundays and holidays and, if this failed to inculcate in them the virtues required for the instruction of youth, they received a series of statutory warnings before they were expelled. Almost the entire endowment of the school went to pay the wages of its teachers, the schoolmaster receiving £10 *per annum* and the usher £5 by two instalments payable on May 31 and November 1. But, in addition to this, both men received free accommodation. At the East end of the schoolhouse the schoolmaster was allowed two rooms for his own use, and at the West end the usher had one and they shared between them the profits of the orchard and garden. Moreover, and this was a concession to the growing possibility of employing married teachers, the corporation provided two houses in the town which it promised to maintain in good repair. There was even the tacit promise of a pay rise:

> and as it shall happen the lands hereafter to be increased by virtue of the said licence and by diligence of the above named bailiffs and burgesses, so the wages and salary of the schoolmaster and usher to be increased as shall be convenient from time to time.[15]

Having agreed to all of these conditions, as well as to six months' notice of severance, the masters were required to take an oath before the Archbishop of York or his deputy:

> I...being elected and named as master or instructor of the King's Majesty's Free Grammar School of East Retford, in the County of Nottingham, from this present time so long as I shall be master of the said school, shall not receive nor take any annual service or yearly salary, stipend, or wages of any person or persons which shall or may be hurtful, prejudicial, or hindrance unto the godly bringing up or virtuous instructing of the scholars of the said school. And, furthermore, I shall not fraudulently, maliciously, nor wittingly of my part neglect or

break any ordinance or statute of the said school lawfully set
forth and made, so far as to me doth appertain. But shall
inviolately observe and keep them, and every one of them, as
near as God shall give me grace, as God help and the holy
contents of this book.[16]

Then the bailiffs and burgesses, or six of them, put the
schoolmaster or usher into possession by delivering to him
the hasp of the schoolhouse door, a removable hasp being a
traditional substitute for a key:

Sir, you are chosen to be schoolmaster [or usher] of this
school, to teach scholars hither resorting, not only grammar
and other virtuous doctrine but also good manners, according
to the intent of the most excellent and virtuous prince King
Edward VI, founder of the same. Whereupon, we assure this
to you a room of perpetual continuence, upon your good
demeanour and duty to be done within this grammar school.[17]

So that the statutes were not forgotten they were to be read in
the grammar school once every quarter.

Having taken such care to select and regulate its teachers
what did the corporation expect these men to instil into local
children? The simple answer to that was Protestantism and
the classics. The statutes were emphatic that the masters:

shall not teach anything to their said scholars which is
contrary to God's most Holy Word, his commandments, or
that may provoke the said scholars to vice or evil manners.

To ensure this a regimen of church attendance, psalm singing
and prayer was enjoined. Like the masters, the scholars were
expected to attend the parish church on Sundays and holidays:

and that those scholars which be apt and meet for the same,
do help in the choir to maintain the divine service there.

Every Sunday one scholar was to read the catechism in
English 'openly and distinctly' between morning prayer and
communion 'as well for their own instruction as for the
instruction of the other young children in the said parish'.
Each morning before the beginning of lessons and when they
had finished in the afternoon the masters:

shall cause the same scholars to say or sing in the said schoolhouse
one psalm of David's psalter such as the said schoolmaster shall
think most convenient to be appointed for that purpose.

In the morning the psalm was followed by this prayer:

> O most merciful God and giver of all understanding which, at the invocation of the faithful, has ever given things necessary for the setting forth of thy glory, as the examples of all ages recordeth, and for because nothing is more needful than wisdom and understanding, we therefore congregate in this place to learn the same, most humbly beseech thee, O Eternal Father, so to illuminate our wits and understandings, that we may have our whole affection upon wisdom in these years of our infancy. And furthermore may ever after receive, love, and embrace the same, and accordingly to the precepts thereof may direct all our acts, and last of all that the true wisdom of God may so shine in all our living, as may be to the glory and praise of him from whom all wisdom cometh. Grant this we beseech thee, O God, for the love of thy most dearly beloved son Jesus Christ, Our Lord and Saviour. So be it.[18]

In the evening the following was said:

> Lighten our darkness we beseech thee, O Lord, and by thy great mercies defend us from all perils and dangers of this night, for the love of thy only son our saviour Jesus Christ. Amen.[19]

If the religious observances seem taxing in themselves, they were only a prelude to the surfeit of classicism which was to follow. In summer, school commenced at 6 am and continued until 6 pm with three breaks: breakfast from 8–9 am, dinner from 11.30–1.00 pm, and 'drinking' from 3.30–4.00 pm. In winter, pupils were not expected to be present until 7 am and they were allowed home at 5 pm: however, for this concession they lost their morning breakfast and the afternoon 'drinking', the only break being dinner which was timetabled as in the summer. Thus, in summer nine hours a day was spent in the classroom and in winter that was only reduced by half an hour. With such long hours being worked, and the statutes make no mention of formal vacations, pupils could be expected to progress rapidly if they had an aptitude to learn. Boys would normally go to the grammar school at the age of seven or eight and in the first form there was an emphasis on ensuring that their reading and writing skills were of a sufficient standard. Having mastered this, they progressed to the declensions of Latin nouns and verbs, and it was expected that by the end of the year the better pupils would have made a start on Tully's *Epistles*. In the second form the vocabulary skills already acquired were used to 'turn sentences from English to Latin', and the boys went on to study some of the harder *Epistles* of Tully and the *Colloquia* of Erasmus. The third form provided further practice of English to Latin translation based on the *King's Majesty's Latin Grammar* and the writings of Virgil and Ovid. By the fourth form pupils were learning to compose verses in Latin and were expected to write a Latin epistle of their own each week. If the schoolmaster was able, the boys should have made their first inroads into Greek and Hebrew at this final stage of their school careers.

The course of study instilled a rigorous intellectual discipline and an intimate knowledge of the doings of ancient Romans, but its relevance to a small market town such as Retford might be seriously questioned. None of the subjects which might have been useful to boys who envisaged a life in commerce, such as law and accounting, were even considered. The curriculum rested heavily on Holgate's received influences of the 'new learning', particularly William Lily's experience obtained at St Paul's, and the highly inflexible rostas of study still followed at the English Universities. The bailiffs and burgesses, who managed the school, must have been totally bemused when it came to what went on inside it, and this was a reservation shared by some of the pupils. James Parnell, a Quaker convert who studied at Retford in the 1640s, said of the grammar school:

> I was sent unto the schools of humane learning for to learn human wisdom, for which the schools are profitable, but for the attaining of heavenly wisdom and knowledge they are as far unprofitable, and many books that are there read are much for the corrupting of youth and the nourishment of the wild, profane nature.[20]

The Protestantism implicit in the school statutes, and enthusiastically upheld by the early masters, must have made an impact on the majority of pupils, if only by force of repetition, but such an inflexible system clearly provided no outlet for those who sought real spiritual and educational liberation. The irony was that true 'puritans', such as Parnell, were likely

39: The arms of Edward VI displayed on the new grammar school buildings (1855).

40: An English grammar school in the sixteenth century: corporal punishment is much in evidence.

to view its classical texts as unscriptural and libertine, liable to provoke the 'vice and evil manners' which Holgate was so scrupulously at pains to avoid.

The major practical problem suffered by the school, however, was the vagueness of its statutes with regard to the management of the endowment by the corporation. Under the grant of 1552 the school lands were 'to be holden by the bailiffs and burgesses of the town of East Retford and their successors for ever', and it was expected that out of these all commitments would be met. It is important to remember that these lands formed a major addition to the town estate which traditionally had been very small. The school possessed over 300 acres of land in villages spread around the Hundred, as well as houses and other properties held on lease.[21] There is no evidence of the corporation diverting these leases to its own members (as with other areas of the town estate), but the endowment was, nevertheless, a temptation to the dishonest and the desperate. Before long, it seems, the school's lands merged inseparably with the other properties of the corporation and, while the basic obligations were honoured and indeed added to in a modest fashion, the real value of the school lands to the town soon came to outstrip the remuneration actually offered to the school. As early as the reign of Elizabeth there was a case before the Court of Requests prompted by the unlawful sale to John White of the school's Tuxford estate in 1583.[22] With this precedent in mind, and following the collapse of the church tower in 1651, the corporation sold the entire grammar school endowment to John Holles, 2nd Earl of Clare, in order to raise money for the restoration.[23] It was, no doubt, argued that the school lands, being located outside the town boundaries, created problems of management, and so long as the statutory obligations were honoured it mattered little where the money came from. The decision, however, heralded an era of intense strain between the school and the corporation which culminated when Henry Boawre, the schoolmaster, complained against the corporation in Chancery in 1699 alleging misappropriation of the school's revenues.[24] The complexities of that case are outside the scope of this study and are amply covered elsewhere,[25] but the fact that the situation ever arose is a further indictment of the Edwardian founders who paid scant attention to practicalities, carried along as they were by a zeal for the reformed faith and conventional educational priorities. The problems suffered by Retford grammar school in the seventeenth century were perfectly predictable in the sixteenth to anyone who had a working knowledge of late Medieval institutions, religious or educational, and it is difficult to see why Holgate, in particular, could not have foreseen them.

The date when the new school commenced work is uncertain, but the first schoolmaster, Christopher Say, was in the town in 1558 when he served as a juror on a coroner's inquest on two men who had the misfortune to be struck by lightning.[26] Sir John Hercy continued to be the main patron and provider. In 1553 he made grants of property in Retford and Gringley, including the burgages on Churchgate, near the parish church, where the school was located, and in 1562 he remitted a debt of £70 owed by the town on condition that the corporation contributed £10 *per annum* for four years to the school.[27] In his will, made in 1570, Hercy continued his benevolence. The schoolmaster received a legacy of 3s 4d and the usher 2s 6d but, more important, a new piece of land was provided to give annual pay rises of 5s and 3s respectively. Out of £16 owed to him by the town Hercy directed £14 to provide exhibitions for three poor scholars 'which shall come out of the school...and which be apt to go to the University of Cambridge', the scholars being selected by George Nevell Esq, the bailiffs, schoolmaster and vicar. Finally, he directed 'to every scholar that shall be in the school of Retford at the time of my death, praying for me before, 4d'.[28] The school never again had such a munificent patron before the Civil War, though other townsmen strove to emulate Hercy's example. In 1562 William Rossell II, tanner, and James Holmes, fishmonger, made a further grant of property in Churchgate, and in the following year Gilbert Sawrbie, yeoman, contributed 'to the furnishing of the school one tree which lieth in the market place'.[29] After the 1560s donations lapsed until 1587 when Thomas Salmon, tanner, left 3s 'for the repair of the schoolhouse of the town', and over the next 25 years Simon Pettinger and John Coulbie left small legacies to the schoolmaster and usher.[30] Gifts to the school were, therefore, comparatively rare, but in spite of this the corporation had raised the master's salary to £12 5s 0d and that of the usher to £6 3s 0d by 1600: by the 1630s the differential between the two teachers was widening with the master paid £19 and the usher £7.[31]

The men who were induced to serve for these salaries were eminently well qualified for their posts, particularly the better paid schoolmasters, though the tendency for both schoolmasters and ushers to take on ecclesiastical livings in addition to their teaching duties must raise the question of whether or not the strict routine of Holgate's statutes was actually enforced. The first two schoolmasters, Christopher Say (oc 1558-1588) and George Turvin (1588-1605) were also vicars of East Retford, though Turvin was forced to resign in 1605 when he proposed to take over the rectory of Babworth as well. In an attempt to save the vicar from possible financial embarrassment the corporation promised to restore him to the mastership should he be displaced from Babworth within a given period 'in such plight as he now is'.[32] Turvin's successor, Thomas Cooper (1605-1627), was curate of Ordsall between 1624 and 1626, but Nicholas Dickons (1628-1637) and Thomas Stacey (1638-41) appear to have concentrated on their teaching commitments and avoided outside involvements, reflecting, perhaps, a greater demand for education by the townsmen as the 1630s progressed: Stacey, indeed, was the first schoolmaster who is known not to have been ordained. The most shortlived appointment was that of Roger Manners who briefly preceded Stacey in 1637. Manners had been vicar of Headon since 1626 but his appointment to the vicarage of Helmsley, in North Yorkshire, caused him swiftly to cut his links with the town.[33] All of these early masters were graduates of Cambridge, and in 1564 Archbishop Young's examination of schoolmasters stated that Christopher Say had an exact knowledge of Latin: that he could translate Latin authors: and that he had a good understanding of Greek and was able to translate it. Moreover, he approved of the doctrine of the church and was willing to subscribe to the articles of faith.[34] Say was in some ways an unusual choice, and he stood out when compared with his successors. His degree was in law, not arts, and he finally took orders in 1573 when he was 49 years old. By contrast, all of the other schoolmasters came to Retford as young men, married and raised families there: all, except Stacey, were ordained early in life. Nicholas Dickons is remarkable because he was born into a prominent Retford burgess family in 1597 and probably studied at the grammar school before he went on to Cambridge.[35] Most of them, therefore, were able to harness the energies of youth and a knowledge of Protestant doctrine tempered by their experiences at England's most radical University: Turvin is certainly likely to have taken an advanced form of Protestantism into the schoolroom, and the children brought up in his charge, during the 1590s, must have played their part in moulding the religious attitudes of the town in the years before the Civil War.

It is less easy to be precise about the ushers since their lower pay and status caused them to figure less prominently in records. There may well have been problems of supply and discipline, especially in the early years of the school. In 1577 John Hay was presented to the Archdeacon's court for 'teaching children without licence',[36] and in 1584 another schoolmaster, Robert Dixon, was cited for fornication with Anne Smyth: the erring pedagogue failed to appear for the second hearing of the charge and on the third hearing it was stated that he had 'gone out of the town'.[37] The Archdeaconry Call Books, which name masters and ushers from 1609 (with gaps), note no usher in office between 1638 and 1641, which implies that Thomas Stacey was running the school single-handed. The only names to appear consistently are those of Gervase Jepson (c1612-13) and Roger Jackson (c1629-37), though the standards of recording in this source are not good.[38] The other possibility, of course, is that the school was so poorly supported that it lapsed from time to time for want of pupils though this seems unlikely, even in Retford, during an age of 'educational revolution'.

How did the townsmen view this instrument of enlightenment cast into their midst? Donations to the school, as already noted, were rare, and only a few burgesses took the trouble to specify in their wills that their children should receive a formal education. William Rossell II, for example, requested that his son be 'brought up and trained in good learning and discipline', and Thomas Dames instructed his wife 'to educate and bring up all my children with meat, drink and clothing, and further to

41: Sidney Sussex College, Cambridge: the grammar school sent at least two pupils here to study as undergraduates.

42: Part of the new grammar school erected in 1855 in Tudor style.

bring them up in learning'.[39] But learning was often equated with 'some honest science', and Robert Denman only considered education appropriate until such time as his son could be apprenticed.[40] Progress to University appears to have been rare, and Grounds cites only two firm examples of Retford scholars who went to Cambridge during this period, both of them being admitted to Sidney Sussex College in 1642. One was John Thornhaugh, son of Sir Francis, late sheriff of the county, and the other was Peter Lanfitt, son of a Retford glover.[41] There were, doubtless, other graduates whose identity is uncertain, but if the norm was attendance at the school as a preparation for an apprenticeship and a life in commerce, what evidence do we have of the educational levels of the town as a whole? The best indication is the scope of literacy indicated by signatures in a sample of wills between 1600 and 1642, a period during which the first generations of pupils would be active adults in the town.[42] Amongst testators the literacy level is 42%, a poor guide since many will makers were incapacitated by the time they came to subscribe and may well have made a mark when in better times they would have signed. Amongst witnesses, who were normal healthy adults, the literacy rate rises to 65%, compared with an average of 50% at York, Chester and Gloucester during the same period.[43] Retford was, therefore, more educationally advanced than some larger urban communities, though the benefits of education, in all cases, were clearly slanted towards a particular section of the population.[44] The Retford figure says nothing about the literacy of women, who never witnessed wills and were excluded from the benefits of the grammar school anyway, or indeed of the poor who were rarely summoned to subscribe to testaments. However, amongst males of the burgess class the grammar school had undoubtedly played its part in raising basic standards of education by the middle of the seventeenth century. Even if boys did not go on to University in large numbers, they were provided with the intellectual equipment with which to study their Bibles and other devotional works and also to take higher standards of expertise into their working lives. Coupled with an egalitarianism that joined together the sons of knights and glovers in the schoolroom, this was the measured achievement of Archbishop Holgate's Protestant vision and Sir John Hercy's more practical support.

FOOTNOTES AND REFERENCES

1.   N. Carlisle, *A Concise Description of the Endowed Grammar Schools in England and Wales* (1818), 2, p. 282.

2.   *CCR, 1392-96*, p.135, NAO, DDA/10/20.

3.   RM, Ancient Deeds, 1518. Thomas Gunthorpe was possibly a nephew of the man of the same name who was Prior of Newstead (1467-1505).

4.   Grounds, pp.15-17. Thomas Magnus, who founded a grammar school at Newark, also had links with the town.

5.   RM, Ancient Deeds, 1535.

6.   PRO, C 151, 972/65-66.

7.   *TTS*, 17, p.160.

8.   BI, PR 13 f.524.

9.   Grounds, p.22.

10. E. Arber (ed.), *Sermons of Thomas Lever*, English Reprints (1870), p.4.

11. BI, PR 19 f.482.

12. *CPR, 1550-53*, pp.47/8, Grounds, pp.24/5.

13. For the fate of the chantry lands, see Chapter 8, pp.229-30.

14. The following account is based on the version of the statutes in Archbishop Holgate's Register, BI, AR 29 ff.53-56. There is a printed version in Carlisle, 2, pp.280-88.

15. Carlisle, p.286.

16. *Ibid.*, pp.286/7.

17. *Ibid.*, p.287.

18. *Ibid.*, p.282.

19. *Ibid.*

20. J. Parnell, *Fruits of a Fast* (1655). James Parnell was born in East Retford in 1639 the son of Thomas Parnell and his wife, Sarah Ward (NUCLH, FRF). He was converted when he was fifteen through contact with a Seeker congregation at Tickhill under Thomas Farnsworth and disowned by his family. He encountered George Fox at Carlisle and evangelised in Cambridgeshire and Essex in 1654/55. He died in prison at Colchester in 1656 before he was twenty. C. F. Smith, *Life of James Parnell* (1906). I am grateful to David Bewley for his observations on this man.

21. Carlisle, p.280, Piercy, pp.126-31.

22. PRO, *Proceedings before the Court of Requests*, 7, 2 158/170 (69/28), 3 258/18 (69/28): Piercy p.129: this case was still going on in 1602, JA, RB2 ff.162/3.

23. Grounds, pp.56/7. This was the same man who, as Lord Haughton, had been one of the town's MPs in the 1620s.

Leases of school lands had already been used to gratify some of the aristocratic families who were attempting to exert influence in the town, notably the Earl of Kingston (1638) and Marquis of Dorchester (1647), Piercy, p.130.

24. PRO, C 93, 45 no 26.
25. Grounds, pp.63-70.
26. *Coroner's Inquests*, p.330.
27. RM, Ancient Deeds, 1553, Grounds, pp.43/4. The school was apparently adjacent to a malting: in 1627 William Thornton mentioned a lease of a kiln house 'of the backside the school'. NAO, Wills (William Thornton, 1627).
28. BI, PR 16 ff.482/4. Hercy's phraseology is interesting here. The idea of prayers in this context implies a man of conservative disposition, but Hercy hints that the prayers should have been delivered *before* his death thus avoiding an outward expression of popery.
29. *Ibid.*, 17 f.121, RM, Ancient Deeds, 1562. This implies that building work was still in progress. In 1563 John Twels left 3s 4d 'to the poorest scholars of the grammar school'. BI, PR 17 f.294.
30. BI, PR 23 f.734, 26 f.582. NAO, Wills, (John Coulbie, 1613).
31. Grounds, p.50.
32. See Chapter 6, p.174. *TTS*, 21, p.4.
33. Venn, *Alumni*. For Manners, see also BI, Subscription Book 2, f.140, *TTS*, 20, p.102. I am grateful to Sarah Chamberlain for drawing my attention to this hitherto undiscovered schoolmaster.
34. BI, RV1, A, f.71.
35. Venn, *Alumni*.
36. NAO, DDTS, 2 ff.33/4.
37. *Ibid.*, 24 ff.86, 101, 111. It is not absolutely certain that these men were ushers: there might have been another school in the town. However, the stated hypothesis seems most likely.
38. NUMD, Arch. CL 175.
39. BI, PR 21 f.295, 23 f.91.
40. *Ibid.*, 16 ff.144/5, NAO, wills (Robert Denman, 1637).
41. Venn, *Alumni*, Grounds, p.52.
42. This is the same sample of 107 wills used to calculate the statistics given in Chapters 4 and 5.
43. Barry, pp.230, 271. York (53%): Chester (48%): Gloucester (49%).
44. See, for example, the literacy levels of churchwardens in Chapter 9, p.238.

Chapter 8

THE END OF THE OLD ORDER
1520 – 1558

*To the honour of God and the health of my soul ... and for all
of the souls that I have faren better by.*[1]

On the eve of the Reformation Retford possessed three parish
churches but lacked any foothold in the town for the regular
religious orders, the nearest monks being the Gilbertine canons
of Mattersey, five miles to the North along the river Idle. Friars
from the Carmelite and Franciscan houses at Doncaster preached
in the market square from time to time, but their stay was no more
than temporary. More permanent was the propertied stake that
several monastic landowners had in the town, the most substantial being Worksop priory which owned the manor of Welham
and the Bolham mills in Clarborough parish, and also tenements
in East Retford, spread over all of the main thoroughfares.[2]
Welbeck abbey came a close second, and indeed outstripped
Worksop if only town property is considered. Welbeck's power
rested on its four mills on either side of the Idle at Bridgegate,
rented from the crown in 1227 and valued at £17 10s 0d in 1535:
in addition to this, the convent held burgages and lands in East
and West Retford, and the canons thought it worthwhile to
support a bailiff with a salary of 2s to watch over their interests.[3]
Of the other Nottinghamshire monasteries Wallingwells, Rufford
and Mattersey all had smaller footholds in the town, as did the
Lincolnshire houses of Torksey and Swineshead, but none of
these was a major landowner.[4] If the townsmen saw little of
monks and friars, except perhaps to pay their rents, their parish
churches were a more potent focus of spiritual loyalty. St
Swithun's, East Retford, is still, at heart, a substantial perpendicu-
lar town church, despite damage caused to it in the mid-seven-
teenth century and an extensive Victorian restoration.[5] The
complete rebuilding of the church soon before the Reformation

indicates a period of comparative prosperity for the town, based on the burgeoning wool trade, and a commitment on the part of its leading citizens to the mores of international Catholicism. Although many features have now disappeared, such as the heraldic glass in the great West window which Thoroton viewed in 1677, enough survives to give an impression of a church which was both spacious and well planned, hardly comparable to the great parish churches of Newark, Melton Mowbray and Grantham but, nevertheless, substantially adequate.[6] By contrast, the churches of St Michael the Archangel at West Retford and St John the Baptist at Clarborough were classic 'village' churches, not conceived on such a grand scale and not reconstructed with any determination during the later Middle Ages. St Swithun's thus stood out as the major religious landmark of the area, central to the town as well as to the Deanery which took its name.

The high regard in which parishioners held their parish churches, even the more modest ones, is reflected in wills of the early sixteenth century. Money left to 'kirk work' is commonplace, as is money, or wax, left to the various 'lights', many of them associated with the lesser guilds: in the 1520s, for example, West Retford church supported lights of Our Lady, the Holy Rood, St Saviour, St Christopher and St Bee.[7] There was a figure of St James at Clarborough and an image of St Audrey at East Retford with an associated light.[8] Thomas Sawman, who died in 1519, had a special devotion to St Audrey before whose image he wished to be buried: moreover, he bequeathed two pounds of wax to her light and for some reason, well known to him but not to us, he described her as 'my saviour'.[9] Other parishioners made similar small gifts to the church or to its images: 'a board cloth of twill and a towel', 'a harnessed girdle' for Our Lady, or 3s 4d 'to buy some manner of ornament'.[10] But interest in the church was greatest when major building works were on hand, and that was the situation at East Retford in the early 1520s when the improvements commenced in the fifteenth century were still not complete. In 1516 George Smyth left to the church 'my best brasen mortar towards the making of a bell', and in 1521 John Dolkar bequeathed specific sums 'to the building of the North aisle', to the stalling of the church and to the rood loft 'when they do make it'.[11] Three years later the concern of William Rossell I was for the paving of the church and also:

> that my executors cause a window of three lights to be glazed in the North aisle...and to lay upon my body and Alice, my wife, a convenient trough of stone, and the old trough to be taken away or else to plaster and board the four windows in the steeple.[12]

Although the preoccupation with the parish church was most commonly seen in terms of lights, ornaments and building works, one testator, at least, showed himself to be thinking along the lines of some of the more advanced Catholic reformers of the time, placing emphasis on the quality of the clergy who served the church rather than the visual decoration which festooned it. In 1516 George Smyth, a successful mercer, having appointed feoffees to oversee his estate, stated that in the event of the death of his heirs his property was:

> to be applied to the augmentation and maintaining of a secondary priest to sing in the church of East Retford for ever.[13]

It never came about, but it was a noble thought worthy of Colet, Fisher or More.

St Swithun's, in fact, had had a number of priests associated with it for many years, though only one vicar was lawfully responsible for the cure. The major chantry chapels of St Trinity and St Mary had been established in the parish church towards the end of the fourteenth century and placed under the supervision of the corporation, the priests sharing an annual stipend of £16 8s 0d. Each year on December 4 the chaplains were required to celebrate a special obit in conjunction with the vicar, with *placebo* and *dirige*, for which the vicar received 6d and the chaplains 3d each.[14] This approximated to the annual civic service and was, no doubt, an occasion of some local importance. Beyond that the chantries may well have had some educational role, though there is no direct evidence for this before the corporation attempted to formalise such a link in the 1530s.[15] The *Valor Ecclesiasticus* stated that there was once four chantries, but none has been traced other than St Trinity and St Mary.[16] Certainly, the presence of two chantry priests, or possibly four, within the town must have taken some of the pressure off the vicar in his task of ministering to the spiritual needs of the community, though George

Smyth clearly believed that even this potential manpower was not sufficient or could not be relied upon.

The St Trinity and St Mary chantries were not destroyed by the 1528 fire but they were seriously damaged by it. Piercy suggests that by then the chapels themselves had become decrepit and were either pulled down or drastically altered, and certainly the last incumbents, Richard Beyoke and Robert Mowbray, found their houses burned and much of the endowment on which they depended reduced to ruin.[17] This endowment consisted of ten messuages and five tofts 'in divers and sundry places' in the parish.[18] After discussions with the corporation it was agreed that the employment of the chantry priests should be suspended, and an experiment was embarked upon 'for a certain time' by which the bailiffs and burgesses administered the endowment under licence from the Archbishop of York. An account of chantry lands made in 1547 illustrates the scale of the task faced, since house rents had fallen from 23s 4d to 2s and from 28s to 3s 4d.[19] Although land rents remained fairly consistent, overall income had collapsed from £13 8s 0d (before the fire) to £5 15s 5d (in 1547), with an expectation of raising £17 6s 8d 'when the decayed houses are reedifyed'. The wills of Robert Cutler (1540) and Thomas Marshall (1542) record that they were both lessees of chantry property from the town, and in each case the land had been developed from its ruined state and the last rents due were to be given to the support of the church and chantries, possibly a general condition of these transactions. Certainly the activities of Cutler and Marshall confirm the statement of the corporation in 1547 that 'the most part thereof [are] reedifyed now by the said bailiffs, burgesses and commonality'.[20] Out of the income thus received the town paid a new priest a reduced salary on condition he took on the obligation of schoolmaster as well as looking after the chantries.[21] There was also some rationalisation of the ever growing number of obits, because in 1535 the terms of employment for the new chantry priest/schoolmaster stated that he should only be bound to perform four, on February 14 (St Valentine's Day), May 15, August 9 and November 12. An income of £12 was attached to these obits, and on each occasion small payments were made to the clergy of the town, the staff of the parish church and the corporation bellman. But they were also occasions from which the poor profited, since money was expended on the 'most needy' people, there was a dole in 'silver, bread and ale' and the residue, clear of all expenses, was distributed 'in sake of charity' by the vicar and bailiffs.[22] There was a vague implication that the old priests would be restored in due course as things improved, but Mowbray, at least, was quite well provided for since he was also vicar of Kneesall and received a pension as a vicar choral of Southwell Minster.[23]

The religious guilds and confraternities, which existed independently of the chantries, provided another dimension to the spiritual life of the town. In East Retford six guilds existed in 1513 (Corpus Christi, St Lawrence, St Mary, St Crux, St John and St George) and across the river in West Retford there was another four, or possibly five:[24] two wills of 1521 mention the guilds of St Crux, St Saviour and St Bee, and the guilds of St Mary and St Christopher receive one mention each.[25] The St Mary guild of East Retford was probably that of Our Lady of Pity which received a generous gift in 1516 and was mentioned in a deed of 1537,[26] but the Corpus Christi guild was easily the most important and it received consistently larger bequests than the others, 2s as opposed to 6d or 4d. It is likely that these sums represented unpaid subscriptions, indicating that the Corpus Christi guild was certainly the preserve of the wealthier citizens. The guild had its own priest and was administered by lay 'proctors' drawn from amongst the membership. Its functions were both religious and social. The priest kept a 'mass book' recording the names of brothers and sisters of the fraternity for whom he had to pray, and the procession on Corpus Christi Day (the first Thursday after Trinity Sunday) was another major social occasion in the town.[27]

In 1499 William Brokshaw gave a jewelled necklace for the image of the Virgin when it was carried in procession and also for use in the performance of the mystery plays, especially the play of 'Mankind'.[28] Thomas Gunthorpe's agreement with the corporation in 1518 included the purchase by him of:

> a new shrine or ferratory to be substantially and properly made and gilded...in the honour of God and the solemn feast of Corpus Christi.[29]

During the annual procession the shrine was to be borne by two 'honest priests' nominated by the vicar, and four poor

43: The font of St Swithun's: one of the best survivals from the late Medieval rebuilding of the church.

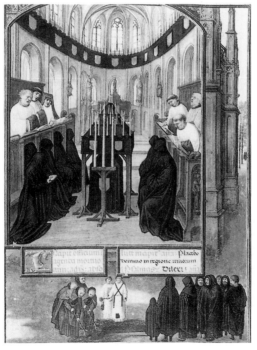

44: Elaborate funerary rites were one of the major expressions of religious sentiment prior to the Reformation.

men were to follow it about the town praying for the souls of Gunthorpe and all members of the fraternity.[30] David Palliser paints an evocative picture of the Corpus Christi celebrations in sixteenth-century York, which cannot have been very different to those in Retford:

> On Corpus Christi Day the craft gilds between them performed the 52 plays of the great York cycle of mystery plays. On the morrow of the feast the consecrated elements, housed in a jewelled silver-gilt shrine were carried in procession...led by the clergy of the Corpus Christi Gild, but the mayor, city councillors, and craft gilds also took part, and the householders along the route were expected to decorate their house fronts with bed-coverings and to strew rushes and flowers before their doors.[31]

Underlining the social functions of the guild, which must have been considerable, Gunthorpe also ordered that the proctors should arrange for loads of coal to be purchased for the poor and distributed by the vicar and chantry priests for ten years after his death. Thus, there was considerable inter-relationship between the various religious agencies of the town, but the Corpus Christi guild should be seen as of prime importance in co-ordinating initiatives and encapsulating the religious aspirations of the burgesses. Some townsmen, their horizons broadened by the contacts of commerce, could afford to look beyond the little world of Retford. In 1516 George Smyth bequeathed 52s 8d to the Fraternity of St Thomas at Canterbury and five years later Richard Oldfield left 13s 4d to the Boston guild 'to be brother of the same'.[32] Smyth and Oldfield were clearly amongst the more pious citizens of the town, because Smyth also left money to the Franciscans of Doncaster, to St Margaret at Ketsby and to the Rood at Boston, and Oldfield to the Cistercian monks of Roche abbey.[33] Pilgrimage to local cult centres such as the shrine of Our Lady at Doncaster must have been a regular feature of life even for the poor, but it has left no record in the surviving sources. Indeed, the town had its own attractions in the form of two holy wells, one on 'Spaw Lane' in Retford which 'was very famous for the cure of sore eyes and numerous other complaints', and the other at Welham, known locally as St John's well. Both of these sites commanded a minor cult following as late as the eighteenth century when the Retford well was covered and drained off because 'several nuisances were committed near it'.[34]

If devotional practices pursued during life are sometimes shielded from us by the nature of our sources, the same cannot be said of the cult of the dead since it figures so prominently in wills, many of which have survived. Before the 1530s Retford wills followed a more or less consistent pattern, the testator beginning with a commendation of his or her soul:

> I give and bequeth my soul to Almighty God, to the blessed Virgin his mother, Our Lady St Mary, and to all the holy company in heaven.[35]

After that instructions were given for burial; for the payment of a mortuary; and for a contribution to the 'high altar' to cover tithes 'negligently paid' or 'forgotten'. Almost all testators showed some concern for the manner of their internment and the welfare of their soul after death, but here wealth and personal predilection entered into the equation to determine the degree of opulence which might be achieved. Funerals were invariably conducted with the rites of *placebo* and *dirige*, and candles were lit around the hearse for which testators provided quantities of wax varying from one to three pounds: in 1524 William Rossell I specified how this wax was to be divided up, one pound for the 'cross candle' and two pounds for 'tapers'. He went on to bequeath 4d:

> to every light in East Retford church set and burned around my body, my brotherhood and every priest at my said *dirige* and mass of requiem.[36]

After the rituals were complete the body would be laid to rest in the chosen place—sometimes the fashionable Lady Choir of East Retford church — and doles of money would be distributed amongst the poorer mourners, many of whom will have attended specifically for this consideration.[37] In 1542 Alexander Witton of Moorgate, doubtless aware of the problems of transport to the outlying church of Clarborough, had the circumspection to offer 4d to four men 'to bear me to my parish church to be buried' and a further 4d 'to them that make my grave'.[38]

But once in the grave the journey of the soul was just beginning, and the support of the priesthood was needed to ensure that it reached its desired destination unscathed. As many testators as were able made some provision for 'an honest and discreet priest' to say or sing masses for their souls and often for the souls of others too: frequently these masses were specified as 'trentals', and on one occasion in 1521 as the 'five masses of the five wounds'.[39] The desire to get the most for one's money, and to provide insurance against shady deals done in the past, is well illustrated in the will of William Rossell I: he requested masses in St Swithun's church for six months:

> to the honour of God and health of my soul, my father's and my mother's soul, my wives, Alice and Agnes, my father-in-law, Saville, and Lord Saville, and for all the souls that I have faren better by, and for all Christian souls.[40]

There was no fixed charge for this service and the 'honest priest' simply had to be contracted by the executors to do the job for the sum available: indeed, there is likely to have been some competition between the town clergy leading to under cutting, since only occasionally do testators specify the person they would like to do the work for them.[41] In 1512 and 1542, for example, 10s was left for a trental, and in 1519 and 1522 £4 13s 4d and £4 were left for a whole year of masses.[42] Thomas Sawman, putting the matter in the hands of his executors, in 1519, hoped that enough would be raised from the residue of his estate to provide masses 'as long as they will', but quite clearly nothing specific had been worked out.[43] By contrast, in 1521 John Dolkar offered what must have been a plum contract when he left the princely sum of £10 6s 8d for a mere six months of masses in East Retford church.[44]

Over a longer period of time a deceased person might wish to be remembered in an annual obit and this invariably involved a landed endowment and a proper contract, perhaps drawn up by 'learned counsel'.[45] John Dolkar made such an arrangement when he charged the inheritor of his house on Bridgegate to:

> make or cause to be made yearly...a solemn obit to the full value of 5s by year for the health of my soul and my wife for ever more, so to endure as long as the belonging of the said messuage doth last, yearly in the same day that it shall happen me to depart.[46]

Although Retford endowments tended to be related to houses, there was a contract struck at Clarborough in 1520 which involved land in the open field. Robert Stirrup willed to the vicar:

> One rood and a half of land lying in the church furlong to pray for my soul and all Christian souls in the bede roll...I bequeth to the high altar two mets of barley growing of the rood, and half that is bequethed to the bede roll, the residue of the barley to the guild of St John Baptist.[47]

Arrangements such as these, be they for trentals or obits, depended on trust and co-operation between clergy and laity and a confidence that both sides in the contract were getting value for money. Generally, there seems to be little hint of dissatisfaction, except for one comment in the will of that hard-nosed businessman, William Rossell I, made in 1524. Rossell passed on property in Chapelgate and Newgate to his son Humphrey, part of the arrangement being that Humphrey should arrange for an annual obit 'to be done, sung or said' on the feast of St Mary Magdalen. The endowment was supposed to raise 3s 4d *per annum* and Rossell specified that out of this the vicar was to be paid 6d, the parish clerk 6d 'for ringing and singing', and 2d was to be spent on wax: the remaining 2s 2d was presumably to be bestowed on church funds. If the vicar of East Retford did not like this arrangement the bailiffs were to be instructed to give the whole amount to the poor.[48] The comment implies some concern about the fate of monies derived from obits, since it seems that Rossell himself was no stranger to sharp practice. Interestingly, it also represents a half-way house between the preoccupations of pre-Reformation Catholics and their Protestant successors later in the century.

This traditional pattern of devotion was seriously shaken by Henry VIII's Supremacy Act of 1534 whereby the King became 'Supreme Head of the Church in England'. Although the authority of the Pope was thus removed, and the monasteries dissolved between 1536 and 1540, Henry's personal beliefs remained rooted in Catholicism and despite the Protestant reforms initiated by Cromwell and Cranmer little had altered in the localities by the time of the King's death in 1547. In Retford the last reference to mass and *dirige* was made in a will of 1536, but bequests to lights remained fairly consistent until 1545 and the use of candles and tapers at funerals appears to have passed out of fashion at about the same time.[49] Prayers for the dead saw a similar lingering demise, the last example in the town being the 10s given to Richard Barneby by John Otter 'to pray for my soul and all Christian souls' in March 1547, soon before the passing of the Chantries Act made such devotions illegal.[50] Despite the survival of all of these non-Protestant religious practices right up to the time of Henry VIII's death there is a distinct feeling, from reading a number of wills, that they were being pursued with considerably less enthusiasm than in the 1520s. Wills now have a more pragmatic feel to them, the new relationship between church and state being spelt out by increasing use of the royal titles in the dating process:

> Our sovereign lord King Henry VIII...Defender of the Faith and on earth the Supreme Head of the Church of England immediately next under God.[51]

This was a transition well illustrated by the changing customs of mortuary payments to the clergy. In the 1520s testators invariably gave 'my best beast' or 'as the custom of country requireth'.[52] By 1536 mortuaries were given 'after the laudable use of the church', but in the 1540s 'according to the last Act thereof made' or 'as the custom of England requireth'.[53] These were rapidly changing times, and it was a fact well known to the population of Retford that the Pilgrimage of Grace had been halted at Doncaster less than twenty miles from the town.

The crisis must have caused some heart searching, because on the one hand the burgesses were well aware of their status as a 'royal' borough, with its consequent expectation of loyalty, but on the other hand, deep down, they probably sympathised with the conservative objectives of the pilgrims. An analysis of will preambles in the basic categories of 'Catholic', 'Protestant' and 'neutral' reveals only one will in the latter two categories between 1520 and 1546.[54] Not included in this is an interesting transitional preamble to come from Clarborough in 1537 in which Robert Witton stated:

> I give and remit my soul unto the hands of Almighty God, trusting steadfastly in the merits of Christ's passion, requiring to be with the holy company of heaven, and I will after my departing my body to be brought unto the church of

Clarborough and there to be buried afore the image of St James and my mortuary to be paid according to the King's statutes.[55]

There were Wittons settled in Moorgate at this time, but since Robert cannot be definitely linked with the suburb he has not been noted as Retford's first identifiable Protestant. That distinction must go to Thomas Marshall of Moorgate who made his will in 1542 and died in the following year:

> First, and before all things, I give and bequeth my soul unto Almighty God, creator of heaven and earth, in whom I trust only to have remission of all my sins, by the blood of his only begotten son our Lord Jesus Christ, and after this life to reign with him and his elect saints in joy and felicity world without end.[56]

Marshall described himself as husbandman but, clearly, he was a well connected man in the town and had interests in malting and gloving as well as more conventional farming. How he discovered Protestantism at this early date given the conservative proclivities of the local clergy is not clear, but he must have been a man of some determination to enunciate his views before a cadre of contemporaries who still instinctively looked to the past in matters of faith.

With the accession of the Protestant boy-King Edward VI in 1547, and the advent of the English Prayer Books of 1549 and 1552, Retford's Protestantism began to take on a rather more visible aspect. Between 1547 and 1553 the neutral preambles rise to nine and the Protestant ones to five, the two Catholic preambles of these years being associated with the more conservative suburb of West Retford and both being dated in 1547.[57] The advent of Protestantism to the town is to be linked with Robert Reveley, a curate who was active between 1549 and 1553 and who was the witness and author of several wills.[58] Reveley's form of preamble, which must have been approved by the parishioners who used it, is illustrated by an early and a late example from his curacy. In 1549 William Thompson, yeoman, recited the royal titles and then stated:

> First, I give and commit my soul to the mercy of God and Christ my saviour and redeemer and to the holy host and company of heaven with whom mine assured hope is to be partaker and felloer [*sic*] in the fruition of the deity.[59]

45: Sir Philip Hoby: Tudor courtier and diplomat who gained title to the small properties of Torksey priory in Retford.

46: William Cavendish, 1st Earl of Devonshire, who obtained the rectories of Clarborough and East Retford and firmly established a family interest in the town.

Four years later, in 1553, Alexander Day, husbandman, also recited the royal titles and stated:

> I bequeth my soul to the mercy of God and to the holy fellowship in heaven in sure hope that my said body shall rise again at the last day and accompany my soul to receive judgement of my Lord Jesus Christ and then to enter with him and his elect into his kingdom and glory for ever.[60]

By 1553, therefore, Reveley's churchmanship had developed to embrace the Calvinist concept of the elect, and some of his parishioners seem to have understood sufficient of this to permit the reference to be included in their wills. Other Reveley wills display similar radical terminology. In 1549 William Thompson desired burial 'in the burial place for the Christian congregation commonly called the church or church yard', and in 1550 Thomas Howes referred to 'the house of common prayer, commonly called the church'.[61] Residues of goods were given 'to God's glory, as he thinketh convenient'.[62] With the town under national scrutiny because of the foundation there of an Edward VI grammar school in 1551 these must have been heady days indeed for the small but expanding Protestant community of Retford. The question must be asked, of course, to what extent was Reveley reflecting the view of the testator in his preambles, and to what extent was he imposing the rhetoric of his own doctrinal preconceptions? This is a real problem, and arguments have been put forward both ways in this respect. However, it appears from a full analysis of Reveley wills that the curate had no off-the-peg format and that he was just as capable of composing bland and neutral preambles as he was Protestant ones:[63] indeed, even his Protestant formulae differed in quite considerable detail as is noted above.[64] Therefore, it seems fair to assume that there was, in reality, a growing Protestant sentiment in Retford during the reign of Edward VI, a sentiment strongest amongst property owning individuals such as Thomas Howes and William and Joan Thompson whose unusually detailed wills provide an impression of their position in the community.[65]

Edward VI's premature death in 1553 and the failure of the Duke of Northumberland to place Lady Jane Grey on the throne led to the accession of the Catholic Mary Tudor and, in theory at least, a return to doctrinal practice as it had existed before the breach with Rome. However, the damage done to the infrastructure of the Catholic church by Henry VIII and Edward VI was considerable and that ensured that the clock could not be turned back without serious difficulties. The absence of the religious orders, especially the friars, and the chantries, meant that popular piety could never be as it was in the 1520s, and changes in the Catholic church, initiated by the Council of Trent, rendered that style of pre-Reformation devotion questionable in any case. In a small way all of these trends were reflected in Retford. With Reveley safely removed and a conservative vicar installed in the person of Nicholas Holme, the restoration of Catholic forms could get under way. Will preambles for this period (1554-59) are solidly Catholic with only five testators failing to recite the old invocation to the Virgin and saints.[66] Small gifts once more begin to show a rekindling of interest in the fabric of the parish church which had totally lapsed during the later years of Henry VIII and the reign of Edward VI. In 1556 Henry Marshall, tailor, gave to the high altar 'one towel to be used about the administrations there', and in the same year Henry Boxton gave 3s:

> to be bestowed of a coverlet for folks to kneel upon the day of their espousal before the high altar and to be used and occupied there about other administrations.[67]

In 1558 at West Retford Thomas Bowringe gave 20d towards the repair of the leads, and Janet Braithwaite gave 'my best kerchief to cover the cross withall'.[68] Out of 40 wills for the Marian period, however, the number of requests for mass and *dirige* for the soul is comparatively small, suggesting that the chantries legislation had left its mark: a habit of long standing had been dislocated and the priests who had serviced this market had died or had been dispersed. Nevertheless, certain townsmen were still prepared to do things in some style. In 1557 Richard Booth gave every poor man in East Retford ld on the day of his burial:

> to be distributed unto every one of them at the church door after *dirige* and mass are done for the health of my soul and all Christian souls.[69]

Indeed, those testators who bothered to make arrangements for traditional obsequies often followed Booth in linking them with payments to the poor. In 1555 Margaret Marre stated 'I will there be dealt for three years 8s to poor folk to pray for me': and in 1557 Vincent Seyton gave 20s to the poor 'for my soul's health and for the health of all Christian souls'.[70] Elizabeth Backhouse was one of the last of this new generation preoccupied with her passage through purgatory. In September 1558, less than two months before Queen Mary's death, she gave to Robert Beighton 'to make my grave 12d and a load of wood to pray for me'.[71]

If some of these bequests look like attempts to obtain salvation on the cheap, soliciting paupers and grave diggers to do the job once done by chantry priests, it should be remembered that the vast majority of these Marian wills were made during the devastating plague years of 1557/58. Many were made by persons of less substance than those who normally left wills — because the disease threatened to carry away younger people whose worldly affairs might not have been settled — and the circumstances of death would not permit plans for prolonged or elaborate ritual: even the vicar perished during these years.[72] Our sample for Mary's reign, therefore, may not be a typical one, but it does highlight the fact that the Catholic revival of the 1550s was different in tone to the 'traditional' Catholicism of the 1520s. This had something to do with changed perceptions of doctrine, which shifted piety away from the sort of areas likely to be recited in wills, but it was also connected with the positive achievements of the Protestants, be they constructive (as in the case of education and evangelism) or destructive (as with the dissolutions). By 1559 Retford was no stranger to both of these trends. As the town recovered from what was possibly its worst mortality since the Black Death, Protestant survivors must have murmured and blamed such horrors on the restoration of popery. On January 11 1559, when it was still by no means clear in which direction the religious policy of Elizabeth I was to develop, the wealthy mercer William Dawson sat down to write his preamble:

> I bequeth my soul to the mercy of my saviour and redeemer Jesus Christ, trusting thereby to rest in the fellowship of our Blessed Lady and all the holy company of heaven.[73]

It was a strange bet-hedging sort of formula, but it must have typified the uncertainties which beset the town as the new reign dawned.

As well as initiating a crisis of faith the Reformation saw also the redistribution of the monastic and chantry property. The beneficiaries of these changes, in the first instance at least, tended not to be townsmen but those with influence at court and sufficient money to be able to afford the large packages of property of which the Retford estates usually comprised merely a small part. In October 1537, soon after the dissolution of Rufford abbey, George, 4th Earl of Shrewsbury, received a grant of all of its property which may well have provided him with his first foothold in the town, a situation which the Talbots were to exploit over the next hundred years. Similarly, in November 1539, Anthony Nevell, Esquire of the Body, was granted the entire property of Mattersey.[74] The Nevells could be accounted a local family and the Talbots almost so by virtue of their strong connections in Derbyshire and South Yorkshire;[75] however, the Rufford and Mattersey properties which they obtained in the town were comparatively unimportant. More significant, and also 'local' by a stretch of the imagination, was Robert Swift of Rotherham who, in conjunction with his son William, received substantial grants of Worksop and Welbeck lands in 1544 and 1553 which included property in Retford. Swift was a successful mercer who married the widow of a prosperous London brewer, thus enabling him to invest heavily in the monastic land market: the connections of his eldest son, Robert, with the Earls of Shrewsbury may well have opened up connections at court and eased his way into the town. The Swifts had a closer link with Retford in the person of Robert's brother, Alexander, who was a burgess and became bailiff in 1531, but following Robert's death in 1561 at the advanced age of 83 licences were applied for by his son to alienate the town property to Francis Wortley.[76] A monument still exists to Robert Swift in Rotherham parish church, a scroll emitting from his mouth with the inscription 'Christ is our life, And death is our advantage'. The epitaph goes on to annunciate the virtues of this archetypal beneficiary of monastic lands, explaining how Swift and his wife:

> lived many years...in virtuous fame, great wealth and good worship. They were pitiful to the poor and relieved them liberally and to their friends no less faithful than bountiful.

> Truly, they feared God who plenteously poured his blessings
> upon them.[77]

Other new landowners in the town had equal cause to give
thanks to the Almighty. Richard Audley, Equerry of the Stable,
received a 21-year lease of one of the Welbeck mills in 1546, and
further grants of Welbeck property in West Retford were made
to John Wright and Thomas Holmes of London in 1553.[78] The
small properties of Torksey were included in an extensive
package granted to the courtier and diplomat Sir Philip Hoby in
1544, and those of Swineshead in another sold to the Lincolnshire
gentlemen Nicholas Girlington and Robert Broklesby in 1546.[79]
The chantry property was incorporated in a single grant to Sir
Michael Stanhope, First Gentleman of the Privy Chamber, in
1548, and as late as 1575 the lands of Wallingwells priory in
Welham were leased to Richard Pype, an alderman of London.[80]
It is clear, therefore, that the main beneficiaries of church lands
were those who held privy chamber office at court or who had
contacts with the city of London. The only grant made at first
hand to a local person was a lease of some Welbeck and Worksop
property to Edward Southworth of Clarborough in 1562, though
this was specifically stated to be in a condition of great decay.[81]

Despite the initial advantages enjoyed by the rich and influential, local people were able to do better at second and third
hand, buying or leasing property from the principal grantees
once it had been broken down into smaller units. The Retford
corporation soon obtained the Idle mills from the Swifts, on
payment of the accustomed rent to the crown, and by 1554 part
of the property was in the occupation of William Dawson,
mercer, who was accused of allowing the mill house to become
ruinous in that year.[82] This transaction was, no doubt, prompted
by the influence of Alexander Swift and it brought the town
considerable benefits in future generations. But the clearest
example of transfer of property involved the chantry lands. By
1548 Sir Michael Stanhope had passed on his interest to Robert
Thornell of Walkringham who, in that year, sold it to John
Stanley of Thoresby, and John Wymoke and William Rossell II of
East Retford for £103.[83] Wymoke and Rossell were leading
burgesses who were acting on behalf of the corporation, and the
transaction illustrates how property could change hands from
courtier to local speculator remarkably quickly. Wymoke, in-

deed, occupied one of the chantry houses himself, underlining the point that many local people remained as tenants in occupation just as they had done under the old order.[84] More mysterious is the fate of another twelve chantry houses, itemised in the corporation account of 1547, but not included in the formal chantry certificate or the grant to Sir Michael Stanhope in 1548. These houses may well have been associated with the chantries which 'vanished' before 1535 rather than the better documented St Trinity and St Mary chantries, and as such they may have become an undisclosed perk of the corporation or certain prominent members of it.[85] If that was so the perpetrators of the fraud escaped scot free, since no action for 'concealed' land was brought in the town except for a grant involving some property of Mattersey priory in 1574.[86] For the people of Retford, therefore, the grants of church lands made by the crown were often of marginal importance since the initial grantees did not always represent the final beneficiaries: certainly, the property transactions brought about by the Reformation led to less perceptible dislocation than the attack on Catholicism, the guilds and the ornamentation of the parish churches.

For the people of the town the events of the Protestant Reformation undoubtedly brought a mixed legacy. The corporation was strengthened by the permanent annexation of the chantry lands, and the long standing uncertainties over education were finally laid to rest with the refoundation of the grammar school in 1551, another measure which compelled the bailiffs and burgesses to take a more active role in local affairs. Yet it is interesting to note how much of this change was already under way before Henry VIII's breach with Rome and owed its origin to the fire of 1528 rather than the King's much publicised matrimonial difficulties: indeed, the borough was compelled to begin to put its own house in order *before* direction to do so came from above. In other areas it is notable how the town scrupulously followed the lead given by the legislators in matters of faith, invariably reflecting national policy as it veered first one way and then the next between 1534 and 1558. This may have had something to do with Retford's self perceived status as a 'royal' borough, or may be there was just too much to do repairing the damage of the great fire. All of the magnates who had a measure of influence in the town at this time, the 4th and

47: Robert and Anne Swift from their brass in Rotherham church (1561): the Swifts were the major beneficiaries of monastic lands.

48: The site of the Idle mills: Welbeck abbey property which fell into the hands of the town after the Dissolution.

5th Earls of Shrewsbury and the lst and 2nd Earls of Rutland, were notable conformists, and their example goes further to explain the religious standpoint adopted by the burgesses. Most people accepted Catholicism in the 1520s as the only faith they knew and they gave to their churches as much out of habit and mechanical piety as any real sense of religious commitment. Certainly their priests appear to have done little to inspire them, a failing which had its roots in the distant past. An apathetic conservatism was the order of the day rather than the virulent popular piety suggested by Eamon Duffy's recent research: had there been a marked grass roots enthusiasm for Catholicism it is difficult to see why the townsmen did not do more to defend it.[87] Only the demise of the Corpus Christi guild in 1547 created a vacuum which needed to be filled in some other way and for which there was no obvious replacement. With hindsight, it is tempting to see the beginning of a positive alternative in the reign of Edward VI with the work of Robert Reveley, particularly the new attitudes to charity and the endowment of the grammar school, but one is left with the feeling that had Queen Mary lived longer the story may well have been very different. As ever, the historian is the prisoner of sources which say very little about what ordinary people actually felt and believed, but it is difficult to resist the conclusion that in matters of faith Retford quickly, and readily, responded to direction from above.

FOOTNOTES AND REFERENCES

1. BI, PR 6 f. 287.
2. *Valor*, 5, pp.174/5, PRO, LI, S(upplementary) S(eries) 3, pt3, 414.
3. *Valor*, 5, pp.170/1, PRO, LI, 553, Pt3, 411.
4. *Valor*, 5, pp.172, 178/9, PRO, LI, 553, pt3, 406, 415, 259, *CPR, 1572-75*, p.515, *LP, 21 pt2*, p.332.
5. 'Big, but also unrewarding' is Pevsner's patronising conclusion. Pevsner, p.295.
6. R. Thoroton (and J. Throsby), *The Antiquities of Nottinghamshire* (1790-96), 3, p.277.
7. BI, PR 9, ff.230, 372. St Bee, or St Bege, was a seventh-century Irish nun, and an unusual choice for a guild and associated light at West Retford.

8. *Ibid.*, f.85, 11 ff.259, 362.
9. *Ibid.*, 9 f.85. Perhaps he had been a pilgrim to the shrine of St Audrey, or Etheldreda, at Ely.
10. *Ibid.*, 9 ff.230, 249, 11 ff.663/4.
11. *Ibid.*, 9 ff.37/8, 183.
12. *Ibid.*, f.287.
13. *Ibid.*, ff.37/8.
14. *CPR, 1381-85*, p.465, Kidson, pp.11, 16, Piercy, p.97.
15. Grounds, pp.15/16. See Chapter 7, p.196
16. Unless there is a confusion here with the guild priest of Corpus Christi who also had the function of a cantarist. However, it is unlikely that his role could be said to be suspended in 1535. 'St John's Street' raises a suspicion of a vanished dedication in the town, especially since it links with 'Chapelgate'. *Valor*, 5, p.180, Kidson, pp.13/14, 52.
17. Piercy, pp.96/8, *TTS*, 17, p.160.
18. *Valor*, 5, p.180, *TTS*, 17, pp.159/60, *CPR, 1381-85*, p.465. There are minor variations regarding the value and location of this property: the *Valor*, for example, suggests that it was spread over East Retford, Ordsall, Gringley and Bolham rather than centralised in the town. The account of chantry lands in 1547 itemises 22 houses rather than ten, and this may be explained by the addition of the property of the 'vanished' chantries and/or properties connected with obit endowments or the Corpus Christi guild. JA, RB1 (Chantry lands).
19. *Ibid.*
20. *Ibid.*, BI, PR 11 ff.514/5, 666.
21. *TTS*, 17, pp.113/4.
22. RM, Ancient Deeds, 1535. The vicar received 12d at each obit: every priest 'doing daily service within the said church' 8d: the parish clerk 12d: the ringers 4d: the bellman of the town 6d: candles at each obit 2d. £1 3s 0d was distributed in charity, plus the residue after repairs to property.
23. *TTS*, 17, p.160.
24. BI, PR 9, f.74.
25. *Ibid.*, ff.206, 217.
26. *Ibid.*, f.37, RM, Ancient Deeds, 1537.
27. RM, Ancient Deeds, 1518.
28. Kidson, p.12.
29. RM, Ancient Deeds, 1518.
30. *Ibid.*
31. Barry, p.212. The growing popularity of the Corpus Christi cult in fifteenth-century York is to be seen in E. White, *Bequests*

in York Wills to Religious Guilds, 1365-1549, unpub Borthwick Index, 1983.

32. BI, PR 9 ff.37, 243.
33. *Ibid*. Ketsby near Alford, Lincolnshire, where there is the site of a church dedicated to St Margaret which was the centre of a minor cult. See B. Spencer, *Salisbury and South Wiltshire Museum: Medieval Catalogue*, 2 (1990), pp. 55/6.
34. JA, BB ff.173/4, Piercy pp.242/3.
35. BI, PR 9 f.111.
36. *Ibid.*, f.287.
37. *Ibid.*, ff.111, 183, 287. The only surviving monument from this period in the marble tomb slab to Henry Smyth, mercer, who died in 1496, possibly the father of George Smyth noted above. An even more impressive monument to John Rowley who died in 1454 existed when Piercy was writing in 1828, but this was dismantled in 1840 to make more room for the Archdeacon's Visitation Court. For the majority of testators, however, the final resting place was the churchyard. Piercy, pp.109/10, Kidson, pp.75/6.
38. BI, PR 11, f.663.
39. *Ibid.*, 9 f.243. A trental was a series of 30 requiem masses.
40. *Ibid.*, f.287.
41. *Ibid.*, f.230, 11 f.625.
42. *Ibid.*, 9 ff.80, 222, 249, 11 f.664.
43. *Ibid.*, 9 f.85.
44. *Ibid.*, f.183.
45. *Ibid.*, f.372.
46. *Ibid.*, f.183.
47. *Ibid.*, 10 f.41.
48. *Ibid.*, 9 f.287.
49. *Ibid.*, 11 ff.233, 309, 362, 664, 772, 13 f.81.
50. *Ibid.*, 13 f.163.
51. *Ibid.*, 11 ff.514, 663/4.
52. *Ibid.*, 9 ff.111, 122.
53. *Ibid.*, 11 ff.235, 666, 13 f.524.
54. See Appendix, Table 6.
55. BI, PR 11, f.259.
56. *Ibid.*, f.666.
57. See Appendix, Table 6.
58. BI, PR 13 ff.648, 732, 779, 926, 1022.
59. *Ibid.*, f.648.
60. *Ibid.*, f.1022.
61. *Ibid.*, ff.648, 732.

62. *Ibid.*, f.779.
63. For example, PR 13 ff.779, 926. For a discussion of the importance of will preambles in the city of Lincoln, see Mary Lucas, 'The Methodology of Will Analysis in determining the Religious Opinions of the City of Lincoln during the Reformation', *East Midland Historian*, 1/2, 1991/2.
64. For example, PR 13 ff.732, 977.
65. BI, PR 13 ff.732, 647/8.
66. See Appendix, Table 6.
67. BI, PR 15A f.145, 15B f.132.
68. *Ibid.*, f.246, 15C f.423.
69. *Ibid.*, 15A f.308.
70. *Ibid.*, 15B ff.252, 359.
71. *Ibid.*, 15C ff.429/30.
72. *Ibid.*, f.407.
73. *Ibid.*, f.431.
74. *VCH, Nottinghamshire*, 2, pp.104, 141.
75. Anthony Nevell does not appear on the Nevell of Ragnall pedigree submitted at the 1569 Visitation of Notttinghamshire. *The Visitation of Nottinghamshire*, pp.64-66.
76. RM, Ancient Deeds, 1532, *CPR, 1563-66*, pp.263, 298.
77. J. Hunter, *South Yorkshire* (reprinted 1974), 1, pp.204/5, 2, p.18, *LP, 19 pt2* p.319, *CPR, 1553*, p.294.
78. *LP, 21 pt2*, p.436, *CPR,1553*, p.325.
79. *LP, 19 pt1*, p.276, *21 pt2*, p.332.
80. *CPR, 1547-48*, pp.391/4, *1572-75*, p.515.
81. *CPR, 1560-63*, p.528.
82. JA, RB 2 f.85, BI, PR 15C f.431. The lease is mentioned in Dawson's will (1559) and raises the question of whether the mill was used for fulling.
83. RM, Ancient Deeds, 1548. The purchase price was to be paid in two instalments, £60 'at and upon the font stone in the Cathedral church of St Paul's in London' and £43 'at the house of William Dawson in East Retford'.
84. *CPR, 1547-48*, p.391.
85. JA, RB1 (Chantry property), *CPR, 1547-48*, pp.391/4, *TTS*, 17, p.113.
86. *CPR, 1572-75*, pp.363/5. This was part of a grant made to Alexander Rigby and Percival Gunson.
87. E. Duffy, *The Stripping of the Altars: traditional religion in England, c1400-c1580* (1992).

Chapter 9

PROTESTANT CONFORMITY 1559–1642

I commend my soul unto God's mercy undeniably believing
my remission of sin in Christ, my saviour, and my body to
be buried...near the communion table, in my grandsire's time
called the high altar.[1]

After 1559 the challenge facing the Elizabethan government was to inculcate the message of Protestantism into a
population which, but for a few short years during the reign
of Edward VI, had been nominally Catholic since before the
Norman Conquest. In this task their main allies in the
localities were the clergy who, by preaching and example,
could break down old patterns of 'superstition'. But the
government also looked to its secular parochial officers, the
churchwardens, to work in conjunction with the ministers
and church courts to punish breaches of the Elizabethan
settlement and also to impose on the populace habits of
Christian morality and neighbourliness.[2] Churchwardens
were, therefore, men of critical importance in their communities and, indeed, had been so since the Middle Ages. The
wardens were elected annually and sworn before the archdeacon at his visitation. Each parish had two of these officers and
at East Retford they were assisted in their work by an unspecified number of sidesmen.[3] At West Retford the wardens
appointed layers to help with the levying of church rates, but
whether these officers were synonymous with sidesmen is
not clear.[4] All of the parishes also had a clerk to assist the
minister with the singing of the responses, to teach the
catechism to children and to keep the register in good order.
For these services clerks were paid a small wage out of
parochial funds, though this was sometimes difficult to extract and non-contributors were prosecuted from time to

time.[5] One of the few parish clerks about whom information survives is Oliver Baxter, labourer, who held office at Clarborough under Nicholas Watkins and Nathaniel Hunte. He was appointed in 1591 at the age of 24 and served in the parish until his death in 1624.[6] In normal circumstances literacy would be a basic requirement of the post, and Baxter seems to have matched up to this even though his will is attested by a very shaky signature. This probably had more to do with his impending demise than his rudimentary mastery of the pen, because he was buried only three days after having signed the document.[7] Another clerk, William Lambart of East Retford, received from his vicar, Edward Hodgson, his second best gown and a loose coat as a legacy in 1565, indicating the relationship of deference which usually existed between clerks and parish clergy.[8]

Churchwardens, by contrast, were drawn from the solid middle class of the parish, though there was no reason why they should have been venerable men or have resided there for very long. In fact, the opposite was often true. Charles Oxenforth, churchwarden of Clarborough in 1611, was 36 years of age and had lived in the parish for only three years.[9] Many of his counterparts were, in fact, much younger than this. Examining the names of churchwardens recorded in the Call Books of the Retford Deanery (1609-1642) it is plain that in all three parishes there was a broad range of families represented, with prominent local names such as Cosin, Parnell, Bellamy and Earle appearing frequently at St Swithun's.[10] Yet there was no requirement that a churchwarden of the 'corporation church' should also be a burgess, and out of six wardens traced between 1623 and 1625 (when we have a more or less complete listing of burgesses) only three were freemen of the town.[11] It was, therefore, one of the offices to which elements of the 'commonality' could aspire to help influence local affairs. Clearly, there was no shortage of men willing to do the job, since only rarely were wardens required to serve more than once.[12] In East Retford, in particular, the office was viewed as a useful stepping stone for the ambitious and upwardly mobile and was usually held as a prelude to the more important civic offices of chamberlain and bailiff.[13] At Clarborough the situation was different, since the 'country' families of Southworth and Otter were invariably well represented, though not to the exclusion of families such as the Parnells and Childers who came from the urbanised part of the parish. However, once a Moorgate man was accepted as a churchwarden he tended to serve more than once, suggesting that that part of Retford lacked men with the substance or inclination to involve themselves determinedly with the management of the rather distant mother church of the parish.[14] Basically, the selection of churchwardens was most broad based in East Retford and least so in Clarborough, with West Retford sitting somewhere between the two.

Presentment bills and bishop's transcripts, both of which were signed by the churchwardens, provide an opportunity to assess the levels of literacy amongst these officers, particularly in the 1620s and 1630s. However, analysis of these produced an unexpected complication since it was quite common for the same man to attest one document with a fluent signature and another with a mark.[15] The explanation could be that some people were genuinely inconsistent in the way in which they subscribed to documents, or that, on occasion, literate friends or colleagues 'signed' on their behalf. However, what is clear is that at East Retford and Clarborough, even allowing for these vagaries, literacy levels amongst churchwardens were very high indeed, with 89% and 90% respectively being able to sign. At West Retford, where the survey was based on presentment bills alone, literate wardens came out at 37% confirming that this was an educationally disadvantaged part of the town. Doubtless, the same could be said for Moorgate and Spital Hill, though here a high proportion of the wardens came from outside the urban area or were drawn from a narrow range of the more substantial suburban dwellers. Nevertheless, taken as a whole, a churchwarden literacy rate of 72% outstrips the average for the town by 7%, indicating that the wardens were selected from amongst the better educated sections of the community.[16]

It was the duty of the churchwardens to care for the fabric of the parish church (with the exception of the chancel which was the responsibility of the rector), and to act as the eyes and ears of the archdeacon in the parish by presenting to the church courts all of those who infringed the law of God and the Queen's *Injunctions*. In this there were certain offences which went back to the Medieval period — such as sexual malpractice — and others which owed their origins to the drive for Protestant conformity after 1559. Offenders from Retford were likely to be summoned before the Archdeacon of Nottingham's court meeting at Mansfield, Newark, Southwell or Nottingham in the 1570s and 1590s. During the 1580s and early 1600s the court sat closer to home in St Swithun's church hearing cases for the whole Retford Deanery, which must have made life easier both for the town's churchwardens and the unfortunate malefactors called to answer. On occasion, special sessions were convened in the houses of the prominent local oligarchs David or Nicholas Watson, and on one occasion in 1603 an afternoon session was held in West Retford church after a morning meeting across the river.[17] When the court convened out of town hearings were irregular, but at Retford a monthly session was the norm. These variations were dictated by the attitudes of different court officials, Thomas Pettie and Michael Purefoy being the surrogates responsible for the more businesslike approach which prevailed in the 1580s and the early seventeenth century. This was a structure the churchwardens were expected to use both to justify their own tenure of office and to maintain the harmony of a community living at peace with itself and with God.

From the records of the Archdeaconry of Nottingham Research Unit details of all cases, both criminal and civil, were extracted for the three parishes of the town between 1565, when the Act Books commence, and the resignation of Archdeacon King in 1610. This span of 45 years saw two contrasting Archdeacons of Nottingham, John Louth (1565-90) and John King (1590-1610), and it covered also the vital formulative years of the Elizabethan church settlement.[18] Table 7 shows the result of a survey of 349 *ex officio* defendants during these years, dividing their cases into four basic categories.[19] From this it can be seen that the major preoccupation of the churchwardens was with moral crimes — mainly sexual ones. This was rather more so in East Retford and Clarborough than it was in West Retford, but the concern was nevertheless universal. An attempt to enforce church attendance, and later sabbatarianism, accounted for 17% of prosecutions, and offences against the effective running of the ecclesiastical jurisdiction comprised 13%. Only 5% of defendants had offended directly against the canons of the Anglican settlement, and 3%, mostly churchwardens themselves, had failed in their obligations to maintain church property. In all three parishes there was an irregular, but steadily rising, pattern of business which is plotted on Graphs 7, 8 and 9.[20] From these it can be seen that some years were much more fertile for prosecutions than others, but there is no discernable pattern to this except to note that in all parishes after 1600 non-sexual cases came to comprise an increasingly significant proportion of the whole, these additional cases being largely related to the drive to enforce sabbatarianism. Many factors could be at work to explain these variations, such as changing levels of deviance within the parishes: the attitudes of different court officials: and, of course, the determination of the churchwardens themselves to root out and present their erring neighbours.

A further dimension to these statistics is provided when we introduce a gender based analysis. Overall, men figure in church court prosecutions in a ratio of more than 2:1, 66% of offenders being male and 34% female. In all categories in Table 7 men exceed women, the gap being widest in jurisdictional cases and those concerning the maintenance of church property. In the area of moral crime the gap closes to a mere 10%, though even here it is significant that women, conventionally lambasted by Calvinist divines as wanton temptresses, still remain less commonly prosecuted than men. Only in the small sub-section of non-sexual moral crime do women take the lead, largely because of their perceived penchant for scolding, though here the numbers are so small as to be of little statistical value. Basically, the survey would seem to indicate that the town churchwardens, who were exclusively male, did not employ overt sexual prejudice in the pursuit of their offices. The same could be said of the court officials, who were fairly even-handed about the sort of punishments imposed upon male and female offenders. If there were distinctions between the sexes, they were to be seen in the increased ability of men to buy commutations of penance and to move out of the area if and when the performance of such a punishment looked inevitable.

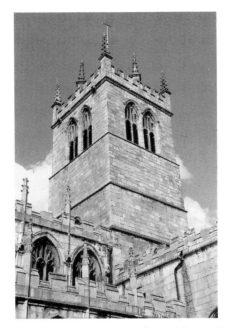

49: The tower of St Swithun's, incongruously rebuilt with stone from Roche abbey following its collapse in 1651.

50: Edward Manners, 3rd Earl of Rutland, prays at the tomb of his father (1563): as high steward he no doubt worshipped at St Swithun's.

If the period of Louth and King represented the highwater mark of the old Elizabethan Calvinist consensus, how did things change with the advent of Arminianism in the 1620s and 1630s? To answer this question a survey was made of all *ex officio* business conducted during the years 1631-40 under Archdeacons Richard Bailey (1627-35) and William Robinson (1635-42), when Edward Mottershead, a prominent Laudian, served as official in Nottinghamshire. As a comparison a similar survey was conducted for the years 1591-1600, two periods divided by a generation of townspeople. The results are presented in Table 8.[21] Firstly, it is notable that in the 1630s many more cases were brought (134 as opposed to 79), and that when numbers of defendants are counted this differential expands even further (199 as opposed to 105). Secondly, there are far fewer cases of an unspecified nature in the 1630s (three as opposed to fourteen), suggesting a more rigorous approach to record keeping on the part of the court officials. Thirdly, and most interesting, the priorities of prosecution had shifted decisively. Whereas in the 1590s cases of sexual immorality accounted for 55% of identifiable cases, by the 1630s this had dropped to 27%. The deficit was made up by a dramatic increase of cases involving the enforcement of attendance at church, 8% of the whole in the 1590s but 40% in the 1630s. Although in areas other than sexual immorality and church attendance the proportion of cases is comparable in the two decades, closer examination reveals new priorities, particularly the much greater number of prosecutions for failure to pay church rates in the 1630s (seventeen as opposed to two). The contrast is, therefore, fairly marked. On the eve of the Civil War people in Retford were almost twice as likely to be haled before the Archdeacon's court than those of their parents' generation; non-attendance at church, illicit sex and failure to pay church rates being the most likely charges, in that order of importance. Fathoming out the underlying reasons for this change is rather more problematical. Over half a century of Calvinism in the town may have begun to stem the flood of incontinence amongst the young, or it could be that churchwardens were simply less worried about it because of the improved economic position of the 1630s. The desire to enforce church attendance, especially in the face of the alternative delights of the alehouse, was very much a Laudian preoccupation pursued by clerics fearful of subversive opposition to the crown during the delicate years of Charles I's personal rule. Church rates was an issue close to the hearts of the East Retford wardens in particular, for reasons which will be explored below. Thus, it was a combination of factors — social, political and economic — which dictated the changing pattern of court activity within the town, but change it did, and it would be difficult to believe that people were more endeared to the robust ecclesiastical jurisdiction of 1640 than that of 50 years earlier.

The churchwardens themselves were closely watched by the clergy and by individual parishioners, all of whom had it in their power to make a complaint to the court if they suspected unfairness or dishonesty. Money, as might be expected, was often the problem. In 1581 Thomas Sampson and Robert Wharton, the East Retford wardens, were accused of detaining money rightly belonging to one of the old wardens, Martin Billiald, and they were ordered to pay it to him before Michaelmas on pain of £10.[22] Similarly, in 1602 Thomas Horsefole and Thomas Brookes of East Retford had failed to make an account, a case which resulted in their excommunication; and in 1626 the wardens for 1623, William Ratcliffe and Samuel Bellamy, were brought to court because they had 'sold and disposed of the church goods and specially lead amounting in the value to £4 or thereabouts'.[23] An insight into the sort of breakdown in relations which led to accusations such as these is provided in West Retford over the winter of 1583/84. Here the churchwardens, Alexander Denman and Richard Kitchen, fell out with their layers, John Leggett and Robert Golland, who they alleged were not assessing the church rate properly.[24] Golland, moreover, was accused of stirring up trouble by scolding with the wardens, but he quickly hit back by accusing Kitchen of fornication with an unspecified female by the name of Mary. Both men successfully purged themselves of these accusations, Golland by producing four compurgators and Kitchen on his own oath.[25] No sooner had the dust settled on this controversy than the wardens found themselves jointly in court, this time for failing to present bowlers during service time.[26] Kitchen responded angrily that he had not had a chance to make a presentment, and the wardens pointed the finger once more at John Leggett suggesting that he had failed to inform them of what was going on. When it emerged that Kitchen and Denman had been absent from church themselves on the critical day (possibly with the bowlers), the judge imposed a fine of 6d each upon them to be paid to the poor box.[27] The presentment of the churchwardens duly arrived naming three bowlers during evening prayer, all of whom received the same penalty as Denman and Kitchen.[28] The incident must have been a major talking point in West Retford, and it dominated parish affairs for six months. It should have reminded prospective wardens that once they were in office they became very easy targets for malicious accusation and, therefore, they had to tread with great care to avoid the risk of an unpleasant scandal. In fact scandals such as these were rare, and the churchwardens of all three parishes appear to have undertaken their duties with a tolerable degree of circumspection, knowing, no doubt, that they were likely to be victims themselves if they stepped too far out of line.

The major financial commitment of the parish was the maintenance of the church. Prior to the Reformation this was a cause which evoked considerable popular enthusiasm, but the Protestant purges of ornaments in the mid-sixteenth century and the altered priorities of the 1559 Prayer Book, with regard to the orientation and furniture of worship, caused churches to be viewed increasingly as austere and practical places rather than objects of communal pride. No new building is recorded in any of the parishes after the 1520s except for a vestry 'newly built' at St Swithun's in 1638.[29] But, more worrying, old buildings were not being properly maintained. In 1595 the church porch of Clarborough was in a state of decay, and in 1603 West Retford church was presented as being in disrepair:[30] both churches occasionally lacked prescribed books and both had churchyards which were not always properly fenced.[31] Under the close scrutiny of Edward Motterhead, Clarborough was presented in 1638 because its stalls were 'generally ununiform', the leads were in decay, and there was no 'decent cover' for the font.[32] In 1636 swine were wandering in West Retford churchyard, and in 1638 the church itself received an even more swingeing indictment:

> The aisles of the South choir are not even paved. The minister's seat is indecent and pulpit not sufficient. Mr Spivall's seat is not so in form. The windows are not sufficiently glazed. There are divers loose stones in the church. The poor man's box hath neither lock nor key. The East side of the churchyard is unfenced. There wants a pulpit cloth and the cushion is not sufficient. There wants a pewter flagon. The cloth for the communion table is of old buckrum. There wants a Bible of the last edition and a book of Homilies and a book for the names of strange preachers. There is no register book in the church and the North porch is in decay.[33]

But these defects were possibly less serious than the ongoing problems encountered at East Retford, particularly evident to the officials since they themselves sat regularly in the church and therefore suffered its discomforts at first hand. As early as 1579 the church was in decay, charges which were repeated in 1594: the lack of proper fencing for the churchyard was causing particular offence 'so that swine do greatly dig and root it up'. On the latter occasion the churchwardens, Walter Day and Henry Parnell, twice failed to appear in court to answer the charge and consequently spent the months between February and April 1595 under excommunication.[34] In 1625 the churchyard was still not fenced,[35] but by then the major area of concern had shifted to the chancel which, on several occasions, was stated to be ruinous both in its fabric and its windows, and to contain irregular seating. The churchwardens were less sure who was responsible. Under normal circumstances it would have been the rector — in this case the Cavendish family or their farmers — but the wardens prevaricated by blaming the vicar, John Watt, 'as we think', or stating that the decays were 'in the fault of the parish'.[36] On the eve of the Civil War the problems had still not been rectified, and in October 1651, during a great storm of wind, the central tower of the church collapsed destroying most of the defective chancel and causing damage estimated at £3,400:

> the church of East Retford by reason of the fall of the steeple and the five choirs thereof is now become very ruinous and made a heap of stones.[37]

The collapse of the tower required the corporation to take the matter out of the hands of the churchwardens and take drastic, and illegal, steps in an attempt to raise the money needed for repairs.[38] But the problem clearly was the result of many years of neglect and the inability of the wardens to raise the money needed for running repairs from normal parochial funds. Lack of churchwardens' accounts prevent us from knowing much about the traditional sources of income on which the wardens depended: doubtless there was a St Swithun's Day feast, or church ale, and certainly the church owned some property which was let out on lease.[39] What the wardens could not depend on after 1559, however, were the generous legacies to the 'kirk work' which had been a characteristic of the pre-Reformation period. Some testators still left specific gifts to the church, now of a distinctly Protestant character. Nicholas Dickons in 1597 gave 10s to West Retford 'towards the buying of a Bible', and in 1628 Thomas Bate gave East Retford 20s 'to buy [an] hour glass and a frame of brass for it to stand on the pulpit'.[40] John Wymoke's legacy to repair windows at East Retford in 1560 may well have been a specific response to damage to 'popish' stained glass wrought by iconoclasts in the wake of the 1559 Visitation.[41] In 1582 John Wilson, a Lincoln alderman living in retirement at Retford, left the church works of St Swithun's a generous gift of £10, but this was not matched by natives of the town who were not lacking in money.[42] What few gifts there were to the three parish churches during the Elizabethan period were invariably small — 3s 4d was about average — and they gradually died out altogether in the early years of the seventeenth century.[43] However, just as cash legacies were falling out of fashion, four parishioners attempted to create ongoing endowments as a lasting solution to an age-old problem. The draper William Spivy established the trend in 1602 when he left St Swithun's 8s 8d *per annum* over 21 years, a total of £8 16s 0d 'to be bestowed on the most needful places of the said church'.[44] In 1613 John Coulbie, tanner, endowed East Retford with a further 5s and West Retford with 1s 8d out of his lands in the town, and in the following year Clarborough similarly received 3s 4d from Avery Keyworth of Moorgate.[45] The idea evidently appealed to the Keyworths, who had suffered the headaches of the churchwardens office themselves, because in 1625 Thomas Keyworth, Avery's son, added 2s to his father's endowment out of his property in South Leverton and Cotham to be paid bi-annually 'so long as the world endureth'.[46] The experiment, which could hardly be termed significant in its scope, lasted only for a quarter of a century and was probably driven by the same Protestant impulse which tried to circumscribe more clearly payments to the poor, avoiding the vague 'prodigality' of earlier days. It was possibly the resentment against Arminian 'idolatry' which prevented these long term acts of benevolence being carried through into the 1630s.

The lack of cash legacies going to the parish churches after the mid-sixteenth century is probably connected with the growth of the church rate — the 'laye' or the 'cess' as it is frequently termed — as a means of funding church repairs and business. Once a person felt he or she was 'rated' there was little impulse to individual acts of benevolence, though whether the rate was a response to a decline in generosity, or *vice versa*, is impossible to determine. The difficulties of setting a rate have already been encountered in the problems faced by the churchwardens and layers of West Retford in 1583, and the situation repeated itself because in 1606 Robert Bend, another West Retford layer, had to appear before the archdeacon to explain why his account was not up to date.[47] Many people were, evidently, behind in their payments or had not paid at all, and if they failed to respond to informal approaches by the parish officers they could be summoned before the court and ordered to pay. At the end of the day the archdeacon had no powers of compulsion in this respect, but an admonition frequently seems to have done the trick. All parishes had a constant procession of non-payers of rates appearing before the court, though the problem was worst at East Retford during the 1620s and 1630s when the pressure was on to do something about the crumbling fabric of the parish church. Sums owed ranged from a few pence to the 9s 4d owed by Robert Parnell, alderman, in 1639,[48] which raises the question of why people chose to hold out in this way. For some, poverty may well have been a consideration, and others objected to the fact that they could not get a seat,[49] but that did not apply to Parnell and his like who may have withheld their rates for reasons of conscience, disapproving

51: The church courts made a major impact on everyday life: an ecclesiastical judge and an apparitor discuss the fate of a female defendant.

52: An alehouse keeper and a cook lamenting the limitations placed on their livings by Sabbatarianism (1641).

of the church, or vicar, and what went on inside it. Certainly the whole business could evoke heated passions. At Clarborough in 1625 Katherine Carr made 'unreverend speeches against the churchwardens...for demanding the church layes', and in 1637 William Pocklington called one of the wardens ' "Rogue" divers time together at such time as the churchwardens did make demand for the church duties'.[50] It was, undoubtedly, one of the most thankless aspects of a churchwarden's work and, if the case of East Retford is anything to go by one of the least successful.

Another perennial difficulty was enforcing attendance at church. Even if Elizabeth I did not desire to 'make windows into men's souls' and penetrate the inner sanctum of their belief, she *did* demand outward conformity to the rites of the Church of England, a preoccupation which grew as the 'threat' posed by Roman Catholic recusants and puritans was believed to expand in the 1580s and 1590s. Consequently, all three parishes prosecuted comparatively large numbers of 'negligent comers to church' or, more specifically, those who failed to attend the Easter communion, a more potent test of loyalty than the ordinary weekly services. Some offended only once, but others were more redoubtable such as Edward Emerson who was continually in trouble for missing church in the 1620s and 1630s but was never regarded as seriously subversive.[51] The reasons for such behaviour were many and varied, work, recreation and laziness being the most commonly encountered explanations. But there were unusual variations. In 1583 four Clarborough parishioners accused of not attending the Easter communion replied in their defence 'that the vicar is the occasion'. Nicholas Watkins duly appeared and confessed that he had turned away these individuals, as was his entitlement, because of suspicion of 'evil life' or not living 'in charity' with one another.[52] Similarly, Richard Fletcher was barred from communion at St Swithun's in 1587 for 'not being in perfect love and charity with some who slandered his wife', actions on the part of the clergy which must have created some difficulties at a time when the central government was increasingly keen to identify Roman Catholics.[53] At East Retford in 1608 William Billiald admitted that he had missed church on two Sundays 'by reason he was in danger of being arrested', an excuse which earned him a 2s contribution to the poor box.[54] Geography might also be held to blame. At the Archbishop's Visitation in 1637 William Childers of Moorgate explained his absence from Clarborough church in the following terms:

> That he being 63 years of age and living a mile and a half from his own parish church and about a quarter of a mile from Retford church; and that when he is able to go to his own parish church in summer, and in winter he doth duly repair to Retford church.[55]

A similar defence would probably have been voiced by another Clarborough parishioner, Henry Cromwell, who evidently found it more convenient to attend West Retford church in 1609.[56]

Cromwell's case was dealt with with some severity, which underlines the point that in some cases the court may have been privy to information that we are not aware of. In 1593, at the height of George Turvin's vestiarian troubles, Nicholas Denman was cited for not receiving the Easter communion. Three times he failed to appear before the court and he was excommunicated before he finally took the sacrament in February 1595 after a full year of procrastination. As a member of one of the town's most prominent families, with strong Protestant connections, Denman's protest was quite possibly the result of conscience rather than apathy.[57] Similarly, Anne Southworth was presented for not receiving communion for twelve months at Clarborough in 1620:[58] the fact that she was sister to Thomas and Edward Southworth, who were puritan exiles in Leyden, hints strongly that this too may well have been a protest against the established church. Although people of this sort were never formally cited as 'puritans' the circumstances of their cases imply that they were. No such sensitivities protected those whose non-attendance at church was rooted in Roman Catholicism, though these were exceedingly rare in the town. After 1610 the Archdeacon's court cited only three 'popish recusants', all of them female, and in 1632 a further four were called before the Quarter Sessions, two of them, Thomas and Anne Gilby of West Retford, probably being related to the recusant Lady Elizabeth Gilby of Hayton.[59] Also minimal in its apparent impact on Retford was sorcery and magic, another area of 'superstition' disapproved of by Protestant reformers but difficult to penetrate because of the nature of our sources. Retford did not produce a witch in the period under review, but the countryside around has its fair share of 'cunning folk' and in 1585 Henry Townrowe was accused of 'seeking unto wise men'.[60] Townrowe was a glover who made a perfectly conventional Protestant preamble to his will in 1590, though the fact that he had a 'little wench' in his house, possibly a dwarf, may have excited the suspicion of his neighbours.[61] Similarly, when Isabel Calton of Hayton was called before the Quarter Sessions accused of 'using charms' in 1608 Thomas Calton, a Moorgate husbandman, was one of her sureties.[62] The incidents prove just how close the new beliefs were to the old and the diverse ingredients which went to make up the popular religious psychology.

Failure to attend church became closely linked with the notion of 'profaning the Sabbath', in other words that the Sabbath was a special day, decreed as such in the Ten Commandments, and that on that day God's work alone was to be done. This was not a peculiarly Protestant phobia, but it was, nevertheless, viewed with increasing seriousness towards the end of Elizabeth's reign. People had always been obliged to attend church on Sunday, but the implication before the 1590s was that if they did so the rest of the time was their own. Now simple church attendance was not deemed enough: the rest of the day had to be spent in appropriate godly pursuits. People became culpable for profaning the Sabbath during service time, the more serious accusation, and also for engaging in unauthorised pursuits at other times during the day. After 1600 numbers of cases of 'Sabbath breaking' began to increase sharply, with work, such as baking, milling, or keeping open shop, providing the main category of offender.[63] When a servant was detected in an illicit pursuit his or her master was held to be responsible. More heinous than work were the pleasure related pursuits of bowling, and gaming, carding and drinking in the numerous alehouses of the town.[64] Usually only small groups of people were involved — less than half a dozen being typical — but presentments continually stress the 'disorder' and

drunkenness associated with these gatherings and the offence they were believed to give to God.   Yet drunken
parishioners were probably safer in the alehouse than they
were in the parish church.   Humphrey Barton of West Retford
was a notorious tipler 'of many Sabbath days', but when he
decided to attend East Retford church in 1625, doubtless the
worse for drink, he struck George Woodrough 'most violently with his foot and would have knocked him down but
for one George Bingham'.[65]   In 1638 William Hill stumbled
into West Retford church 'distempered with drink', and there
were always the more mellow brethren, like William Markham
and John Richardson of Clarborough, who slept through the
services once they got there.[66]

The clergy clearly regarded drink as a disruptive influence
and one which closed men's ears to the word of God.   The
irony was that most of the churchwardens who attempted to
enforce these rules were themselves no strangers to the inside
of an alehouse or to Sabbath day activities, but they had to
repress these instincts, at least for their year of office, even if
it sometimes meant presenting friends or close relatives.
Original Steele, a Clarborough churchwarden in 1625, had
himself been prosecuted for gaming 'both at morning and
evening prayer' in his youth, and in 1620 Thomas Keyworth
was one of the wardens who presented his own brother,
Childers, for being absent from church for a month.[67] William
Ingleby, a Clarborough warden in 1637, was a prominent
alehouse keeper frequently in trouble before both church and
civil courts for unlawful brewing and 'disordered company'.
When he was lambasted as a 'rogue' by William Pocklington
during his year of office, there was probably more than a grain
of truth in the accusation.[68]   Parochial administration was
therefore a very intense affair, not without real tests of
honesty and loyalty, but the community appears to have
policed itself *as a community*.   There is little to be said for the
notion, fashionable amongst some historians, that churchwardens were an elevated Calvinist *élite* who used their
positions of authority to terrorise and 'control' their poorer
neighbours. Though the first part of that hypothesis might be
upheld, the second part could not.   The lack of social polarity
in Retford, and the checks and balances built into the system,

ensured that the Reformation worked its course broadly as central government would have wished.

A legalistic view of the Reformation, based on church-wardens' presentments and the workings of the canon law, gives only a very limited picture of how a movement such as this altered people's doctrinal horizons. As we have seen, it is difficult to extract from 'negligent comers to church' any notion of whether we are dealing with non-conforming zealots or simply sluggards. So what sources are available to assess the growth of Protestantism amongst the folk of Retford? The evidence we have comes largely from wills which means we have a narrow and socially exclusive sample to deal with; moreover, the usefulness of some of that evidence, notably from preambles, is debatable. One thing which does emerge from this source, however, is the increase in Bible ownership after the 1580s and the passing on of a Bible to a child or godchild almost as a talisman. Thomas Wentworth, chandler, left his cousin 'my little English testament in token of my goodwill unto him', a clear reference to the Geneva Bible beloved of English Protestants.[69] In 1600 Margaret Towers, a widow who was related to the Protestant Sloswickes, passed on to Anne Denman a gold ring with the posie 'Let virtue be thy guide', good advice to the woman who was to become the scourge of the turncoat vicar, George Turvin.[70] Robert Speighte in 1592 preferred to leave legacies to children 'that I witnessed for at their baptism', rather than use the term 'godchildren', which to some advanced Protestants was anathema.[71] A survey of Christian names in the parish registers provides further tentative evidence of an expansion of Protestant feeling. Despite a very wide spread of names in the town, and the continued popularity of old favourites such as William, John, Anne, and Elizabeth, two classes of name make their first appearance or grow in popularity in the early seventeenth century. The first are virtue names applied to girls — Faith, Grace and Prudence. The second are scripture names, often from the Old Testament, such as Obediah, Isaac, Rebecca and Ruth. It would have needed a particularly well informed Biblical scholar to have discovered Bathsua and Mered from the Old Testament and Dorcas and Christian from the New, yet these were all names that were used in Retford prior to the

Civil War.[72] The Geneva Bibles, which crop up in wills from time to time, were clearly doing good service amongst the populace and were probably more widespread than we can ever be sure of.

But the main evidence is that drawn from preambles. Table 6 shows the portion of wills incorporating four basic preambles (or lack of a religious preamble) in four period blocks between 1559 and 1642.[73] Clearly, what can be seen is that the proportion of Protestant preambles, with testators seeking salvation through the death of Christ alone, increases substantially after 1580 and always outnumbers the neutrals. By 1642 for every testator who took refuge in a bland but nevertheless religious form of words, two proudly proclaimed their Protestantism. As a pointer to the future the first wills also appear after 1600 which contain no religious preamble at all though, as yet, these are restricted to very small numbers. All this is to be seen in sharp contrast to Palliser's findings on York.   Here, during the Elizabethan period, devotion to Catholicism lasted longer and neutral preambles consistently outnumbered Protestant ones.   Retford, by contrast with its larger neighbour, had become a distinctively Protestant community by the end of the sixteenth century.   In relating the preambles to the clergy who wrote the wills it has been discovered, as with the pre-1559 period, that there was indeed a tendency for certain clerics to favour particular forms of words.   Francis Denman, rector of West Retford, could be recognised by something like this, used in the will of Christopher Gowland in 1585:

> And first, as fruits of my faith, I commend my body to the earth from whence it came and to be buried at the discretion of my friends in full and perfect belief of the rising again of the same at the latter day. And my soul I commend into the hands of the living God, unto the latter coming of my Lord and Saviour Jesus Christ at which time I believe verily to be saved, not for any worthiness, merits or deservings in me, but only through the death and bloodshedding of my Lord and Saviour Jesus Christ.[74]

Nicholas Watkins, vicar of Clarborough, also had a recognisable style, represented in an advanced form in the will of William Carter of Moorgate in 1607:

> First, I give and bequeth, commit and commend, my soul into
> the hand and safe keeping of the Almighty and most merciful
> God, in persons three but in substance one true and everlasting
> God, even God the father who made it, God the son who
> redeemed it, and God the Holy Ghost who sanctified it. And
> my body I commit and comend unto the earth to be buried
> after the manner of Christians, in hope that it shall arise again
> at the last day to eternal and immortal bliss and possess again
> my soul, and both together dwell with God for ever in his
> glorious kingdom. And that through the mercies of God the
> father, the passion, death and merits of Christ my only and
> alone saviour, and the grace of the Holy Ghost working true
> faith in my heart whereby I shall be partaker of all the graces and
> favours of God in Christ, and repentence for dead works to
> serve the Lord always wherein I desire to live and hope to die.[75]

It seems unlikely that someone unsympathetic to Protestantism
would have sanctioned these lengthy, if somewhat stereotypi-
cal, statements of faith. Nor is it likely that someone hostile to
religion would have summoned the rector or vicar to his death
bed in the first place: there were plenty of wills made without any
clerical involvement at all. But final proof is provided by the fact
that both of these verbose clerics, like Robert Reveley, were
capable of penning quite neutral preambles when the situation
demanded it, Denman in the case of Edmund Oxenforth in 1586
and Watkins in the case of Gregory Childers in 1590.[76] Clearly,
preambles are a more useful source of information than some
historians are prepared to admit.

On the other hand, some Protestant preambles were written
without apparent clerical prompting, and these, even more so
than the first category, provide an insight into the beliefs of men
and women of the town. In 1638 Robert Denman stated:

> First, and principally, I commit my soul unto the hand of
> Almighty God, by the merits of his most blessed son Jesus
> Christ, my only Lord and Saviour, to have a joyful habitation
> in his eternal Kingdom: and my body I commit to be buried
> in the parish church of East Retford, in the steadfast hope to
> a joyful resurrection at the coming of the Lord Jesus Christ.[77]

In 1639 George Brown opened his will with the following words:

> I commend my soul (my precious soul) into the hands and
> safe custody of Almighty God, my creator, by and through

the merits, bitter death and passion of whose son, my dear Lord and Saviour Jesus Christ, I trust assuredly to be saved, and by the sanctifying of the blessed spirit of grace.[78]

Rosamund Fletcher, spinster, wrote in 1632:

First, I commend my soul into the hands and tuition of God, most humbly beseeching him from the bottom of my heart to forgive me all my sins and offences for his son's sake, Jesus Christ, by whom my faith is most steadfastly to be saved and that it may please him in this my sickness to assist me with his holy spirit, that whether I live or die I may be one of his flock and chosen children, and made partaker of that heavenly kingdom which is prepared for all believers through the only merit of Christ my Saviour. The burial of my body I leave to the discretion of my executor, not doubting but that he do convey it to the earth as the body of her that at the last day doth most constantly believe to see her saviour and redeemer, and to be made partaker of his glorious resurrection.[79]

These were the words of confident and well informed people who, in the last analysis, had no need of a priesthood either to pen their wills or to help them to the afterlife. The Calvinist idea of predestination, clearly expressed in the will of Rosamund Fletcher, was repeated by various testators between 1559 and 1642 'trusting and faithfully believing that...I am one of the elect and chosen of God'.[80] This was never a widespread claim, indeed, with the exception of Rosemund Fletcher, it was made only ten times before the Civil War.[81] However, it was made, invariably, in the context of the wealthiest and most influential families of the town, the Whartons and Parnells in the seventeenth century and the Masons and Rossells in the sixteenth. The brotherhood of the elect in Retford was based on hard cash and political influence: poorer people appear to have been excluded, or at least to have lacked the confidence to make such bold statements on paper.

But the most extreme statement of Protestant belief was made by those who deliberately detached themselves from the rites and ceremonies of the Church of England and, as a last resort, went overseas to seek freedom of conscience. Separatism was illegal after 1593 and it is difficult to penetrate because of its clandestine nature, but that should not disguise the fact that inhabitants of the town and its neighbourhood were, on occasion, prepared to take this important risk to life and property. The religious crisis associated with George Turvin's incumbency

MEETING for **SUFFERINGS**
was formed 1675 to record + alleviate
the sufferings of Friends

JAMES PARNELL
after great suffering
died in Colchester
Prison 1656
aged nineteen

Be willing that self
shall suffer for Truth + not the Truth for self

Yorkshire "I must and I will see George Fox"
Dales Notts
Kendal Leeds
Cumbria
Sheffield
Retford

53: James Parnell: the town's most celebrated religious radical and a pupil of the grammar school.

54: Protestant dissidents emigrating to the continent in the belief that religious 'persecution' at home was too harsh to endure.

undoubtedly deepened the sense of disillusionment which many more advanced Protestants felt with the established church, and a small minority proved that they were prepared to take action. Firstly, it is likely that some people from the town became actively involved with John Smith's Gainsborough congregation or Clifton and Robinson's Scrooby group both in operation before 1607.[82] Secondly, dissent continued in the area after these major separatist groups had departed for the Low Countries, a fact underlined by Peter Haworth's letter to Matthew Dodsworth in 1609.[83] Soon before that letter was written, in April 1608, it was reported to the Quarter Sessions that Robert Garth had spoken unspecified words against the King: it was ordered that two Retford artisans be called before Thomas Symcock to be examined as to the words spoken, one of them, Nicholas White, painter, sharing a surname with a prominent family of exiles.[84] In 1611 a dissenting congregation was discovered in the house of Michael Murre at Clarborough, and it is possible that John Broome and his wife of Babworth, cited as 'Brownists' in 1617, were members of the same group.[85] By August 1608 Richard Jackson, William Brewster's supporter in the Scrooby conventicle, had moved to Tickhill and it may be no coincidence that James Parnell, the Retford Quaker, was converted by dealings with a separatist group in the same village after the Civil War.[86] Given the continuation of the separatist tradition around Retford, it seems likely that contacts were maintained with members of the exiled congregations by virtue of the trade links which the town must have had with Leyden 'the centre of the textile trade' in the United Provinces.[87] Humphrey Denman, son of the puritan dissident John Denman, was living in Amsterdam in 1634 when he received a legacy from his uncle Walter Travers.[88] By 1610 Elizabeth Pettinger was at Leyden, and by 1613 she had been joined there by her sister Dorothy, along with Thomas and Edward Southworth.[89] The Southworth brothers were sons of Richard Southworth of Clarborough, yeoman, born in 1583 and 1585 respectively,[90] and, although the parentage of the Pettingers has not been established, they clearly stemmed from the West Retford clan of the same name which had close connections with the puritan Denmans and Sloswickes. Dorothy Pettinger of East Retford was cited before the Archdeacon's court as a 'recusant' in June 1610: she failed to appear and was excommunicated, and it is possible that she and her sister took the decision to emigrate soon after.[91]   Dorothy settled in Leyden as the wife of John Jennings, a fustian worker, but nothing further is known of her sister or of Thomas Southworth.   Edward Southworth, the younger brother, died at London in 1620.[92] However, Edward's widow, Alice, emigrated to America aboard the 'Anne' or 'Little James' in 1623, and in the same year married William Bradford as his second wife.[93] Bradford, who came from Austerfield, and was an admirer of Richard Clifton, was a leading figure in the Scrooby congregation and was many times governor of Plymouth, New England, prior to his death in 1657. Retford, therefore, can claim a distinguished place in the ancestry of North American Protestantism. It is notable the extent to which these feelings of religious radicalism were restricted to a small and inter-related group in the town and stretched back to the earliest years of the Reformation in the person of William Denman. The departure of the Pilgrims was no casual whim, but a deep-felt Protestant commitment rooted in the family traditions of North Nottinghamshire.

As in the early years of the Reformation Retford, for the most part, set a commendable example of conformity in the years after 1559. The churchwardens, of course, were beset with the usual problems of enforcing the settlement; in other words, combating widespread apathy when it came to attending services and paying for the maintenance of churches, or failure to treat the Sabbath with the respect that it was believed to deserve. All of these areas represented breaches with earlier traditions, and the Protestant cult of individualism meant that corporate initiatives were more difficult to mount: certainly there was no replacement for the quasi-spiritual fellowship of the Corpus Christi guild which probably helped convince people to give more generously to their churches and to take some pride in attending them for worship. When the Laudians attempted to bridge this gulf with greater use of legal sanctions, rather than communal initiatives, the resentment felt against the church authorities was deep and bitter. Yet, despite these problems, which were by no means peculiar to the town, a distinct Protestant awareness had developed amongst many of its citizens by the end of Elizabeth's reign, and practical devotion to the old faith was all but dead: in 1602 William Spivy could comment, quite casually, on his best chair with four cushions 'made of vestments'.[94] If, for the majority of townsmen, the mechanical Catholicism of the 1520s had been replaced by an equally mechanical form of Protestantism, there was in Retford a godly Calvinist minority and an even smaller fraction of that minority prepared to secede from the Church of England in support of its beliefs. For the origins of this Protestant extremism we might look to the ministries of preachers such as Clifton, Denman and Turvin; to the town grammar school; or even to the hallucinatory effects of the extensive hemplands of North Nottinghamshire. Whatever the reason, by 1642 the religious zealots of the town looked overseas to the United Provinces and to New England rather than to Rome and the fellowship of St Thomas at Canterbury. It was a sea change that brought with it significant shifts in attitude, documented meticulously at Dorchester and no doubt evident, albeit to a lesser degree, in Retford too.

FOOTNOTES AND REFERENCES

1. NAO, Wills (Mary Luddington, 1637).
2. For the best modern studies of the church courts during this period see, R. A. Houlbrooke, *Church and People during the English Reformation* (1979), M. Ingram, *The Church Courts, Sex and Marriage in England* (1987).
3. NUMD, Arch. PB 341 (1637).
4. NAO, DDTS 23 ff.152, 159.
5. For example, Thomas Calton at Clarborough (1597) and Bernard Sutton at East Retford. *Ibid.*, 6 ff.108, 118, 121, NUMD, Arch. A 42 f.258.
6. He married Euphan Taylor at Clarborough in 1599. NAO, CPR (1599), BI, CP H 660.
7. NAO, Wills (Oliver Baxter, 1624).
8. BI, PR 17B f.458.
9. *Ibid.*, CP H 660.
10. NUMD, Arch. CL 175.
11. William Ratcliffe, Henry Atkinson and George Kirke were burgesses in the 1624 listing; Samuel Bellamy, Thomas Parnell and Thomas Cade were not. *Ibid.*, Cl. LP. 52.
12. For example, Richard Reynolds at East Retford (1636 and 1638): Richard Farmery at West Retford (1627 and 1638): and Robert Staniland at West Retford (1609 and 1615). Piercy's list in JA, RB 1 (Churchwardens) implies considerably more repetition, but the list is unreliable when compared with the Call Books and signed BTs.

13. See Chapter 2, p.52-3. Burgesses only, of course, were eligible for these offices.
14. Long serving Moorgate wardens were Richard Childers (1612, 1618, 1623, 1638) and Richard Parnell (1617, 1624, 1643). These men can have had no ambitions in civic government since they lived outside the borough.
15. Four examples of this practice were encountered involving Francis Wilson and Robert Smeeton of East Retford; George Harrison of Clarborough and John Goodlad of West Retford.
16. For the purposes of this study wardens who 'signed' *and* made marks were deemed to be illiterate.
17. David Watson (1592/95): Nicholas Watson (1603/5).
18. See Chapter 6, p.179-86. Processed case data can be viewed at NUCLH.
19. See Appendix, Table 7.
20. See Appendix, Graphs 7, 8, 9.
21. See Appendix, Table 8.
22. NAO, DDTS 22 f.147.
23. *Ibid.*, 7 ff.114, 124, NUMD, Arch. PB 339 (1626).
24. NAO, DDTS 23, ff.152, 159. The second named warden is called Thomas Kitchen in some of the records, though clearly the same man is intended: the Richard Kitchen who is mentioned in the will of Christopher Kitchen (1578) is probably the right man. BI, PR 21 f.295.
25. NAO, DDTS 23 ff.166/7, 175, 184.
26. *Ibid.*, ff.205, 212, 219.
27. *Ibid.*, f.229.
28. *Ibid.*, ff.233, 236.
29. BI, V 1636, CB f.444.
30. NAO, DDTS, 5 ff.169, 171, 174, 177, 7 f.190.
31. *Ibid.*, 8 f.190, 10 f.19, BI, V 1600, CB 2 f.31, 33, NUMD, Arch. PB 341.
32. *Ibid.*, PB 341 (1638).
33. BI, V 1636, CB f.444, NUMD, Arch. A 45 (3/9/1638). Mr Spivall is probably a mistake for Mr Spivy.
34. NAO, DDTS 5 ff.143, 167, 172, 186, 226.
35. NUMD, Arch. PB 339 (1625). In this case the churchwardens were accused by George Malin, the apparitor.
36. *Ibid.*, A 42 f.274, 45 f.186, PB 339, 341.
37. Kidson, p.19.
38. See Chapter 7, p.204. Eventually a brief was issued in June 1658 authorising a collection in Nottinghamshire, Lincoln-shire, Yorkshire and London for the repair of the church and in the same year the work was carried out by John Boulton of Firbeck, using stone from the ruins of Roche abbey. W. A. Bewes, *Church Briefs* (1898), p.137, Kidson, p.22.
39. BI, PR 15C f.434. St Swithun's day was on July 15, though in 1536 Convocation ordered that all dedications were to be

celebrated on the first Sunday in October 'and upon none other day'. Kidson, p.131.

40. *Ibid.*, 26 f.582, NAO, Wills (Thomas Bate, 1628).
41. BI, PR 16 ff.144/5.
42. *Ibid.*, 22 ff.423/4.
43. For example, BI, PR 23 f.734, 25 f.1135, 26 f.582.
44. PRO, PROB 11/101.
45. NAO, Wills (John Coulbie, 1613: Avery Keyworth, 1614).
46. *Ibid.*, (Thomas Keyworth, 1625).
47. NAO, DDTS 10 ff.141/2, 149.
48. For early examples of non-payment see, DDTS 2 f.51, 10 f.188, 11 f.210: for the 1620s and 1630s, see NUMD, Arch. PB 339, 341.
49. *Ibid.*, A 47 f.57.
50. *Ibid.*, PB 339 (1625), 341 (1637).
51. *Ibid.*
52. NAO, DDTS 23 ff.19, 20, 41, 50.
53. T. M. Blagg (ed.), *A Miscellany of Nottinghamshire Records* Thoroton Society, Record Series, 11, 1945, p.35.
54. NAO, DDTS 11 ff.136, 142.
55. BI, V 1636, CB f.432.
56. NAO, DDTS 11 ff.202, 207, 233. Cromwell's will (1617) describes him as husbandman of West Retford and gives no hint of radical belief: Thomas Bishop was named as one of his supervisors. How the confusion arose about his place of residence is not clear. Wills (Henry Cromwell, 1617).
57. *Ibid.*, DDTS 4 ff.248, 261, 5 ff.4, 11, 112, 176. It is not clear whether this was Nicholas Denman son of William Denman, rector of Ordsall; or Nicholas Denman son of Alexander Denman.
58. NUMD, Arch. PB 339 (1620).
59. *Ibid.*, PB 341, A 39 f.14, 42 f.274, 44 f.79, 47 ff.52, NAO, QSMI/7. The only 'established' townsman was Childers Keyworth of Moorgate in the 1632 Quarter Sessions list: Elizabeth Man, a negligent comer to church in 1638, had graduated to a 'popish recusant' by 1639, an illustration of the fine line dividing these offences.
60. *Ibid.*, DDTS 22 ff.8/9.
61. BI, PR 24 f.416.
62. NAO, QSMI/2.
63. See for example, DDTS 6 f.269, 7 f.134, 10 f.227, NUMD, Arch. PB 339, 341.
64. See for example NAO, DDTS 6 f.273, 11 f.174, 12 ff.162, 164, 168, NUMD, Arch. PB 339, 341.
65. *Ibid.*, 339 (1625).
66. *Ibid.*, 341 (1638): NAO, DDTS 2 f.205, 3 f.102.
67. *Ibid.*, 11 ff.17, 35, NUMD, Arch. PB 339 (1620).

68.   Ingleby had moved to Clarborough after he had been disfranchised as a burgess in 1625: his notorious conduct evidently continued in Moorgate. See Chapter 2, p.54. NAO, QSMI/10, NUMD, Arch. PB 339 (1637).

69.   BI, PR 27 f.659.

70.   *Ibid.*, 28 f.297.

71.   *Ibid.*, 25 f.1135.

72.   John and Anne Denman, notable puritans, produced children with the names of Humphrey (1600); Elizabeth (1602): Bathsua (1604); and Hannah (1607). NAO, ERPR, NUCLH, FRF.

73.   See Appendix, Table 6.

74.   BI, PR 23 f.507.

75.   NAO, Wills (William Carter, 1607).

76.   BI, PR 23 f.320, NAO, Wills (Gregory Childers, 1590).

77.   *Ibid.*, (Robert Denman, (1638).

78.   *Ibid.*, (George Brown, 1639).

79.   *Ibid.*, (Rosamund Fletcher, 1632).

80.   BI, PR 23 f.851.

81.   By John Wymoke, drover (1560); William Rossell II, tanner (1578); Thomas Stockham, mercer (1584); Edmund Mason, tanner (1588); William Spivy, draper (1602); John Wharton, woollen draper (1631); Ann Parnell, widow (1634); Saville Wharton, gentleman (1637); Dorothy Wharton, widow (1639).

82.   The prosecution of William Brewster and other Scrooby separatists by the York High Commission is noted in BI, HC/AB 15 ff.115, 116, 118, 177.

83.   See Chapter 6, pp.184-5.

84.   NAO, QSMI/2. The other was Thomas Holland, petty chapman: the Whites were a pilgrim family related to the Carvers and Robinsons. J. W. Tammel, *The Pilgrims and other people from the British Isles in Leiden, 1576-1640* (1989), p.10.

85.   NAO, QSMI/3, 5.

86.   BI, HC/AB 15 f.177. For James Parnell, see Chapter 7, pp.202, 210.

87.   Tammel, p.5.

88.   NUCLH, FRF.

89.   Tammel, pp.210, 211, 248. Edward Southworth is described as 'say worker': traditional Retford skills were readily reusable in the Low Countries. There are other local names amongst the Leyden exiles — for example, Jepson and Bishop — but relationships are not easy to establish.

90.   NCRO, CPR (1583, 1585), NCLH, FRF.

91.   NAO, DDTS 12 f.152.

92.   Tammel, p.136.

93.   *Ibid.*, p. 8. Alice Southworth's maiden name was Carpenter.

94.   PRO, PROB 11/101.

Conclusion

When we look at Retford in the context of the debate between continuity and change discussed in the Introduction it soon becomes plain that elements of both were present, though perhaps not quite in the measures suggested by Clark and Slack. In most areas of day-to-day life the 'inherited framework', as it is described by Palliser, was much the same for ordinary citizens in the fifteenth century as it was on the eve of the Civil War.[1] The basic layout of the town had not changed, and the landmarks were the same though significantly altered, the Moothall rebuilt because of fire, and St Swithun's church shabbier and less well cared for, perhaps, than it had been in the past. Indeed, the town must have taken on the aspect of a permanent building site, the impact of three major conflagrations having left long lasting devastation in their wake. People needed to work hard to earn a living, but doubly so to repair damage resultant from this unhappy by-product of the urban economy. The energies sapped by this vital restoration work may well have prevented the inhabitants from being as commercially innovative as they might have been had not these constant demands been placed on their purses and persons. Nevertheless, the town expanded into the areas of Moorgate and Spital Hill and there is evidence to support Sjoberg's view that the poor, along with offensive tradesmen, tended to be marginalised in these suburbs.[2] Although the market place and some of the main thoroughfares were being paved, pigs continued to roam the streets and root in the churchyards and attitudes towards sewage and refuse disposal are likely to have remained unaltered for generations. The old hazards of plague, flood and fire were every bit as dangerous in 1600 as they had been in 1400.

Within this traditional context life went on much as it always had done. People gravitated towards their family groups, though with an awareness of a 'cousinage' constantly expanded by the ever-growing interrelationship between townsmen and their immediate rural neighbours. There seems little evidence for the more patriarchal society which is sometimes argued to be one of the results of Protestantism. Despite obvious disabilities (lack of burgess rights, for example) women were accepted as a significant force in the town, possibly because they had always formed an active and important element in the workforce by way of the fabric and retail trades. Those trades were already well established by 1600 and there was nothing new about the 'specific' economic orientation of the town in the sixteenth century. Medieval charters underline a long succession of shoemakers, tanners, ropers, and dyers, confirming the fact that Retford's market town role, combining the general and the particular, had very ancient roots. Nor was there anything new about depression and crisis and the resultant problems of poverty, since the textile trade had always been notoriously volatile and the period of the Hundred Years War had taught the town that it needed to cope with bad times as well as good. The recession of the 1620s might have been an unpleasant reminder of this, but it is unlikely to have been unprecedented. For Retford people, the really important things of life — what they ate and how they earned their livings — continued regardless of dynasties and were impacted upon only by external forces well outside of their control.

The major institutions of the town were similarly firmly rooted in a bygone age. Urban government owed its privileges to the expansive years of the thirteenth century and it is significant that the only year in which the town returned its own citizens to Parliament was in 1315. In the seventeenth century there is some evidence that these municipal privileges were used to pursue paupers and other undesirables to the non-corporate suburbs, but there is likely to have been a similar response to the problems of vagrancy and immorality which had characterised the years before 1350. Just as corporate privilege was long established by 1642, so was the power of faith. The basic provision of one ill-paid vicar to serve the town went back to the twelfth century when the tithes had been expropriated to enrich the collegiate foundation of St Sepulchre's, York. Although fashions in religion came and went — and this can be seen in the Middle Ages, quite apart from the major shift of Protestantism — it is often forgotten that the basic moral precepts of the faith remained largely unaltered: people worshipped the same God in the same church, they baptised their children in the same font, and they struggled to meet the same moral standards required by the clergy and the canon law. And if morality was by no means a monopoly of sixteenth-century Protestants, no more so was a belief in the efficacy of preaching or the benefits of education. Retford had a grammar school long before the reformers took the idea on board, and no doubt children from the town and surrounding countryside learned good lessons there. Many of these points would need to be substantiated by more detailed research on the Medieval town, but the initial reaction would be to agree fully with MacCaffrey's comment on the 'continuity of Medieval custom' at Exeter or the 'administrative and social conservatism', noted by Dyer at Worcester.[3] Socially, economically and institutionally Retford was deeply rooted in its past.

But it would be wrong to go on from this and suggest that nothing had changed: on the contrary, the inherited pattern was assaulted by two forces in the sixteenth century which were to help dictate the development of the town for the next three hundred years, culminating in East Retford being pilloried as one of the classic 'rotten boroughs' at the time of the Reform Bill. The first was Protestantism, which had the effect of reducing the number of clergy in the town, redistributing monastic and chantry property and dissolving the important Corpus Christi guild in 1547. In time a very different type of cleric was to emerge, committed to the new faith and looking towards the community of the elect in this world as an embodiment of those saved in the next. This stood in stark contrast to the broad-based fellowship of Corpus Christi, with its colourful pageantry, praying for the souls of long dead townsmen as it provided comforts for the living. The problems of emotional and intellectual adjustment to this new and stark form of religion must have been very considerable, yet there is an argument that it had a special appeal to townsmen (particularly the wealthier ones) and its impact cannot be denied in Retford.[4] The success of Protestantism in the town was to be closely linked with the refoundation of the grammar school in 1551 which drew income from dissolved chantries and utilised the labour of some of the 'reformed' clerics already referred to. The impact of all of this was considerable since by 1600 Retford was a relatively well-educated community and its doctrinal horizons had shifted, in many ways an embodiment of the godly and well ordered market towns seen by the reformers as one of the necessary prerequisites to the 'conversion' of the realm. How all of this effected the majority of townsmen in their working and family lives is more difficult to determine, but some clues are provided by the changing nature of church court business between 1565 and 1642. Certainly, like Dorchester, the town had its minority of puritan zealots who no doubt worked hard to improve the moral tone of the community, as they saw it, and faced with disillusionment were sometimes prepared to risk life and property in the dangerous journey to the Low Countries or to America.

The second factor, which was closely linked with Protestantism, was the growing influence of great families in the town, particularly the Earls of Rutland, Shrewsbury and Devonshire. These families first became apparent in the sixteenth century by exploiting the traditional office of high steward and the monastic land market. The prize they sought was patronage in the form of town offices and lands but, more important than this, the domination of the two Parliamentary seats of the borough, revived in 1571. Their motive in this was simply to heighten their profile in national affairs and if opposition was encountered it was not likely to come from the burgesses of the town, who were too weak to resist, but from rival magnates. The 1590s, which saw a major clash between the Manners and Talbots, saw an associated conflict in Retford, a quiet community with a long tradition of sorting out its own affairs. The dispute seemed to hinge on questions of law and possibly economics, but it is difficult to resist the conclusion that the hidden agenda was an attempt by the magnates to procure a corporation which was more tractable and amenable to guidance from above. The 1607 charter, which was the upshot, restricted the role of the burgesses in local government and tightened the existing 'inner ring', but it did not create the closed and dominant oligarchy beloved of Clark and Slack.[5] A superficial examination of the evidence might liken Retford to Basingstoke where a 'family party' came to rule the corporation after 1641, but in reality the oligarchs were fairly easily penetrated by newcomers and the 'family party' was the family of the town, because almost everyone was related and most who wanted to had the chance to join in. To have denied this would have created further disorder which is what the formulators of the new incorporation were principally at pains to avoid. Change was therefore evident after 1520, but it was change set firmly in the context of extant institutions, the church and corporation. The traditional life of the town had been amplified rather than fundamentally altered, yet in this amplification some freedom of action had undoubtedly been lost. The measure of this is the fact that in 1640 the Cavendish family could nominate the town vicar, occupy one of its Parliamentary seats and command leases of the town estate, a dominance never before achieved by a single grouping.

The abiding impression of the society which succumbed to these pressures, be they from godly ministers or ambitious magnates, is of an open and conforming community — hence its vulnerability and readiness to adapt to change. Open, because of the ease with which newcomers moved in and out of the town and participated in its civic affairs, and also because of the accountability of all citizens to the presentments of their neighbours. Conforming, because of the marked reluctance to stray far beyond the expectations which central government had of its subjects in both a political and religious context. Whether it was a community which was 'rural' or 'urban' is a question that would not repay the energies spent debating it, since the two were so inextricably mixed as to make the distinction virtually meaningless. Retford people invariably had family roots in the countryside and they looked to the country for their prosperity and survival, despite the fact that the town in which they lived emulated larger centres, such as York, for many of its institutions and social mores. The important point is that Retford strove to work and behave like the much-idealised community of neighbours, an aspiration which was just about attainable because of its smallness, its lack of sharp social distinction, and the fact that the burgess dynasties rarely lasted for very long.[6] The corollary of this, of course, was that the town was a constant prey to outside forces who sought to over-awe and exploit it for their own interests. This was a major complaint of the burgesses to the Earl of Rutland in the 1590s which might be seen as a critical decade in both the civil and ecclesiastical life of the community. It could be argued that the political seeds of the rotten borough were sown then, although they matured in the fertile soil of the Medieval past.

In so far as any small community can be deemed 'typical' Retford could be said to have many of the characteristics which extended to English small town life as a whole. Despite a certain Ruritanean quality implicit in its top-heavy corporation and pompous sounding functionaries, the town was, at heart, a tolerant and conforming place in which people got on with their own lives and work. The very lack of drama in Retford's history betrays its essential Englishness. It was also an exceptionally resilient community, because its survival through the various crises of the sixteenth and seventeenth centuries — plague, fire and economic depression — must have tested the courage and morale of its people to the limit. The fact that the town survived, and enjoyed something of a Renaissance in the eighteenth century with the redirection of the Great North Road and the building of the Chesterfield Canal, owed much to the refusal of its citizens to give up when things looked to be at their worst. Thus, although Retford might have been pilloried as a rotten borough by the political commentators of the nineteenth century, they failed to perceive the human qualities which underpinned its political facade — or, more positively, they saw those qualities and determined that they should have full representative expression. Though the timbers of the corporation might have been decayed, the society they purported to uphold had survived in a much healthier state, the product of many years of experience and adaptation to changing circumstances. This theme can hardly be unique to Retford, and it serves to underline the basic qualities of ordinary folk in countless communities throughout the land over and above those who seek to govern and control them.

FOOTNOTES AND REFERENCES

1. Palliser speaks of a continuity of 'assumptions, relationships and physical surroundings' in Tudor York. Barry, p.242.
2. *Ibid.*, pp.166-205.
3. W. MacCaffrey, *Exeter 1540-1640* (1958), p.281, A. D. Dyer, *The City of Worcester in the Sixteenth Century* (1973), p.256.
4. For Gloucester, Clark argued: 'To civic leaders trying to govern a community beset by rising population, economic instability, widespread poverty and other social and political difficulties, puritanism, with its emphasis on public control and godly discipline, had a powerful appeal'. Barry, p.268.
5. Clark and Slack, p.25.
6. It might be argued that there were psychological reasons for this sense of tolerance too. Shoemaking was traditionally the 'gentle craft', and the soporific hum of the spinning wheel, laden with narcotic hemp, might have engendered a mild sense of euphoria.

Map 1: Retford and the surrounding area

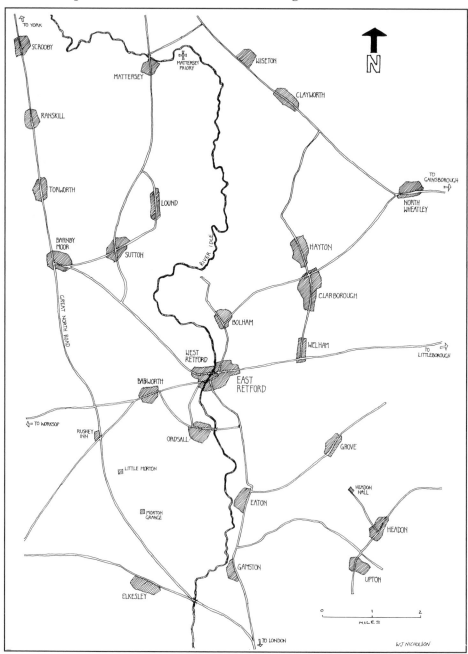

W.J. NICHOLSON

Map 2: Retford: the urban core

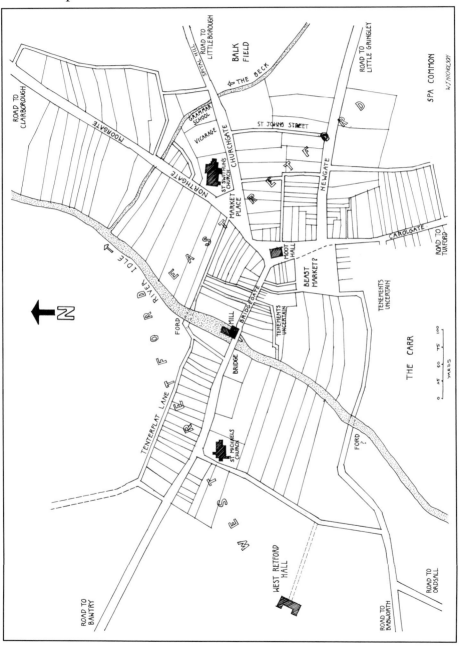

Table 1:   Bailiffs, 1503-1642[1]

1503	Richard Kytteson John Wymoke	1571	Mr Bailiff Rose [William Rose?]
1518	Christopher Eykring John Dokker Thomas Barker	1584	John Sloswicke* Ralph Wyndell
		1585	Edmund Spivy* Martin Billiald
1519	Richard Kydson John Smyth John Broxshawe	1586	David Watson+ William Smyth+ William Thornton
1520	Richard Kytteson William Rossell	1588	John Cobb
1524	Robert Bolloge Richard Gedling	1590	David Watson
1531	Alexander Swift James Hamerton John Wymoke	1591/92	William Thornton John Mason
		1592	Edward Hellabye William Beldon
1536	Robert Holland John Watson Nicholas Wilson	1597/98	Geoffrey Bailey+ Hercy Cobb+
1536	Edmund Samson	1598/99	William Thornton John Mason
1541	John Wymoke John Rossell [William] Tennant	1599/00	John Jepson John Glanville
1548	John Wymoke (?) William Rossell (?)	1600/01	William Woodrough* John Ellis
1545	Robert Gollard John Watson Nicholas Wilson	1601/02	Henry Mason* John Jepson
		1602/03	Richard Elsam+ Thomas Tupman*
1553	John Twels	1603/04	John Sloswicke* Thomas Wharton
1554	Robert Roger Christopher Jackson William Rossell	1604/05	Robert Wharton* Henry Parnell
1556	Hugh Jackson	1605/06	John Ellis Richard Parnell
1562	Hugh Jackson [April] Thomas Stockham John Twels	1606/07	William Thornton Nicholas Watson
1562	John Twels John Holland		

1607/08	William Thornton Nicholas Watson		1629/30	Thomas Dickons Michael Finney
1608/09	Robert Stockham Francis Barker		1630/31	Henry Barthrop Thomas Parnell
1611	John Jepson		1631/32	William Cade Martin Horsefole
1612	Francis Baker William Parnell		1632/33	George Earle William Dunstan
1614	Nicholas Watson Thomas Draper		1633/34	Henry Atkinson William Earle
1616	William Dixon William Chappell		1634/35	Saville Wharton Robert Parnell
1619	William Scrope		1635/36	William Mason William Parnell
1620/21	William Earle John Wharton		1636/37	Francis Moody George Maltby
1621/22	Martin Taylor William Mason		1637/38	Thomas Parnell Alexander Stowe
1622/23	William Dixon Henry Earle		1638/39	George Kirke Henry Johnson
1623/24	William Dickons George Earle		1639/40	William Horsefole Richard Reynolds
1624/25	John Wharton John Earle		1640/41	Robert Parnell Richard Denman
1627	Leonard Cosin Nicholas Colley		1641/42	William Parnell Nicholas Sharpe
1627/28	William Mason Robert Denman			
1628/29	Robert Stockham George Kirke			

* = 'young man'   + = 'ancient'

1.   This list has been derived from Piercy's Mss., Ancient Deeds, Wills, and Miscellaneous sources.

Table 2: Distribution of property in wills, 1600-1642

Proportions of wills making bequests of specific property, divided according to social categories.

G = gentlemen   H = husbandmen/labourers
T = tradesmen   W = women
Y = yeomen   U = unspecified
·········· = overall mean for 107 wills

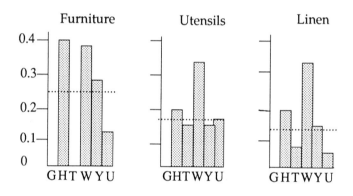

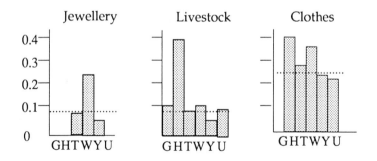

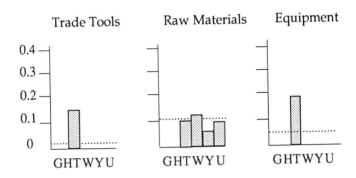

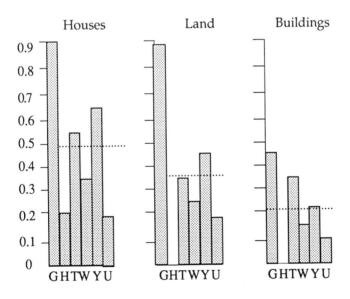

Table 3: Cash legacies, debts and bequests to the poor, 1600-1642.

Status group	Number of wills	Cash Legacies		Debts	Bequests to Poor
Gentlemen	9	Less than £5: £5 - £10: £11 - £20: £21 - £50: Over £50:	1 1 1 0 6	Owed: 0 Owing: 1	7
Yeomen	22	Less than £5: £5 - £10: £11 - £20: £21 - £50: Over £50:	9 0 2 2 6	Owed: 4 Owing: 2	10
Tradesmen	30	Less than £5: £5 - £10: £11 - £20: £21 - £50: Over £50:	6 6 1 3 7	Owed: 6 Owing: 8	11
Husbandmen/ Labourers	6	Less than £5: £5 - £10: £11 - £20: £21 - £50: Over £50:	3 1 1 0 0	Owed: 1 Owing: 0	2
Women	22	Less than £5: £5 - £10: £11 - £20: £21 - £50: Over £50:	2 5 1 3 9	Owed: 8 Owing: 7	9
Unspecified	18	Less than £5: £5 - £10: £11 - £20: £21 - £50: Over £50:	8 3 6 0 0	Owed: 3 Owing: 2	8
Totals	107	93		44	47

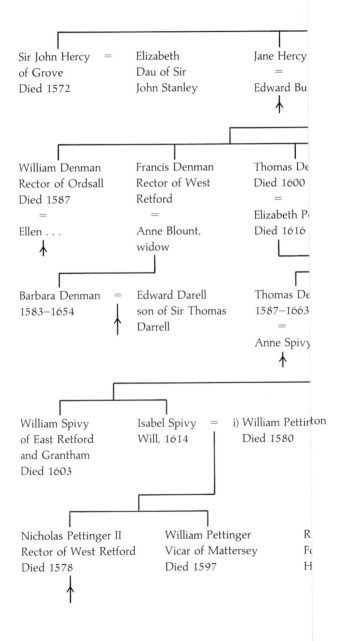

Sir John Hercy = Elizabeth
of Grove   Dau of Sir
Died 1572   John Stanley

Jane Hercy
=
Edward Bu

William Denman
Rector of Ordsall
Died 1587
=
Ellen . . .

Francis Denman
Rector of West
Retford
=
Anne Blount,
widow

Thomas De
Died 1600
=
Elizabeth P
Died 1616

Barbara Denman = Edward Darell
1583–1654   son of Sir Thomas
                        Darrell

Thomas De
1587–1663
=
Anne Spivy

William Spivy
of East Retford
and Grantham
Died 1603

Isabel Spivy = i) William Pettirton
Will, 1614   Died 1580

Nicholas Pettinger II
Rector of West Retford
Died 1578

William Pettinger
Vicar of Mattersey
Died 1597

R
F
H

Table 4: Penances imposed by the Archdeacon's Court, 1565-1610 (M = males F = females)

Parish		Certified	Non-certified	Commuted	Totals
Clarborough	M	3	3	2	8
	F	4	8	2	14
	Total 7		11	4	22
East Retford	M	8	7	8	23
	F	9	11	1	21
	Total 17		18	9	44
West Retford	M	1	4	0	5
	F	3	2	0	5
	Total 4		6	0	10
Totals		(37%) 28	(46%) 35	(17%) 13	76

Table 5: Division of bequests within social groupings, 1600-1642 *A: Immediate family*

	Wife	Sons/ Daughters	Sons-in-law/ Daughters-in-law	Grandsons/ Grand-daughters
Gentlemen	24%	45%	17%	14%
Yeomen	28%	54%	6%	12%
Tradesmen	29%	51%	7%	13%
Husbandmen/ Labourers	30%	40%	10%	20%
Unspecified	32%	52%	4%	12%
Women	-	44%	20%	36%

Table 5, continued   *B: Extended family*

	Father/ Mother	Brothers/ Sisters	Nephews/ Nieces	Aunts/ Uncles	Cousins
Gentlemen	6%	42%	35%	0	17%
Yeomen	8%	46%	38%	0	8%
Tradesmen	21%	45%	24%	0	10%
Husbandmen/ Labourers	0	43%	43%	0	14%
Unspecified	15%	55%	25%	0	5%
Women	6%	31%	42%	0	21%

C: Non-family

	Friends	Servants	Godchildren	Others
Gentlemen	30%	10%	30%	30%
Yeomen	32%	11%	32%	25%
Tradesmen	15%	35%	15%	35%
Husbandmen/ Labourers	40%	20%	20%	20%
Unspecified	8%	8%	8%	76%
Women	19%	38%	5%	38%

Table 6: Will preambles, 1520-1642*

	Catholic	Neutral	Protestant	No Preamble	Totals
1520-1546	39	1	1	0	41
1547-1553	2	9	5	0	16
1554-1558	35	5	0	0	40
1559-1579	2	13	13	0	28
1580-1602	0	17	34	0	51
1603-1624	0	17	22	2	41
1625-1642	0	16	39	2	57

* Based on an analysis of 274 wills.

Table 7: Defendants in *ex officio* cases before the Archdeacon's Court, 1565-1610*

Category of Offence	Male Defendants	Female Defendants	Defendants as a proportion of whole
Morality	55%	45%	62%
a) sexual	[56%]	[44%]	[59%]
b) non-sexual	[20%]	[80%]	[3%]
Ecclesiastical Jurisdiction	94%	6%	13%
Church Attendance/ Sabbatarianism	78%	22%	17%
Conformity	68%	32%	5%
Church Maintenance	100%	0	3%
	65%	35%	

* Based on 349 defendants prosecuted during this period, not on individual prosecutions which might have included more than one defendant. For a guide to the nature of the offences included in the categories, see Table 8.

Table 8A: Numbers of *ex officio* cases, and defendants, before the Archdeacon's Court during two sample periods, i.e. 1591-1600, 1631-1640

(Numbers of defendants are given in brackets)

		1590s		1630s	
Morality					
a) sexual					
Fornication/Incontinence		26	[44]	23	[41]
Fornication before marriage		1	[2]	9	[17]
Adultery/suspected adultery		7	[7]	1	[1]
Carnal knowlege/attempted fornication		1	[1]	1	[1]
Incest		1	[2]	0	
Cohabitation		0		1	[2]
	Totals	36	[56]	35	[62]
b) non-sexual					
Scolding		1	[1]	1	[1]
Usury		1	[1]	1	[1]
	Totals	2	[3]	2	[2]
Ecclesiastical Jurisdiction					
Irregular marriage		1	[1]	1	[1]
Clandestine marriage		2	[3]	2	[3]
Living apart		4	[4]	1	[1]
Harbouring offenders		1	[1]	0	
Not paying church dues		2	[2]	17	[19]
Not paying clerk's wages		0		2	[2]
Failure to present/account		0		2	[4]
Unlawful administration		2	[2]	0	
Standing excommunicated		3	[3]	3	[3]
	Totals	15	[16]	28	[33]
Church Attendance/Sabbatarianism					
Not attending church		0		10	[13]
Not receiving communion		1	[1]	7	[14]
Not attending catechism		0		1	[1]
Not giving thanks after childbirth		0		1	[1]
Not signifying name before communion		0		2	[3]
Profaning the Sabbath		4	[6]	6	[7]
Alehouse in service time		0		22	[39]
Recusancy		0		3	[3]
	Totals	5	[7]	52	[81]

	1590s	1630s
Conformity		
Failure to wear surplice/perform rites	3 [3]	0
Misbehaviour in church	2 [3]	8 [8]
Totals	5 [6]	8 [8]
Church Maintenance		
Church in disrepair	1 [2]	6 [10]
Lack of books etc	1 [2]	0
Totals	2 [4]	6 [10]
Unspecified	14 [14]	3 [3]
TOTALS	79 [105]	134 [199]

Table 8B: Comparison of offences as a proportion of specified cases*

Category of Offence	1590s	1630s
Morality	58%	29%
a) sexual	[55%]	[27%]
b) non-sexual	[3%]	[2%]
Ecclesiastical Jurisdiction	23%	20%
Church Attendance/ Sabbatarianism	8%	40%
Conformity	8%	6%
Church Maintenance	3%	5%

* i.e. 65 in 1590s: 131 in 1630s

Graph 1: East Retford population movement, 1573–1640.

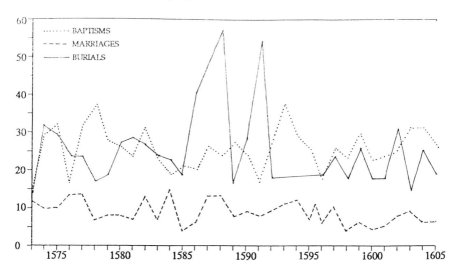

Graph 2: Clarborough population movement, 1567–1640.

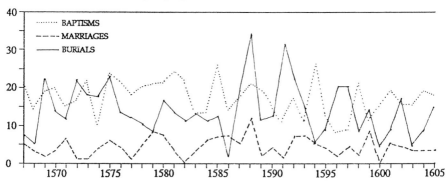

Graph 3: Ordsall population movement, 1538–1640.

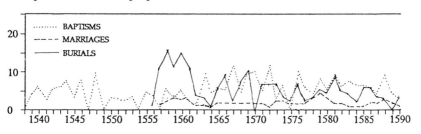

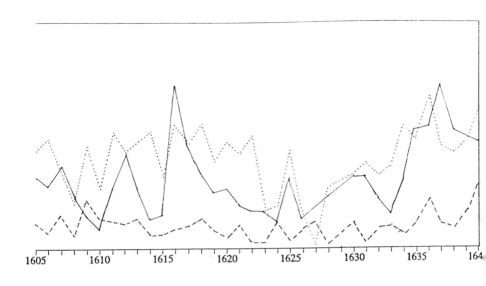

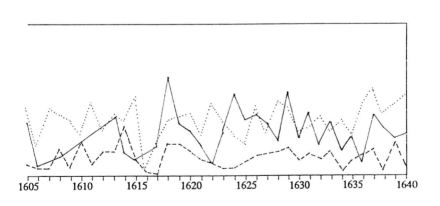

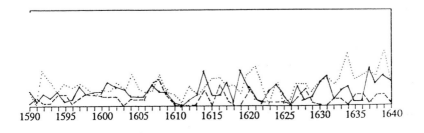

Graph 4: Number of Retford wills (extended town) brought to probate, 1515-1640. Presented in five year blocks.

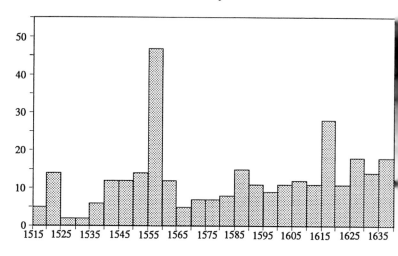

Graph 6: Population estimate (extended town) based on adjusted five year averages, 1576-1640.

Graph 5: Population estimates based on five year averages
(East Retford, Clarborough and Ordsall), 1576-1640.

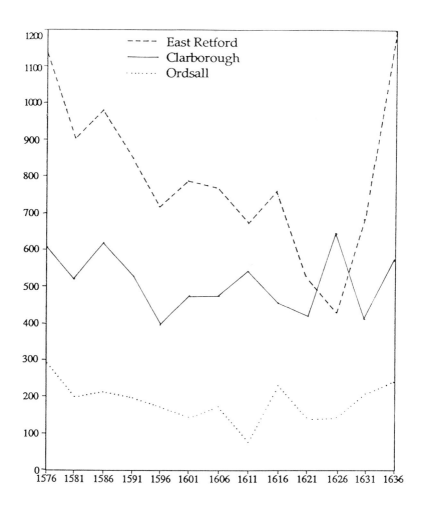

Graph 7: Defendants in *ex officio* cases before the Archdeacon's Court, 1565–1610. East Retford.

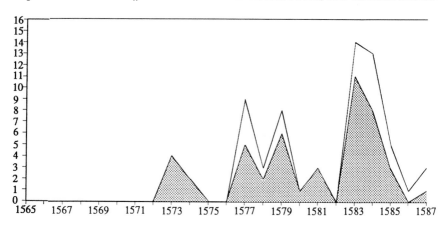

Graph 8: Defendants in *ex officio* cases before the Archdeacon's Court, 1565–1610. Clarborough.

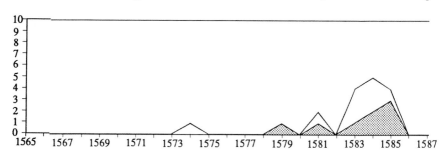

Graph 9: Defendants in *ex officio* cases before the Archdeacon's Court, 1565–1610. West Retford.

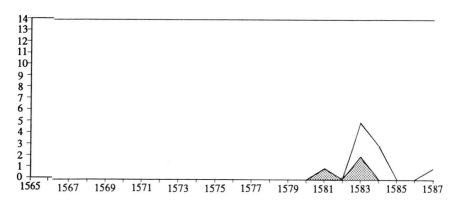

(defendants in cases of sexual immorality are indicated by the shaded graph)

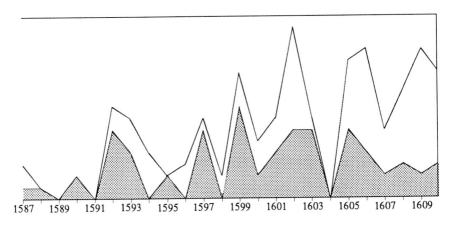

(defendants in cases of sexual immorality are indicated by the shaded graph)

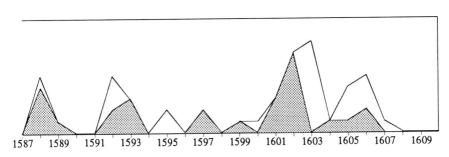

(defendants in cases of sexual immorality are indicated by the shaded graph)

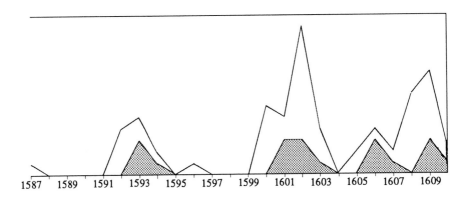

Bibliography

A   MANUSCRIPT SOURCES

1   *Belvoir Castle*

Letters: 26/4/1585, 16/7/1585, 22/9/1586, 24/9/1586, 22/2/1590(2), 31/11/1592, 22/10/1598, 3/11/1598(2).

2   *Borthwick Institute, University of York*

    i)   Archbishop's Registers: 29-32.
    ii)   Archbishop's Visitations: V. 1567/8 CB: 1600 CB 2: 1607 (Misc): 1636 CB.
    iii)   Cause Papers: 1043, H.660.
    iv)   Chancery Wills: 1587.
    v)   High Commission Act Books: 15-16.
    vi)   Probate Documents: 1617, 1618, 1630, 1642.
    vii)   Probate Registers: 9-28.
    viii)   Subscription Book: 2.

3   *Jones Alexander and Co., Retford*

Piercy Mss: Red Books 1-3, Black Book.

4   *Lambeth Palace Library*

Shrewsbury Mss. 708.

5   *Nottingham University Manuscripts Department*

    i)   Archdeaconry Act Books: A39-47.
    ii)   Archdeaconry Call Book: CL 175.
    iii)   Archdeaconry Libels etc: LB 215-228.
    iv)   Archdeaconry Penances: PN 352.
    v)   Archdeaconry Presentments: PB 292-341.
    vi)   Induction Mandates, 1573-1660.
    vii)   Clifton Mss: C. 17, 149, 294, 295, 344, 378, 606, 684, 715: D. 1632: LP. 52.

6   *Nottinghamshire Archives Office*

   i)   Archdeaconry Act Books: DDTS 1-12, 22-25.
   ii)   Catalogue of Mee Mss.
   iii) Parish Registers: East Retford (1573-1642), Clarborough (1567-1642), Ordsall (1538-1642).
   iv)   Quarter Sessions Act Books: QSMI/1-12.
   v)   Wills, 1600-42: East Retford, West Retford, Clarborough and Ordsall.
   vi)   Miscellaneous: DD. 461, 538/1, 1301/5, 509/1, 487/1: HO 13 W56: PR 8024: DP 47/1,2,4,24: DDA 10/20.

7   *Public Record Office, Chancery Lane, London*

   i)   Chancery Records: C93, 45 no.26.
   ii)   PCC Wills: PROB 11/101.

8   *Retford Museum*

   i)   Ancient Deeds, 1518-1658.
   ii)   Orders and Constitutions, 1599 and 1639.
   iii) Ordinances, 1600.
   iv)   Rates of Wages, 1627.
   v)   Charters of Elizabeth and James I, 1562 and 1607.
   vi)   Miscellaneous: 667.85.

9   *Southwell Minster Library*

   Bishops Transcripts: East Retford (1602-42), West Retford (1622-42), Clarborough (1608-42).

10   *York Minster Library*

   Torre Mss.

B   CALENDARS AND PRINTED SOURCES

Acts of the Privy Council, 1586-87.

T. M. Blagg (ed.), *A Miscellany of Nottinghamshire Records*, Thoroton Society, Record Series, 11, 1945.

British Record Society, Index Library, 25, *Wills Proved in the Prerogative Court of Canterbury, 1584-1604*, 4.

British Record Society, Index Library, 43, *Wills Proved in the Prerogative Court of Canterbury, 1605-19*, 5.

British Record Society, Index Library, 52, *Lincoln Administrations: Consistory Court, 1540-1659.*

Calendar of Close Rolls, 1392-96.

Calendar of Patent Rolls, 1381-85, 1547-48, 1550-53, 1554-55, 1555-57, 1557-58, 1558-60, 1560-63, 1563-66, 1572-75, 1575-78.

Calendar of State Papers Domestic, 1581-90, 1595-97, 1598-1601, 1601-03, 1603-10, 1619-23, 1625-26, 1629-31, 1635-36, 1636-37, 1637.

J. Caley (ed.), *Valor Ecclesiasticus*, 6 vols (1810-43).

Catalogue of the Arundel Castle Manuscripts...[and]...Calendar of Talbot Letters, Sheffield City Libraries, 1965.

J. W. Clay (ed.), *Dugdale's Visitation of Yorkshire*, 3 vols (1894-1912).

H. H. Copnall, *Nottinghamshire County Records* (1915).

38th Report of the Deputy Keeper of Public Records, *Exchequer Depositions by Commission* (1877).

C.W. Foster (ed.), *The Parish Registers of Grantham, 1, 1562-1632*, Lincoln Record Society, Parish Register Section, 4, 1916.

J. Glanville, *Reports of Certain Cases...in Parliament, 21 and 23 James I* (1775).

R. E. Glasscock (ed.), *The Lay Subsidy of 1334*, Records of Social and Economic History, New Series, 2, 1975.

Historical Manuscripts Commission, *The Manuscripts of his Grace the Duke of Rutland preserved at Belvoir Castle*, 2 vols (1888-89).

R. F. Hunnisett (ed.), *Calendar of Nottinghamshire Coroner's Inquests, 1485-1558*, Thoroton Society, Record Series, 25, 1969.

W. Jorden (ed.), *Rutland Papers*, Camden Society, 21, 1842.

Journal of the House of Commons, 1.

Letters and Papers of Henry VIII, 1542, 1544, 1545, 1546-47.

T. Lever, *Sermons* (ed. E. Arber), English Reprints, 1870.

C. E. Long (ed.), *Diary of the Marches of the Royal Army...kept by Richard Symonds*, Camden Society, 74, 1859.

PRO Lists and Indexes:
- i) 10, *List of Proceedings of Commissioners for Charitable Uses* (1963).
- ii) 21, *List of Proceedings in the Court of Requests*, 1 (1963).
- iii) 25, *List of Rentals and Surveys* (1963).
- iv) 27, *List of Special Commissioners and Returns in the Exchequer* (1912).
- v) 48, *Early Chancery Proceedings*, 6 (1922).
- vi) 50, *Early Chancery Proceedings*, 7 (1926).
- vii) 51, *Early Chancery Proceedings*, 8 (1929).
- viii) 54, *Early Chancery Proceedings*, 9 (1933).
- ix) 55, *Early Chancery Proceedings*, 10 (1936).
- x) *Index of Chancery Proceedings*, Series 2, 1 (1558-79) (1896).
- xi) *Index of Chancery Proceedings*, Series 2, 2 (1579-1621) (1908).
- xii) Supplementary Series 3, *List of Lands of Dissolved Religious Houses* (1964).

xiii) Supplementary Series 4, *Proceedings in the Court of Star Chamber, 1485-1558*, 1 (1966).

xiv) Supplementary Series 7, *Proceedings in the Court of Requests*, 1 (1964).

L. T. Smith (ed.), *The Itinerary of John Leland*, 5 vols (1909).

A. H. Thompson, 'The Chantry Certificate Rolls for the County of Nottingham', *Transactions of the Thoroton Society*, 17, 1913.

The Visitation of Nottinghamshire, 1569 and 1614, Harleian Society Publications, 4, 1981.

The Visitation of Nottinghamshire, 1662-64, Harleian Society Publications, New Series, 5, 1986.

W. F. Webster (ed.), *Nottinghamshire Hearth Tax, 1664: 1674*, Thoroton Society, Record Series, 37, 1988.

W. F. Webster (ed.), *Protestation Returns 1641/2: Notts/Derbys* (n.d.).

E. White, *Bequests in York Wills to Religious Guilds, 1365-1549*, Unpub Borthwick Index, 1983.

A. C. Wood (ed.), *Manuscripts of the Holles Family, 1493-1656*, Camden Society, 3rd Series, 55, 1937.

C SECONDARY SOURCES

J. Barry (ed.), *The Tudor and Stuart Town: a reader in English urban history, 1530-1688* (1990).

W. A. Bewes, *Church Briefs* (1896).

B. J. Biggs, *Living in Old Retford* (1973).

M. W. Bishop, 'The origins of East Retford', *Transactions of the Thoroton Society*, 82, 1978.

M. Bonsall, 'John Lowth and John King, Archdeacons of Nottingham: a study of ambition and mediocrity in the Elizabethan church', *Bulletin of Local History East Midland Region*, 21, 1986.

B. Brook, *The Lives of the Puritans*, 2 vols (1813).

N. Carlisle, *A Concise Description of the Endowed Grammar Schools of England and Wales*, 2 vols (1818).

P. Clark, K. Gaskin and A. Wilson, *Population Estimates of English Small Towns, 1550-1851*, Centre for Urban History, University of Leicester, Working Paper No. 3, 1989.

P. Clark and P. Slack (eds.), *Crisis and Order in English Towns, 1500-1700* (1972).

L. A. Clarkson, *The Pre-Industrial Economy in England, 1500-1750* (1972).

P. Collinson, *The Elizabethan Puritan Movement* (1967).

Dictionary of National Biography.

E. Duffy, *The Stripping of the Altars: traditional religion in England, c1400-c1580* (1992).

S. Dunster, 'An Independent Life? Nottingham Widows, 1594-1650', *Transactions of the Thoroton Society*, 95, 1991.

E. Ekwall, *The Concise Oxford Dictionary of English Place-Names* (1966).

N. Evans, *The East Anglian Linen Industry, 1500-1850* (1985).

A. Everitt (ed.), *Perspectives in English Urban History* (1973).

J. Foster, *Alumni Oxonienses, 1500-1714* (1891).

V. Gibbs (ed.), *The Complete Peerage*, 13 vols (1910-59).

A. D. Grounds, *A History of King Edward VI Grammar School, Retford* (1970).

P. W. Hasler, *The House of Commons, 1558-1603*, 3 vols (1981).

B. D. Henning, *The House of Commons, 1660-1690*, 3 vols (1983).

R. A. Houlbrooke, *Church Courts and People during the English Reformation* (1979).

R. A. Houlbrooke, *The English Family, 1450-1700* (1984).

R. Howell, *Newcastle-upon-Tyne and the Puritan Revolution* (1979).

J. Hunter, *South Yorkshire*, 2 vols (reprinted 1974).

M. Ingram, *The Church Courts, Sex and Marriage in England* (1987).

A. Jackson, *A History of Retford: the growth of a Nottinghamshire borough* (1971).

N. G. Jackson, *Newark Magnus: the story of a gift* (1964).

A. A. Kidson, *History of East Retford Church* (1905).

S. J. Knox, *Walter Travers: paragon of Elizabethan puritanism* (1962).

M. Lucas, 'The Methodology of Will Analysis in determining the Religious Opinions of the City of Lincoln during the Reformation', *East Midland Historian*, 1/2, 1991/2.

W. T. MacCaffrey, 'Talbot and Stanhope: an episode in Elizabethan politics', *Bulletin of the Institute of Historical Research*, 33, 1960.

A. Macfarlane, *Reconstructing Historical Communities* (1977).

R. Marchant, *The Church under the Law*, (1966).

C. Markham, *Markham Memorials*, 2 vols (1913).

G. Markham, *A Way to Get Wealth* (1611).

R. O'Day, *The English Clergy: the emergence and consolidation of a profession* (1979).

D. M. Palliser, *Tudor York* (1979).

J. Parnell, *Fruits of a Fast* (1655).

N. Pevsner [and E. Williamson], *The Buildings of England: Nottinghamshire* (1979).

C. Phythian-Adams, *Desolation of a City: Coventry and the urban crisis of the late Middle Ages* (1979).

J. S. Piercy, *The History of Retford...[and]...the villages of West Retford, Babworth, Ordsall, Grove and Clarborough* (1828).

N.J.Pike, 'Marriage Formation and Breakdown in Nottinghamshire, 1570-1610', University of Nottingham MA dissertation, 1989.

C. Platt, *The English Medieval Town* (1976).

R. C. Richardson and T. B. Jarvis (eds.), *The Urban Experience. A Source Book: English, Scottish and Welsh towns, 1450-1700* (1983).

J. Roffey, *The Book of Retford* (1991).

J. J. Scarisbrick, *The Reformation and the English People* (1984).

P. R. Seddon, 'A Parliamentary Election at East Retford, 1624', *Transactions of the Thoroton Society*, 75, 1972.

P. R. Seddon, 'The Nottinghamshire Elections for the Short Parliament of 1640', *Transactions of the Thoroton Society*, 80, 1976.

P. R. Seddon, 'Marriage and Inheritance in the Clifton Family during the Seventeenth Century', *Transactions of the Thoroton Society*, 84, 1980.

P. R. Seddon, 'An East Retford Parliamentary Election of 1670', *Transactions of the Thoroton Society*, 88, 1984.

J. A. Sharpe, *Defamation and Sexual Slander in early modern England: the Church Courts at York*, Borthwick Paper, 58, 1980.

C. F. Smith, *Life of James Parnell* (1906).

B. Spencer (ed.), *Salisbury and South Wiltshire Museum: Medieval Catalogue*, Part 2 (1990).

L. Stone, *The Family, Sex and Marriage in England, 1500-1800* (1979).

J. W. Tammel, *The Pilgrims and other people from the British Isles in Leiden, 1576-1640* (1989).

R. Thoroton (and J. Throsby), *The Antiquities of Nottinghamshire*, 3 vols (1790-97).

K. S. S. Train (ed.), *Lists of the Clergy of North Nottinghamshire*, Thoroton Society, Record Series, 20, 1961.

D. Underdown, *Fire from Heaven: life in an English town in the seventeenth century* (1992).

J. and J. A. Venn, *Alumni Cantabrigienses*, Part 1 (1922-27).

Victoria County History, Nottinghamshire, 4 vols (1906).

F. H. West, *Sparrows of the Spirit* (n.d.).

F. and J. White, *History of Nottingham* (1844).

R. F. Wilkinson, *Notes on the History of the Parish of Ordsall* (1940).

C. E. L. Williams, 'The Tanners of Nottingham and their Household Inventories, 1679-1749', Certificate in Local History Dissertation, University of Nottingham, 1983.

E. Wilmshurst, *The History of the Old Hall of the manor of West Retford* (1908).

A. C. Wood, *A History of Nottinghamshire* (1947).

E. A. Wrigley and R. S. Schofield, *The Population History of England, 1541-1871: a reconstruction* (1981).

K. Wrightson, *English Society, 1580-1680* (1982).

INDEX

Information provided in the Appendix has not been included in the Index.

Studies in Local and Regional History

other titles:

The Last Principality: Politics, Religion and Society in the Bishopric of Durham 1494-1660 (ed. David Marcombe)

House of Care: Prisons and Prisoners in England 1500-1800 (J.E. Thomas)

Close Encounters: English Cathedrals and Society since 1540 (eds. David Marcombe & C.S. Knighton)